–

Green
Politics
Two

–

EDITOR
WOLFGANG RÜDIG

–

Green
Politics Two

–

EDINBURGH UNIVERSITY
PRESS

© Edinburgh University Press 1992
22 George Square, Edinburgh

Set in Linotron Joanna
by Koinonia Ltd, Bury, and
printed in Great Britain
by Robert Hartnoll Ltd, Bodmin

A CIP record for this book is available
from the British Library.

ISBN 0 7486 0265 8

Contents

In memoriam Martin Spencer

Editorial

WOLFGANG RÜDIG

Green politics entered a difficult phase in 1991: if 1989/90 was a period of green euphoria, then 1990/91 could be classified as a time of green fatigue. The West German Greens' failure to re-enter the national parliament in December 1990 was perhaps the most dramatic indication of this, and it was, not surprisingly, seen by much of the media as the beginning of the much-prophesied end of the Greens. The Swedish Greens also failed to retain their parliamentary seats in September 1991. In Britain, the public opinion poll standing of the Green Party has declined steadily since its sensational success in the European elections, Green Party membership has been dropping rapidly and the environment appears to have largely disappeared as a major issue of political debate. To some extent, however, failures in West Germany and Sweden were off-set by good election results for green parties in both Finland and Belgium. The Greens have also been doing rather well in German state elections in 1991. Nevertheless, the almost euphoric feeling of 1989 has clearly given way to more sober and self-critical reflections on the future of the Greens in 1991.

The notion that the momentum of the green movement of recent years has come to a halt is not limited to party politics. In virtually all areas of green activity, the heady days of the late 1980s seem to be over. Environmental groups are finding it more difficult to attract new members, retain their current membership levels, and attract financial contributions. Another area to have been hit by disillusionment is consumerism. In the late 1980s, being green and buying green goods seemed to be synonymous. But disillusionment about so-called 'green products' has grown, fuelled by doubt about the veracity of producers' claims concerning the 'greenness' of their products.

How can we explain this apparent downturn in green fortunes? The question, of course, is whether it is only 'up and down' or whether it might be a repeating pattern of 'up, down, and up again'. Indeed, news of environmental problems and catastrophes as well as green activities continues to flow unabatedly and environmental concern generally is still high; environmental issues have not gone away.

There are several possible explanations for the current difficulties of the green movement. On the one hand, one may surmise that it was only to be expected that there would be 'ups' and 'downs' of the fortunes of the green movement. The notion of the 'issue-attention cycle' (Downs) may not be a very convincing model for the explanation of environmental movements as a whole, but as far as the role of the media is concerned, it provides a reasonably accurate picture. After the enormous amount of coverage in 1989/90, it might be seen as inevitable that a saturation effect would set in, with the environment giving way to other issues.

Also, as far as individual commitments to environmental action is concerned, the 'saturation effect' may explain much. To the extent that, for some, 'being green' was a media-induced fashionable attitude, then the apparent crisis of green politics may reflect the disillusionment of such 'shallow' greens; those whose allegiance to the green cause was never more than superficial.

Another possible explanation might be found in the link between economic cycles and the importance of the environment as a political issue. At least in Britain, the rise of the environmental issue coincided with the post-1987 boom years which have now given way to a major recession. In difficult economic times, with rising unemployment this time particularly hitting the affluent south-east and the professional 'middle classes', support for green campaigns and organisations could be expected to be adversely affected.

To blame business cycles and media-issue attention cycles for the current difficulties of the green movement hardly raises any problems which are particularly worrying for the movement. New environmental issues are bound to come up, leading to renewed media interest, and, once the recession is over, the environment could be expected to move higher up on the political agenda again.

But is it really that easy? Are there perhaps other, more fundamental changes in the green movement and its political environment which we have to consider in this context? Environmental groups and green parties have been going through some major changes, and, arguably, some of these changes make them more vulnerable to cyclical fluctuations.

In its formative phase, green politics emerged out of a radical political ecology movement which distinguished itself from other conservation and environmental groups both in terms of its aims and its strategy. Radical ecologists did not see the environment as a 'single issue' area and proposed a comprehensive, alternative vision of a green society. Furthermore, radical ecologists rejected the boundaries of establishment politics and developed a new repertoire of political action which included the mobilisation of members and supporters to take action in marches and demonstrations, boycotts, occupations, civil disobedience and other forms of direct action.

What has happened in the 1980s is that the conditions which applied in the formative period of green politics have largely changed. First of all, the issues have changed. Campaigns of direct action, mass occupations, and similar 'unconventional' forms of public participation were typical of the anti-nuclear movements of the 1970s and early 1980s. Both in the cases of civil nuclear power stations and the stationing of nuclear missiles, movements had specific, physical targets. Their perception as tangible threats helped the mass mobilisation process. In some countries, other projects such as new dams and airports served as mobilisation targets in a similar way. In the 1990s, these types of 'targets' seem to have largely disappeared. Nuclear weapons have virtually ceased to be an issue following the INF Treaty and the disintegration of Communist regimes in Eastern Europe and the Soviet Union. Nuclear power, after making a major come-back as a political issue in the wake of the Chernobyl accident in 1986, has also virtually disappeared as an effective target of mobilisation because no new nuclear power stations are being built.

What about the new environmental issues which arose in the late 1980s, in particular the greenhouse effect and concern about the ozone layer? Significantly, these types of issues do not offer the environmental movement any targets to mobilise people against. There are no grass-roots movements against the greenhouse effect, and not surprisingly so: global warming is an all-pervasive phenomenon which does not manifest itself in an easily recognisable form, its causes do not present themselves as individual targets, convenient for mobilisation purposes. Rather, it is an abstract issue; the perceived threat to the individual is intangible and those to blame are not easily identified. In other words, the mobilisation potential for environmental political action has diminished.

Secondly, the movements themselves have changed. While the traditional conservation and environmental groups have enlarged their repertoire to include more open political campaigning, radical ecology groups have either disappeared or have transformed themselves into professional organisations. Even direct action has become professionalised with the art of the 'media stunt' reaching new perfections. There are still some groups using direct action as a physical challenge to authorities – such as Earth First! in the USA and 'autonomous' groups in Germany – but they mobilise very few people and are increasingly marginalised. Looking at the movement as a whole, there are strong signs that the divisions between the various groups are fast disappearing. Remaining differences are part of a fairly well-arranged division of labour, rather than competition, and do not reflect any significant differences in political outlook or strategy. The old division between environmentalism and political ecology, if still existent on the theoretical level, has largely lost its manifestation in the politics of environmental groups. In other words, we can observe a process of institutionalisation of the radical movements of the 1970s. This has important implications for the role of movement members: they are now largely confined to being supporters, to paying their subscription. Members are expected to be passive and to leave the real campaigning to the professionals.

Where does this leave green parties? Green parties differ from the pressure groups in that they present a comprehensive alternative picture of a green society and they operate in the arena of elections. Nevertheless, we can observe very similar changes within them. Overall, the formation of green parties has to be seen as a part of the institutionalisation of radical ecology movements, turning to a 'conventional' form of political participation, voting, as the instrument of political mobilisation. The prospect of green parties as movement parties, as anti-party parties, seeing their role mainly in the support of extra-parliamentary movements, has clearly failed. As movements have either vanished or institutionalised, there is no significant extra-parliamentary agency with whom to identify or associate. In this situation, green parties cannot escape the pressures of electoral competition and electoral politics. They must maximise their vote and enter into alliances or coalitions with other parties if they want to carve out a meaningful political role for themselves.

Until recently many green parties have found this difficult as they have been functioning with an internal structure dominated by the logic of movement-based parties and the aim to maximise grass-roots democracy and avoid the creation of any party elites. As Herbert Kitschelt has convincingly shown (see the review of his books in the review essay 'Comparing Green Parties' in this volume), such a structure has the opposite effect in terms of democratic decision-making by allowing 'informal' elites a dominant role. At the same time, these structures do not allow for the effective pursuit of a strategy of electoral competition. Unsurprisingly, calls for a greater professionalisation have been forcefully made, particularly in Germany and Britain. A more centralised structure has been demanded along with the creation of a party leadership able to pursue strategies which will maximise the electoral chances of the party and, if such an opportunity should present itself, engage in effective negotiations with other parties about participation in government. Reforms of internal structures enacted in the British and German Green Parties in 1991 seem to go some way towards reaching such an aim.

In many ways, the development of green parties thus mirrors that of ecology movements, particularly in terms of the role of individual members. The commitment of members to green parties and groups is thus mostly limited to subscription-paying, and this offers only a low-key and vulnerable tie to these organisations. As green parties can offer passive members few other tangible incentives, it cannot be a surprise that membership turnover is high, and membership levels highly dependent on their media-standing. Thus, in a country like Britain, membership levels fluctuate strongly, peaking in election years when the party's profile is highest and bottoming out in mid-term periods.

In many ways, the role of individual members in green parties and national environmental groups is similar to that of the green consumer. The only action required is that of the parting with money: you buy 'environmental action', in just the same way as you buy 'green' washing-up liquid. Naturally, the relationship between leaders and members becomes more similar to that between salesman and customer; personal participation in political action is replaced by paying money as the main form of interaction between green group and individual member.

One might speculate that such a change reflects not only the demise or institutionalisation of 'new' social movements but also the life-style changes of movement adherents who had plenty of spare time in their younger and active days, but who have now reached middle-age where occupational and family commitments make activity more difficult. It is this group of people who form what might be called an ecological 'conscience community' – a term first used by John McCarthy and Mayer Zald in the early 1970s, referring to a very similar development amongst former civil rights and anti-Vietnam War activists. These people are still eager to make some contribution to the movement, but are prevented from doing so by their other commitments. One could thus expect that members of this green 'conscience community' are fairly sympathetically disposed towards the idea of contributing financially, and only financially, to the movement.

There will obviously be some variations between individual countries in the developments I have briefly tried to sketch here, but I think that I have represented an overall trend which will affect green movements throughout the Western world. With the latest movement cycle, according to this scenario, having reached an end, it is clear that the new institutionalised green organisations must change their modes of operation. There is a clear dilemma however: on the one hand, green parties are under enormous pressure to demonstrate their responsibility, their ability to operate as seasoned political actors and to exercise some actual influence over government policy. With a passive membership watching, green party leaders have to demonstrate that they are getting somewhere, that supporting the green parties makes a significant practical difference. On the other hand, green parties not only have to contend with a major body of activists who have been socialised within the framework of social movement mobilisation and are thus reluctant to accept steps towards 'professionalisation', but they may also want to keep the doors open to new movement cycles which may well occur. Being just another establishment party may not do them any good in such a context.

Where does this leave green parties? Organisational change is obviously on the agenda, as can be seen by recent debates in Germany and Britain, for example. Green parties are becoming a little more like the established parties. Managerial, pragmatic solutions will be more popular with passive members and the electorate, but grass roots green activists will probably not like it, leading to a possible decline in grass-roots activity. This may well make green parties more 'manageable' from their leaders' point of view but it may also mean that green parties sacrifice a reliable support base in exchange for potentially greater, but more vulnerable support from passive members and voters.

The seven articles as well as the review essays and book reviews brought together in this second volume of *Green Politics* illuminate many of these problems. The mix of the chapters continues our commitment to the broad international treatment of green politics. With the first volume concentrating on green politics in Western Europe, the emphasis of this second volume has shifted more towards green developments in other parts of the world, namely Australia, New Zealand, Brazil and Eastern Europe. I am particularly conscious of the dearth of material on Eastern Europe and what is still predominantly referred to as the 'Third World': future volumes will, hopefully, contain more academic work on these areas. The discussion of green political theory is limited to the review essays and book reviews, no full-length papers of acceptable standard having been submitted. *Green Politics Three* should have more substantial contributions in this area.

Returning to the present volume, the first three chapters deal with politics in Western Europe. (The sequence of chapters does not in any way reflect any judgement on the relative importance of papers or areas of research.) Andrew Flynn and Philip Lowe describe in great detail the development of the British Conservatives' approach to the environment. The chapter sheds new light on the context of Mrs Thatcher's famous Royal Society speech which played such a major role for the greening of public opinion towards the end of the 1980s. The authors show that, in Britain, the environment is a typical 'mid-term' issue in party politics which is demoted to lesser importance by all major parties when a General Election approaches.

Wolfgang Rüdig and Mark N. Franklin then compare the profile of green voters in Britain with those of Germany and France. They find major differences in the political outlook of actual and potential green voters in the three countries: the green potential in Germany is rather limited but stable; France has the greatest potential support for the Greens, but its reliability is questionable; and Britain has the most fickle green electorate with strong indications that 1989's green voters are unlikely to form a strong basis of support in the future. While the green electorate mainly has a leftist orientation in France and Germany, British greens are clearly more centrist.

Russell J. Dalton provides the first comparative analysis of the relationship of environmental groups in ten West European countries to governmental institutions, to trade unions and employers' federations, to the press, and to other political actors. Dalton shows that the level of political integration achieved by these groups is still rather low, as they see most established political actors as more or less hostile to their cause. Alliance opportunities are thus limited, and groups have to rely on building weak and often indirect linkages with polity members on individual issues and campaigns.

Peter Hay provides a fascinating insider view of the 'accord' between green independents and the Australian Labour Party in the state government of Tasmania which was set up in 1989 and lasted for little more than a year. Potentially, this case has major lessons for green parties in Western Europe and elsewhere embarking on a similar course. Hay is particularly scathing about the greens' inability to develop practical policies in the economic field. Placed in a position of influence, greens only have abstract visions of a green society but are at a loss to provide a programme to produce that society.

Stephen Rainbow charts the development of the world's first national green party – the New Zealand Values Party – from its birth in 1972 to its demise and transformation to a new-style Green Party of Aotearoa in 1989. Values did very well in 1975, polling 5.2 per cent of the national vote, for many years the best result ever achieved by a green party. Then, after many years in the doldrums, the new New Zealand Greens scored another major success in the 1990 General Election, polling 6.6 per cent of the total vote.

The fate of the Amazon rainforest has been a major issue of environmental politics for many years, but green activities in Brazil have not received much attention. José Augusto Pádua provides us with a first comprehensive account of the birth of the Brazilian Green Party. Currently represented by one deputy in the national parliament and twelve municipal councillors in eleven cities, it is one of the best-established green parties in Latin America.

Eastern Europe has also been much in the news in the past two years, and new environmental and green parties provided one important force of opposition to the old regimes in these countries. But, as Barbara Jancar shows, once democratisation and economic reform processes had begun, green groups quickly lost influence, despite the massive environmental problems faced by these countries. Jancar tries to explain the development of environmental movements in Eastern Europe with an innovative adaption of chaos and international relations theory, a completely new approach in the analysis of environmental movements.

The seven main chapters of this year's volume are followed by four review essays, covering comparative studies of green parties, contributions to green political theory, and environmental directories. Three book reviews conclude the volume.

I would like to thank everybody who has contributed to Green Politics Two, particularly the anonymous reviewers who helped me in the assessment of submitted papers, and the staff of Edinburgh University Press whose patience was tried particularly hard as one delay chased another.

I would like to dedicate this volume to the one person who contributed more than anyone else to the success of Green Politics, without whom, in fact, Green Politics would never have seen the light of day: Martin Spencer. It was over lunch in Edinburgh in the spring of 1989 that the the idea for Green Politics was born. Talking about various possibilities of books on environmental politics, Martin came up with the suggestion to start a yearbook of green politics. With his usual enthusiasm, he quickly convinced me it was an idea worth pursuing. Shortly afterwards, work started on Green Politics One. Unfortunately, Martin Spencer passed away before the first volume was published. It was a privilege to have known him, albeit very briefly, and I am dedicating Green Politics Two to his memory.

1. The Greening of the Tories: The Conservative Party and the Environment

ANDREW FLYNN and PHILIP LOWE

Bartlett School of Architecture and Planning, University College London, London, UK

Introduction

The 1980s was the decade of the party politicisation of the environment in Britain. The process has been halting and fitful and has yet to achieve its full fruition. Indeed, rather than a gradual and sustained build-up of interest, the parties seem periodically to have rediscovered the environment as a political issue. They have done so, moreover, at recurrent phases of the electoral cycle, namely the mid-term.

In such periods, it seems, environmental enthusiasts within the parties are able to press their claims, and party leaders are more receptive not only to these internal pressures but to popular concerns as well. Mid-term receptiveness, however, does not yield a sustained commitment at the leadership level, and, so far at least, in no general election has the environment figured at all prominently in the campaigns of the major parties.

This periodic engagement with environmental issues – characterised as it has been by a defensive, even cynical, 'testing of the water' – is redolent of a basic scepticism towards the electoral significance of environmental concern coupled with a desire, even so, to cover the party's flank against such an eventuality. It is also symptomatic of difficulties for the major parties in embracing environmental concern, and of their failure to differentiate their positions as the basis for party competition in this field. Superimposed upon the cyclical pattern, however, there has been a cumulative trend which indicates a gathering grassroots commitment that increasingly threatens to engulf the party leaderships, whatever their better judgement.

Thus, each period of heightened political attention has been more intense than the preceding one and has made greater inroads into party policy making. The fringe involvements of the 1970s were followed by the incursions of 1981–2 when, for the first time, the environment entered the parties' mainstream agendas; then came the flurry of activity in 1984–6 which saw all the main parties put out policy statements on the environment; and, most recently, since 1988, there has been a crescendo of interest, with the party leaders and front-bench spokesmen becoming prominently involved and the beginning of conflict between the parties on this issue.

Table 1 below outlines some of the key events in these successive stages. Before examining in detail the response specifically of the Conservative Party, we will consider what unleashed the general process.

The Origins of the Politicisation Process

What were the preconditions for this process of party politicisation of the environment? The main factor was the challenge to existing modes of incorporating environmental interests into policy making established in the late 1960s and early 1970s. In a memorable phrase, Harold Wilson, the then Prime Minister, explained the objective: 'The Polluters are powerful and organised ... the Protesters, the anti-pollution lobbies are less organised, less powerful. Therefore the community must step in to redress the balance' (Wilson 1970). Significantly this was done by setting up various advisory bodies and by according outside groups consultative status in order to draw moderate environmental opinion into departmental (rather than party) policy making (Lowe and Goyder 1983).

Table 1 The party politicisation of the environment: party publications (†) and the formation of ginger groups (*)

The 1970s
* Socialist Environment and Resources Association, 1973
* Liberal Ecology Group, 1977
* Conservative Ecology Group, 1977

1981–1982
† Stanley Johnson, *Caring for the Environment*, Conservative Political Centre and European Democratic Group, 1981
* Socialist Countryside Group, 1981 (formally relaunched 1983). Publications prepared by the Socialist Countryside Group included the following: *National Parks: Space for the People*; *Access to the Countryside*; *Commonplace No More: Common Land in the 1980s*.
† Barry Bracewell-Milnes, *Land and Heritage: The Public Interest in Personal Ownership*, Institute of Economic Affairs, 1982
† Conservative Research Department, 'The quality of the environment', *Politics Today*, January 1982
† Liberal Party, *A Liberal Programme for the Environment*, Liberal Party, 1982

1984–1986
† Tony Paterson, *Conservation and the Conservatives*, Bow Paper, 1984

† Kenneth Carlisle, Conserving the Countryside, Conservative Political Centre, 1984

† Labour's Charter for the Environment, Labour Party, 1985

† Andrew Sullivan, Greening the Tories: New Policies on the Environment, Centre for Policy Studies, 1985

† Social Democratic Party, Conservation and Change: Policy for the Environment, SDP, 1985

† Liberal Party, An Environment for the Future, Liberal Party, 1986

† Conservative Research Department, 'Protecting the Environment', Politics Today, October 1986

1988–1990

† Margaret Thatcher's speech to the Royal Society, September 1988

* Green Democrats, 1988

* Tory Green Initiative, 1988

† Barry Bracewell-Milnes, Caring for the Countryside, Social Affairs Unit, 1988

† Labour Party, 'A better quality of life', Report of the Policy Review Group on the Physical and Social Environment in Meet the Challenge: Make the Change, Labour Party, 1989

† Nicholas Ridley, Policies Against Pollution, Centre for Policy Studies, 1989

† John Redwood, Rebuilding Britain: Can 'Greenery' and Growth be Reconciled?, Conservative Political Centre, 1989

† Tony Paterson, The Green Conservative, Bow Paper, 1989

† Robert Whelan, Mounting Greenery, Institute for Economic Affairs Education Unit, 1989

† Conservative Research Department, The Green Party and the Environment, CRD, 1989

† Susan Owens et al., Green Taxes, Institute for Public Policy Research, 1990

† Richard Ehrman, Nimbyism: The Disease and the Cure, Centre for Policy Studies, 1990

† Labour Party, An Earthly Chance, Labour Party, 1990

† Liberal Democrats, What Price Our Planet?, The Association of Liberal and Social Democrat Councillors, 1990

Radical groups that rejected such incorporation were of marginal significance. They did not turn to the existing political parties which were seen to be too deeply implicated in the destructive growth trajectories of contemporary society. Rather, they pursued various types of fringe alternative politics. One such initiative was the setting up in 1973 of an alternative political party, the Green Party. Despite being the oldest of its kind in Western Europe, for a variety of reasons – including lack of support from the environmental lobby and the daunting barrier of Britain's electoral system – it did not present a significant challenge to the established parties during the 1970s (Rüdig and Lowe 1986). Indeed, unlike many other West European countries, the party politicisation of the environment in Britain has not come about through the established parties having to respond to the threat posed by an ascendant green party. On the contrary, it was the increasing prominence of the environment in mainstream politics that helped the British Greens emerge from their obscurity in the late 1980s.

That politicisation of the environment in the 1980s, in turn, sprang from the mounting frustrations at the diminishing scope for environmental reformism in the late 1970s and early 1980s. The stagflation, recession and mass unemployment of the period undermined the political consensus on which the key post-war policies for social and economic management had been built. Environmental policy did not escape unscathed.

The most general consequence was a slow-down in public and private investments in both pollution control and environmental improvements. Pressure mounted from industrialists for relief from environmental controls, and government showed great reluctance to press clean-up measures on firms hit by recession. Tight restrictions on public expenditure and an unwillingness to see any additional burdens placed on the private sector effectively halted the flow of environmental reforms. Steadily a backlog mounted of recommendations for new measures from various advisory bodies, inquiries and consultative exercises, and in such contexts environmentalists increasingly found a much less sympathetic response to their arguments. Inevitably this provoked some disillusion.

The implementation and elaboration of environmental policies encountered not only an adverse economic climate in the late 1970s, but also the political resurgence of business interests alarmed by the 'limits to growth' debate, and the emergence of 'new right' politicians unsympathetic to business regulation and dirigistic policies of any kind. These counter-pressures had a considerable impact particularly on thinking within the Conservative Party, and the advent of the Thatcher government marked a low ebb in the influence of the environmental lobby (Lowe and Flynn 1989).

The initial instincts of the Thatcher government towards environmental controls were perhaps best captured in leaked Cabinet papers which recorded the intention of her first administration to 'reduce over-sensitivity to environmental considerations' (Sunday Times, 18 November 1979). This largely entailed pressures on regulatory agencies to minimise the burdens placed on business – pressures that were reinforced by cuts in their budget and staff and changes in the composition of their governing councils and advisory boards in favour of business interests. Neo-liberal ideas were most strenuously brought to bear on land-use planning, and here deregulation was explicitly pursued as a political priority. In relation to economic and industrial policy also, there was little sympathy with any controls perceived to obstruct growth or development. As the White Paper *Lifting the Burden* (1985) asserted: 'Too many people in central and local government spend too much of their time regulating the activities of others.' Central units were therefore established in all the major departments to scrutinise new and existing regulations, to report to Ministers on the compliance costs imposed on industry, with a specific Minister nominated in each department to pursue the matter.

Within this adverse political context, environmentalists also faced somewhat diminished opportunities for consultation and reduced levels of formal political access. The early years of the Thatcher government saw the sweeping away of a fair number of the advisory bodies set up during the previous decade to incorporate environmental interests into policy making. These victims of 'quangocide' included the Clean Air Council, the Noise Advisory Council, the Commission on Energy and the Environment, the Water Space Amenity Commission and area archaeology advisory committees. The much-publicised attack on quangos did not, overall, see a massive fall in the number of non-departmental public bodies, but rather some selective political surgery (Hood 1980). The bodies that were wound up were mainly the smaller ones, which although lacking an executive function had often provided points of access for various interest groups. Significantly, across sectors, the culling of quangos was most energetically pursued by the Secretary of State for the Environment (at the time, Michael Heseltine).

Environmental groups responded to this reduction in access and influence by a shift in tactics. In general, they tended to adopt a more populist style of campaigning relying on the strength of their popular support and the media attention they could attract. The newer groups, particularly Greenpeace and Friends of the Earth, led the way in this direction, and profited through strong membership growth. Many of the older conservation and amenity groups also assumed a much higher public profile and adopted more adversarial, media-oriented tactics, while taking care, to varying degrees, not to disrupt their established relationships with government or to alienate the sympathy of their more conservative members.

The somewhat diminished consultation opportunities and reduced levels of formalised access to central government were also offset by the extension of other arenas of influence. The new system of parliamentary select committees introduced in 1979, for example, increased opportunities for groups to promote their views and influence parliamentary opinion. Through the urban greening movement, local government assumed a new salience for environmental lobbying. Key public inquiries assumed even greater significance not only for expressing opposition to controversial developments but also for the opportunity provided to challenge the policies on which they were based. Last but not least, the

European Community provided environmental groups with major new arenas in which to pursue their concerns and exert influence, not only over European policy, but also over the context in which domestic policies would be determined. With many groups thus presenting a much more aggressive and confrontational style, with the general shift towards more open lobbying, with many individual politicians being drawn into environmental conflicts, and in the context of the most highly polarised party politics for fifty years, the scene was set for the party politicisation of the environment.

The Environmental Debate in the Conservative Party

Each party has responded to environmental concerns somewhat differently, though broadly within the temporal pattern outlined at the beginning of this chapter. A full account would want to review these separate responses, but in the rest of the chapter we concentrate just on that of the Conservative Party. This was the party of government during the 1980s, so its response to environmental problems was arguably the most consequential. It was the last party in Britain to seek to identify itself with environmental concern and, in keeping with right-wing and Christian Democrat parties elsewhere, it has experienced some difficulty in absorbing such concern. Nevertheless (or perhaps as a consequence), the Conservative Party has hosted the liveliest debate of any party (with the possible exception of the Green Party) on the desirable means and ends of environmental policy. In so far as the party has also been the vehicle for 'new right' neo-liberalism, whose ascendancy helped to terminate the environmental reformism of the 1960s and 1970s, it is to its internal debates that we should perhaps look for a denouement in the struggle between the advocates of free markets and of sustainability. In examining the evolving debate within the party we will employ the time frame set out in Table 1.

THE LATE 1970S

The 1970s witnessed the development of a fringe involvement with ecological politics in each of the major parties. This was in response to the 'limits to growth' debate. Given the anti-market rhetoric of that debate it is perhaps not surprising that it evoked minimal sympathy in the ranks of the Conservative Party. Thus of the three ginger groups, the Socialist Environment and Resources Association (formed in 1973), the Liberal Ecology Group (1977) and the Conservative Ecology Group (1977), the third one was the last to be formed and was the least substantial, although all three lacked any official status within their respective parties. Arguably, the greatest impact was on the Liberal Party whose 1979 Assembly approved a motion that 'sustained economic growth, as conventionally measured, is neither feasible nor desirable'. The Liberal leadership, however, steered the party away from the idea of a stationary state economy and such radicalism was submerged by the centrist alliance forged in 1981 with the newly formed Social Democratic Party.

The Conservative Ecology Group (CEG) was set up in 1977 by a married couple, Richard and Caroline Williams, who were members of the party in Hampshire. By 1979 it claimed to have a membership of 367 with a core of twenty activists and the support of fifteen MPs and one Peer. The Williamses had previously had some involvement with the Ecology (now Green) Party but saw no prospect of it making a breakthrough in the medium term: 'The initiative for ecological reforms through political action will therefore remain with the ecopolitical groups within the main parties.'[1]

One of the CEG's first actions was to publish an appeal for the Conservative Party to establish a Commission to investigate the claims made in the Limits to Growth book. The Group itself did 'not yet take a dogmatic position on the growth question' although many of its members did 'suspect that growth is probably not sustainable'.[2] It was anxious to stress, however, that:

> We are not anti-capitalist. We believe in a sustainable form of capitalism which will be increasingly sensitive to the constraints of the biosphere. We therefore propose the absolute minimum social change consistent with the need to adapt ... We are not anti-technology, indeed we believe that our society can only be saved by advances in technology, allied to the ecological perspective to use it wisely. We are not advocating a significant drop in the average standard of living. We do not just believe in 'survival' but in survival with comfort.[3]

The CEG's main function was to print and distribute short discussion papers on ecological matters to Conservative MPs and the press. It is difficult to discern any influence it achieved in this regard. The Group's efforts did elicit a message of support from Margaret Thatcher recalling her role as Environment spokesman for the party (in 1974) before becoming party leader. 'I think it is important that Conservatives be identified with pressure to improve the environment,' she averred, but added that: 'Our economic weakness is a hindrance in much that we would wish to do towards improving the environment.'[4] With its ambivalence towards economic growth and its social conservatism ('We do not believe that individuals or institutions should be disturbed any more than is necessary'),[5] the CEG was unlikely to have any impact on the party leadership's gathering neo-liberal radicalism.

The CEG, though, did manage in a minor way to insert a Conservative voice into political ecological circles. Overtures to the Socialist Environment and Resources Association and the Liberal Ecology Group were rebuffed. But the CEG maintained a Conservative presence in such cross-party groups as the Parliamentary Liaison Group on Alternative Energy Strategies and the Green Alliance. Its impact on Conservative opinion, however, must be judged to have been minimal.

1981–2

The early 1980s were not an auspicious period in which to press the priority of environmental concerns within the Conservative Party. The government was forging ahead with its radical economic measures, the economy was in recession, unemployment was mounting, and 1981 saw riots and civil disorder in several cities. The monetarist rigour of the government's fiscal policy caused deep dissension within the party reaching right into the cabinet. The Labour Party was equally divided, and, with a growing polarisation of party politics, the Social Democratic Party was launched with the object of 'breaking the mould'. The argument over nuclear defence reached its height, with the government committed to Trident missiles and the deployment of Cruise in Europe, and a unilateralist Labour Party opposed to both.

A lack of grassroots interest in environmental issues at this time in the Conservative Party can be deduced from the volume of resolutions on the subject to the Annual Conference. Regularly, a handful were put forward from constituency parties covering such topics as protection of the countryside, coastal protection and pollution. In the first few years of the Thatcher government, however, most of the resolutions for debate in the Environment and Local Government section were preoccupied with the financing, expenditure and performance of local authorities. Between 1979 and 1983, for example, there were between 48 and 124 resolutions on local government and between 11 and 26 on the environment.

The government had committed itself, while in opposition, to take action on certain issues where it had been critical of Labour's efforts. The two major outstanding issues in the environmental field were protection for rural landscapes and habitats (where action was also dictated in part by the EC Birds Directive) and the establishment of a National Heritage Memorial Fund (in the wake of the Mentmore débâcle) independent of Treasury control. The National Heritage Act 1980 and the Wildlife and Countryside Act 1981 allowed Michael Heseltine, the Secretary of State for the Environment, to remark: 'Even in our present difficult financial circumstances we have not ignored the need to protect and conserve our environment' (quoted in Johnson 1981, p. 4).

The first of these two measures was well received, but the second provoked considerable criticism from conservation groups. In addition, there was mounting antipathy amongst environmental groups to the consequences of public expenditure cuts (particularly as they affected the work of regulatory agencies), liberalising programmes (especially in relation to the planning system), the abolition of various advisory bodies, and the government's ambitious nuclear programme (it was proposed to build ten reactors by the early 1990s, and to switch to the controversial Pressurised Water Reactor design).

Recognition that a considered response might be needed to the government's environmental critics came with an issue of *Politics Today* on the environment prepared by the Conservative Research Department (1982). It presented a miscellaneous list of policies and actions ranging from reform of the planning system to recreational provision, with no attempt at systematisation. If there was a guiding principle, it was a statement by Heseltine that 'A civilised environment depends above all on the economic base which supports it' (Conservative Research Department 1982, p. 2).

An attempt to forge a more coherent Conservative response to environmental concerns came at this time from outside the party's mainstream. In 1981, Stanley Johnson, a Conservative Member of the European Parliament and former head of the European Commission's Pollution Prevention Division, published *Caring for the Environment: A Policy for Conservatives* which was issued jointly by the Conservative Political Centre and the European Democratic Group. Johnson argued that economic restructuring was both removing some longstanding sources of pollution and generating new industries that were much more environmentally attuned, and that a programme to improve environmental quality could strengthen the nation's economy. But he also sought to link environmental concern with traditional Tory values: 'The sense that we hold land on trust for posterity and that we should not therefore permit random destruction and degradation is very much part of the Conservative spirit' (Johnson 1981, p. 7).

It is evident, however, that Johnson perceived the incumbent leadership to be deviating from that spirit, and in a thinly-veiled attack on the contemporary direction of the party, he commented: 'The provision of a decent environment can be seen – like the provision of health and education – as a goal to which thinking (or "One Nation") Conservatives can easily subscribe' (Johnson 1981, pp. 7–8). 'A laissez faire approach is no more acceptable here than in other areas of policy,' he added (Johnson 1981, p. 11). Rather than attack the government outright, however, he turned to the American Right to challenge their arguments about excessive environmental regulation. Johnson countered that the principle of 'the polluter pays' was consistent with Conservative philosophy and should be widely applied. At present pollution costs were not internalised as a charge on production, but if they were, then the most polluting processes would yield the most expensive products. With its attack on neo-liberal ideas, however, Johnson's critique must be seen as less an attempt to influence the thinking within the leadership, than to signal alternative directions for the party. As such, and coming from a 'wet' MEP, it could hardly be expected to have a significant impact on prevailing party policy, even with a foreword from Michael Heseltine.

A view from a different perspective, and one more likely to command the government's attention, came from Barry Bracewell-Milnes, a staunchly right-wing adviser on fiscal policy, in an Institute of Economic Affairs publication, Land and Heritage: The Public Interest in Personal Ownership (1982). Drawing on traditional justifications of private property, he argued that: 'Among the friends of conservation, the most committed are the personal owners. They have reason to be. Most heritage assets are personal assets and thus more valuable to the owner than anyone else' (Bracewell-Milnes 1982, p. 80). This very much mirrored the stance the government had taken on the Wildlife and Countryside Bill. Bracewell-Milnes advocated additionally that tax burdens and bureaucratic constraints on private landowners should be eased. The exercise of personal ownership could be relied on to mitigate economic and environmental problems. Conflicts of interest surrounding a piece of land, for example, 'can be lessened or even resolved if there is a superior landlord with an interest in the preservation and improvement of the property as a whole' (Bracewell-Milnes 1982, p. 49). Likewise, the key to resolving disputes over externalities, Bracewell-Milnes reasoned, lay in the exercise of property rights. Such disputes could only be solved when one of the parties waives part of their rights; for example, a farmer pays compensation for polluting a neighbouring garden or the neighbour compensates the farmer for not carrying out the activity, the outcome depending on whether the farmer has the right to carry out the operation or the neighbour the right to stop it.

While Bracewell-Milnes was more in tune with the party leadership than Johnson, the lack of political interest in the environment at the highest level at this time is best captured by a throwaway remark made by the Prime Minister at the height of the Falklands War: 'It's exciting to have a real crisis on your hands,' she told the Annual Conference of the Scottish Conservative Party, 'when you've spent half your political life dealing with humdrum issues like the environment' – a reference, it seems, to the months she spent as shadow Environment Secretary in 1974.

1984–6

The first sign of a shift in outlook of the Conservative leadership towards the environment occurred after the 1983 election, in the following year. At this time, Mrs Thatcher's second administration, embroiled in the miners' strike and beset by industrial problems, was attracting much adverse publicity at home and abroad over issues such as acid rain and nuclear wastes. The Royal Commission on Environmental Pollution had accused it of being complacent, and campaigners claimed that Britain was increasingly becoming 'The dirty man of Europe'. Backbench Conservative MPs, especially in the shires, began to signal their unease at the impact of government policies on the environment, particularly in relation to the countryside. A key development was the watering down of two 1984 Circulars

on *Green Belts* and *Land for Housing* after more than sixty Tory MPs had registered their opposition to the first drafts in support of a campaign in favour
of retaining strict land-use controls in rural areas, orchestrated by the
Council for the Protection of Rural England. The Conservative-dominated
parliamentary select committee on the environment, under its chairman
Sir Hugh Rossi, chose to investigate three conservation issues in
succession: the Green Belt; acid rain; and the operation of the Wildlife and
Countryside Act.

In the early summer of 1984, the Prime Minister was widely reported
to be revising her opinion of the political significance of environmental
issues. This followed a trip to West Germany where the Greens had recently
enjoyed an electoral breakthrough and fellow right-wingers warned her
not to underestimate the electoral potential of environmental concern. In
an article headed 'Tories seek to win environmentalist vote', the *Financial
Times* (16 July 1984) speculated that it was only a matter of time before
'green' electoral pressures built up in Britain but that the most likely ben-
eficiary would be the Alliance (between the Liberal and Social Democratic
Parties) rather than the diminutive Ecology Party (as the Green Party was
then known).

The Alliance had not made the electoral gains that it had hoped in the
general election despite polling 25·4 per cent of the vote. Nevertheless, it
was now positioned as the main contender for many Conservative seats
across much of rural and suburban England. One leading Liberal was reported as saying: 'If you take a map and look at the 280-odd seats where
the Alliance came second, you will notice they are almost all in the green
and pleasant bits where the environment is a strong issue. The Tories have
just realised the countryside is no longer entirely safe territory' (*Sunday
Times*, 28 October 1984). The Prime Minister – 'persuaded by party man-
agers and advisors that the Conservative Party should give high priority to
the capture of the "green" vote' (Paterson 1984, p. 3) – convened a series
of ministerial meetings and briefings to examine Britain's environmental
policy. The range of issues covered included acid rain, nuclear power and
rural conservation (*Observer*, 3 June 1984). The government's response concentrated on efforts to improve its image.

Within the Department of the Environment a new conservation policy
propaganda unit was created, modelled on a similar unit dealing with local government issues. The unit was to have three tasks: to co-ordinate government activity on the environment; to alert Ministers about issues affecting their departments; and to identify issues before they came on to the
public agenda (*Financial Times*, 16 July 1984). Internal government discussions centred on 'a more positive and integrated presentation of policy on
safeguarding the environment' and preparing new initiatives 'in areas of
public concern on which some action may be possible without incurring

disproportionate costs'. There was no wish to open up a wide-ranging review of policy that might cause interdepartmental conflict or ministerial squabbling and so the potentially more controversial topics, such as transport and energy, were deliberately sidestepped. A number of initiatives did follow: a unified pollution inspectorate was created (a reform for which the Royal Commission on Environmental Pollution had long been pressing); and the severe budgetary squeeze on the environmental quangos was relaxed.

The most significant changes came in the agricultural field. The Tory Right already had in its targets the extensive supports for farm production, and the Prime Minister was credited with the belief that 'an attack on farmers' privileges is long overdue' (*Sunday Times*, 19 February 1984). Subsequently it was reported that 'Mrs Thatcher has instructed the Agriculture Minister, Mr Michael Jopling, to draw up specific proposals to counter the rapid increase in popular support for the conservation movement' (*Guardian*, 12 April 1984). Some of the early changes included the introduction of Environmentally Sensitive Areas to pay farmers to conserve traditional landscapes, and cuts in farm grants and a shift in their orientation to favour protection of the countryside. An environmental co-ordination unit was set up within the Ministry of Agriculture, and the 1986 Agriculture Act placed new duties on relevant ministers to achieve a balance among the conservation and promotion of the enjoyment of the countryside, the support of a stable and efficient agricultural industry, and the economic and social interests of rural areas.

With the previous indifference to environmental concerns of the Conservative leadership dispelled, pro-environmental elements within the party took heart. The subject, indeed, became something of a rallying ground for those in the party – the so-called wets – who felt unease at the overriding commitment to free market ideas and at the Prime Minister's domineering style of conviction politics. Environmental problems seemed to be the nemesis of such ideas, and the cause of environmental protection seemed to call for a return to a more consensual style of public-interest politics.

1984 saw the publication of two major statements on environmental policy from figures on the left of the party. Both based their argument on claims of a long-standing and deep-rooted affinity between traditional Tory philosophy and conservationists' concerns. As Tony Paterson, a solicitor and parliamentary liaison officer for the Bow Group, put it: 'green voters and Conservative voters share an instinct for preserving what is good and fine and traditional around us. The nature conservationist is a natural Conservative' (Paterson 1984, p. 3). But the party ran the risk of seeming to be divorced from this tradition and becoming too closely associated with development interests. In the words of Kenneth Carlisle, MP for Lincoln and PPS to the Minister of State at the Home Office, 'In the public eye we are too often seen as not really caring for the future of the countryside, and of only taking action when it is forced upon us' (Carlisle 1984, p. 6). The two authors proposed overlapping agendas – including reform of the Wildlife and Countryside Act, changes to agriculture and forestry policies to make them more environmentally friendly, improvements to the planning system, and curbs on the public funding of wetland drainage – to reassert the Conservatives' paternalistic traditions and to counteract growing concern for the plight of the environment.

This gathering consensus on the left of the party did stimulate a response from the right but this in turn revealed the lack of a distinctly new right agenda on the environment. As Andrew Sullivan, author of a pamphlet on *Greening the Tories* for the Thatcherite think tank, the Centre for Policy Studies, conceded: 'To be green is to be wet' (Sullivan 1985, p. 27). Sullivan was a postgraduate student who had recently been President of the Oxford Union and was an occasional leader writer for the *Daily Telegraph*. His analysis borrowed heavily from the paternalistic perspective, emphasising the traditional Conservative links to a national culture that was deeply attached to the past and valued its physical surroundings – 'the small, immediate details of our lives' (Sullivan 1985, p. 6). But in calling for an approach to environmental policy that would 'correspond with conservative sentiments among ordinary people' (Sullivan 1985, pp. 18–19), he sought to associate the preservationist instinct with Thatcherite populism, identifying the extension of private property ownership as 'the best way to combine human nature with environmental protection, to create proper and enduring links between people and their surroundings, and to protect our towns and countryside' (Sullivan 1985, p. 20). Sullivan also sought to distinguish such deep-rooted proprietorial concern – from which perspective the environment was 'not a liberal or intellectual abstraction but a detailed and humane reality' (Sullivan 1985, p. 44) – from the radical green politics of continental Europe. 'The much publicised German "green conscience"', with its 'manic extremes', 'near-fascist sentiments' and its apocryphal visions, he thus contrasted with 'the virtually ignored English "green sensibility"' (Sullivan 1985, p. 14). The latter revealed itself in an ingrained sensitivity 'to our cultural past and present' (Sullivan 1985, p. 17), which fortunately displayed 'no evidence of some sweeping, Teutonic paranoia, or of alternative-lifers concerned with the future of the ozone layer having anything but the mildest influence on popular culture and attitudes' (Sullivan 1985, p. 6). Like the other pamphleteers, Sullivan warned the Conservative leadership of looming electoral problems if it failed to take the environment more seriously. 'In vulnerable, marginal, Alliance-threatened suburbia, the image of a property-developing, polluting government is likely to prove disastrous in an election,' he prophesied, adding that 'The green issue will not go away. The correct and healthy Tory reaction is to expropriate it' (Sullivan 1985, p. 44).

The other parties did perceive the environment as a matter of growing concern. 1985 saw the publication of major statements from the Labour Party and the Social Democratic Party, each attacking the government's record and each setting out an array of alternative policies. The Times described the SDP's document as the 'most complete and coherent set of policy proposals on the environment' of any party (28 August 1985). The following spring the Liberal Party followed suit.

The fact that by now all the main opposition parties had issued policy statements did not elicit an equivalent response from the Conservatives. Ministers and party leaders were conscious of the government's image on the environment and, as we have seen, had taken certain steps to improve that image. An issue of Politics Today reiterated in bullish terms the government's record. But the apparent unwillingness of the party leadership openly to identify with popular concerns in this field led the environment correspondent of the Daily Telegraph (a paper traditionally very close to the party) to bemoan the lack of a clear statement of where they stood (4 October 1986).

The nearest the Conservatives came to such a statement was in the government's formal response to the World Conservation Strategy. The British approach to the environment was said to rest upon three strands:

– the importance of knowledge and a strong science base, coupled with an awareness of our ignorance;

– the need to involve people, to recognise their interests and aspirations and to obtain their willing co-operation;

– and the need for balance and the avoidance of extremes (Department of the Environment News Release 297, 28 May 1986).

The cautiousness evident in this statement of principles reflected a growing defensiveness on the government's part, confronted as it was by mounting pressure in various international fora for demonstrative action on issues such as acid rain, CFCs and the dumping of sewage sludge in the North Sea. The government's general stance belied the accompanying message from the Environment Minister, William Waldegrave, that 'concern for living resources, for the environment itself, must not be a bolt on extra. It must become one of the basic assumptions by which all communities – local, national and international – live.'

It was certainly not apparent that Waldegrave's ministerial colleagues shared this commitment. And if they did, it was not evident at the crucial 1986 party conference when the government renewed its crusading, liberalising zeal, under the banner 'The Next Step Forward'. There were far fewer motions on the environment that year than in 1984 and 1985 and, unlike in those years, the subject was not chosen as a theme for debate.

The omission was critical at a conference that was seen as setting the seal on a new phase of Thatcherite radicalism and as presenting a dress rehearsal for the next general election which was bound to fall during the European Year of the Environment. With inflation at its lowest level for more than twenty years, with the record level of unemployment just beginning to subside, and following a tax-cutting spring budget, the government went to the country in June 1987. The election, which focused on the government's record on the economy and public services, resulted in Margaret Thatcher's third successive victory. Though the environment did not figure significantly in the campaign, all the manifestos covered the respective policies in some detail. Government sensitivity to the electoral consequences of environmental protest was additionally revealed in the decision, hastily announced the month before the election, to abandon the four sites being investigated for their potential suitability for shallow disposal of low-level nuclear waste, all of which were in constituencies held by Conservative Ministers and MPs.

1988–1990

The re-emergence of environmental debate within the Conservative Party during Thatcher's third administration followed a remarkably similar pattern to that during her second administration. As before, after about a year in office, the leadership signalled its recognition of the potential importance of the issue, precipitating a wider debate within the party, including another flurry of pamphlets and motions to the annual conference, but culminating once again in an ambivalent stance by the leadership. There were crucial differences from the second administration, however. First of all, the cycle began this time around with Margaret Thatcher publicly identifying herself with environmental concern, which considerably raised the profile and status of the issue both within and outside the party. This drew some of the party's senior figures into the debate. For the first time, also, the new right was provoked into making a sustained response to the issue. Finally, the focus of the debate was broadened to encompass the global environment as well as the more traditional Tory themes of countryside, amenity and heritage, with Thatcher here too showing the lead.

The speech that Margaret Thatcher gave to the Royal Society in September 1988, therefore, which was greeted as her first on the subject, was an event of considerable significance. Before reviewing the speech, its provenance and its consequences, however, we turn to consider a series of acrimonious exchanges between her Secretary of State for the Environment and one of his predecessors to reveal some of the internal tensions within the party which traditional environmental concerns were engendering.

The Heseltine–Ridley Debate

As the economy boomed, the volume of construction and infrastructural work expanded, in a context in which any semblance of regional planning had been abandoned and in which local authorities, with diminished planning powers, faced strong pressures from central government to be responsive to developers. The sheer scale of development began to provoke a reaction, especially amongst many Conservative supporters in the outer suburbs of the South East and the shire counties. The development-versus-environment controversy within the Conservative ranks became embroiled in a wider debate about the direction of the party, a debate which was implicitly about the party's future course, post-Thatcher.

Foremost amongst the protagonists were Michael Heseltine MP who, having stormed out of the Cabinet in January 1986 in protest against Thatcher's style of leadership, was engaged in an undeclared campaign for the leadership, and Nicholas Ridley, an outspoken free-marketeer and close ally of Thatcher who occupied the position of Secretary of State for the Environment that Heseltine himself had once occupied. To Heseltine, wishing to focus dissent within the party, the cause of protecting the rural environment from excessive development was an attractive issue on which the government was unpopular, not least amongst many of its supporters and backbenchers. To the MP for Henley, a well-preserved commuter town in the South East, the issue was an obvious choice, especially with strong local opposition to proposals for a private new settlement on the edge of the constituency. It was also a ready-made issue through which to signal dissent from Thatcherism without appearing to be overtly disloyal, because it clearly indicated some of the limits of a free market philosophy and was already imbued with alternative visions of Toryism through the efforts of centre-left pamphleteers. And a staunchly Thatcherite Environment Secretary, who had given encouragement to schemes for private new settlements in the South East, presented a suitable surrogate target for criticism.

A series of open letters between the two men began with Heseltine declaring his concern at the action of greedy developers and his fear that the South East was being 'torn up and torn apart' in the building of new towns and villages (Independent, 14 March 1988). Ridley responded by pointing out that Heseltine himself, when Environment Secretary, had raised house-building levels in Berkshire by 8,000 over what the county council had felt was needed and had sought to 'sweep away obstacles to commercial enterprise'. Emphasising the need for additional housing provision in the South East, Ridley declared: 'Housing is not a form of environmental pollution. It is about people and families, where they work and where they live' (Independent, 19 March 1988).

Heseltine was undeterred by such criticism and, in responding, sought to develop an alternative agenda to Thatcherism, one which emphasised a positive role for the state in economic and environmental management by, for example, directing development towards the more depressed parts of the country. Heseltine focused his attack on the operation of the planning system, claiming that when he had been in charge developers had found it less easy to gain planning approval than under Ridley (the chances of a successful appeal against a local planning authority decision had gone up from 30 to 40 per cent). More fundamentally, he charged that market forces could not redress regional imbalance and that government intervention was therefore necessary (*Guardian*, 11 and 12 April 1988).

While Heseltine was establishing his position as a Conservative champion of the environment (*Daily Telegraph*, 21 July 1989), the hapless Ridley was appearing increasingly out of touch with popular sentiments. A backbench group of Conservative MPs, led by Heseltine's lieutenant, Michael Mates, formed SANE Planning to co-ordinate opposition to the Minister's house-building and planning policies for the South East. Ridley also came under attack from environmentalists for his seeming indifference to a number of problems, particularly those highlighted by Britain's failure to comply with European Community directives such as those on drinking water and bathing beaches. With calls for his removal coming from a number of directions, including right-wing newspapers, Ridley was shifted from the Department of the Environment in July 1989. That Thatcher had to take this action against a Minister who was one of her closest allies was in no small measure a consequence of the speech she had made ten months earlier that had focused political attention on the environment and had thus attracted critical scrutiny of her government's record in this field.

Thatcher's Royal Society Speech

The speech that Margaret Thatcher gave to the annual dinner of the Royal Society on 27 September 1988 has subsequently been accorded extra ordinary significance, but at the time it took environmentalists and political commentators completely unawares. Referring to the build-up of atmospheric pollution she raised the possibility that 'we have unwittingly begun a massive experiment with the system of this planet itself ', and declared her commitment to protecting the balance of nature.

Though these remarks were subsequently presented as marking a decisive, even epochal, turning point – 'the moment,' according to Charles Clover of the *Daily Telegraph*, 'when environmental issues truly became part of the mainstream of domestic and indeed international affairs' (30 December 1989) – the circumstances and content of the speech suggest a spirit more of 'testing the water' than of seizing the initiative.

First of all, the speech was delivered not to a political forum, but to a scientific one. Secondly, the environmental pronouncements came in the final quarter of a speech, the bulk of which was devoted to familiar themes concerning the funding of basic research. Thirdly, the Downing Street press office did not give it the advanced billing or treatment that might have been expected of a major speech. In consequence, the following day most of the press gave it little prominence. The Times and the Daily Mail did cover it on the front pages, but only the Daily Telegraph made it the main story, under the headline 'Tories "going for the green vote": Thatcher fears for the future of the planet'. It was thus not until two days after the speech that the press, picking up on the Telegraph's lead, accorded it significant coverage, including a rash of editorials.

Though the speech might be (and have been intended to be) interpreted as a bid to seize the high ground in the environmental debate for the Conservatives, such a gambit was not without risks. First, it presented hostages to fortune, and aroused expectations that the government might find hard to fulfil. In addition, for a self-proclaimed conviction politician as she, there was the double risk that such a major departure would sow doubts about her resoluteness and would not itself carry conviction. As Jonathon Porritt, then director of Friends of the Earth, commented:

> This was not an easy speech for Mrs. Thatcher to make; only a couple of years ago she was referring to environmentalists as 'the enemy within' and will now be hard put to deny suggestions of a major volte-face. What's more, given the Government's record to date, people are unlikely to settle for fine words. (The Times, 29 September 1988)

Inevitably, therefore, there was speculation amongst political commentators about the motives behind the speech. The Times and the Independent, for example, treated it as a spoiler for the address to be given by Paddy Ashdown two days later as leader of the Liberal Democrats (the newly merged centre party) at their first annual conference – Ashdown had already spoken of the importance of the environment for the new party, and in his leadership address he did, indeed, declare that the 'green approach' would be at the core of the party's political identity (Independent, 30 September 1988).

The Financial Times pointed to the extensive media coverage over the summer of ecological stories that had wrong-footed Ministers, such as the seal deaths in the North Sea and the peregrinations of the toxic waste ship the Karin B, but also to internal pressures within the Conservative Party: 'The word is that Mrs. Thatcher was taken completely by surprise by the vehemence of the feeling in her own party about the extent of new development in England's green and pleasant land' (Financial Times, 29 September 1988). There were seventy-three environment motions on the agenda for the forthcoming party conference expressing concern about issues ranging from erosion of green areas to dumping of waste and pollution of beaches. At a fringe meeting, Michael Heseltine was to develop his vision of 'the generous society' including a fairer distribution of wealth and improvements in public service, but also embracing a moral responsibility for the natural world, for, 'Just as our Tory philosophy asserts the obligations of privileged and wealthy individuals towards society, so that same philosophy lays obligations on the more prosperous governments to the planet itself' (Guardian, 12 October 1988). As well as setting out his principles for environmental action, Heseltine implied that it was he who had given a lead to the party on this issue. But Mrs Thatcher was not to be upstaged, and in her address to the conference, she took the protection of the environment as her central theme. Developing the ideas presented in the Royal Society speech, she declared: 'It is we Conservatives who are not merely Friends of the Earth. We are its guardians and trustees for generations to come.'

The specific agenda that Thatcher defined points to other important considerations. The environmental issues to which she referred – the greenhouse gases, the hole in the ozone layer and acid deposition – were all international problems rooted in scientific diagnoses. This agenda, therefore, pitched as it was above the level of domestic politics, simply sidestepped the planning and conservation issues raised by left-wing Tory critics and amplified by Heseltine. At the same time, it underlined both her role as a world leader and her identity as Britain's only scientifically-trained Prime Minister. In the words of a Daily Telegraph editorial, 'Mrs. Thatcher has used the grasp of a former research scientist and her high international standing to deliver, in the right company, a warning to all humankind' (29 September 1988). In this way, her new-found concern could be projected as a high-minded initiative; but it was also a natural progression, with the defence of the global environment, which she herself declared to be 'one of the great challenges of the late Twentieth Century', offering a suitably bracing prospect for her as she approached her tenth anniversary in office confident of having tackled Britain's own economic and social malaise.

The 1980s had seen a gathering tide of international diplomacy on the environment culminating in June 1988 when, at the Toronto summit, Mrs Thatcher along with other western leaders had endorsed the Brundtland report (of the World Commission on Environment and Development) and its concept of sustainable development. There was a sense, though, that Britain was being overtaken by the pace of events, and Thatcher's Royal Society speech, which reiterated her government's commitment to 'sustainable economic development', can be seen as part of a more general response by the British government in seeking to regain the initiative where it had gained a reputation for procrastination. In international negotiations on issues such as acid rain and CFCs the British government had indeed held out for more conclusive scientific evidence before sanctioning action, and even then had sought to establish looser targets and timetables than had other countries. Environmentalists had become increasingly critical of what they saw as a tendency to prevaricate – to use scientific uncertainty as a pretext for political inaction in defence of vested industrial interests – and even the Prince of Wales had voiced his disquiet (at the North Sea Summit in November 1987).

Not only was there a general need to restore Britain's credibility, but on the looming issue of global warming a rearguard stance was less of an option than for previous problems. An international scientific consensus was gaining momentum more rapidly, with British scientists playing a leading role, and, though the implications were much more profound, Britain did not find itself so much on the defensive. As one environmental campaigner has put it, 'Margaret Thatcher was able to hoist the Union Jack on the issue of global warming because, unlike acid rain, sewage or water pollution, Britain's emissions of greenhouse gases had not yet got it into serious trouble with its neighbours or the rest of the world' (Rose 1990, p. 265). But the phenomenon of global warming was also a complex scientific problem and this enabled Mrs Thatcher to restate a traditional theme: 'We must ensure,' she told her Royal Society audience, 'that what we do is founded on good science to establish cause and effect.'

The reaction to the speech was a mixture of astonishment, praise and scepticism. Both the Guardian and the Daily Telegraph characterised her shift of attitude as Damascene. But talk of a conversion and general applause for the Prime Minister's expressed sentiments were accompanied by questioning of her motives and her sincerity. Environmentalists (with the notable exception of Greenpeace) gave the speech a guarded welcome, hoping that the indifference, even apathy, previously shown by ministers to many of their concerns, would at last give way to a more sympathetic attitude. Nigel Haigh of the Institute for European Environmental Policy commented: 'Up till now being an environmentalist in Britain has been like being a Christian in Rome when his religion was proscribed ... But now environmentalism is official' (quoted in the Independent, 29 September 1988).

There seemed to be no doubts that the speech had raised the environment to the top of the political agenda, with significant implications for government policy and for Britain's stance in various international negotiations. From scientists and environmentalists, in particular, there were calls for the Prime Minister's words to be matched with resources and action. As Jonathon Porritt, remarked, 'It is important that she is concentrating on climate change because it implies wide-ranging policy changes' (quoted in Daily Telegraph, 28 September 1988).

But such a profound shift of outlook arguably also needed fresh leadership to carry it through. As the Guardian observed, 'if Mrs Thatcher really means business, Mr Ridley looks more than ever like the wrong man for the job', not least because of his 'record of long disdain for environmental campaigners' (29 September 1988). But such a remark could have been made of Thatcher herself, and indeed the speech immediately drew the fire of all the other parties, pouring scorn on the government's record in this field and accusing the Prime Minister of cynical posturing. Perhaps the most acerbic criticism came from the European Commissioner on the Environment, Stanley Clinton Davies (a former Labour MP). Accusing the Prime Minister of 'gesture politics', he complained that throughout his term of office in Brussels the British government had been 'leading from the rear', deploying 'any excuse to avoid or delay progress', even on the issues that she had singled out (*Guardian* and *Independent*, 6 October 1988). The reaction of environmental leaders also began to harden as both Thatcher and Ridley made follow-up speeches and interviews in which they defended the government's record on the environment and criticised environmentalists for being too often alarmist, unscientific and backward-looking, especially in rejecting nuclear power (*Guardian*, 12 October 1988, *The Times*, 26 October 1988). In February, Friends of the Earth put out an 86-page review of the government's record on the environment. The claim by Ministers that the British government had generally taken the lead in environmental matters was dismissed as 'absurd'. FoE concluded: 'it has always been necessary to drag it, kicking and screaming, into every single one of the few measures it has taken to improve the state of the environment'. A more positive approach would require the government to reassess some of its cherished ideologies, including its faith in market forces, its commitment to privatisation and deregulation and its antipathy towards precautionary action. As a *Daily Telegraph* editorial observed, 'there is still scepticism – which we do not share – about the Prime Minister's conversion to green policies' (28 April 1989). An article in the *Financial Times* concluded: 'this may turn out to be an issue that the Conservatives cannot win' (14 July 1989).

From Ridley to Patten: Changing Directions within the Party

With problems of credibility mounting, the need for a clear political line became more acute. Nicholas Ridley took the initiative with a pamphlet issued in June by the Centre for Policy Studies, in which he roundly rejected the prevalent view of Britain as the 'dirty man of Europe'. The pamphlet accepted pollution control as an essential role of the state in protecting the public interest against particular interests. It then adduced various principles on which control should be based. Some of them – including the need for a sound scientific basis for controls, for concerted international action and for the pursuit of the best practical environmental option – bore the hallmark of civil service thinking and, indeed, echoed an Environmental Charter produced by the DoE in March 1988.

Two free-market principles were also elaborated. The first, which was traced back to Adam Smith, was the need to separate production from regulation so that the public interest could be clearly represented, and the example of the National Rivers Authority was given to show how this principle had been pursued in the Tories' privatisation programme. What the pamphlet omitted to point out was that the government's original proposal had been for responsibility for pollution control to rest with the privatised water companies. And it was only after legal opinion, obtained by the Council for the Protection of Rural England, that this could run counter to European Community law, that the government agreed to the creation of an independent regulatory body.

Ridley's second proposal involved a significant extension of the 'polluter pays' principle to suggest that 'the polluters' customers must pay'. It was, he declared, government policy that 'prices to consumers should reflect the cost of provision including the need for investment in environmental protection'. It was this broad principle that Conservative politicians seized upon as the basis of their proclaimed approach to 'green growth' or 'sustainable development'. Both the Prime Minister and her Environment Secretary made several speeches stressing the point that consumers demanding a better environment must accept the costs involved. And Professor David Pearce, Britain's leading environmental economist, was pressed into service to suggest practical ways in which this could be achieved. Evidence that the government may have raised expectations that it could not fulfil came with the European elections in June 1989, which saw the spectacular breakthrough of the British Green Party. Overnight, with 15 per cent of the vote, the party was catapulted from being the lame duck of the European green movement to becoming its rising star. Political commentators and journalists were truly taken aback. In its sixteen-year history, the party had never before achieved more than 1 or 2 per cent in parliamentary elections.

Though the Greens drew their support from all the parties and from first-time voters, the largest block (29 per cent of the total, according to post-election opinion surveys) were former Conservative voters. Throughout southern and eastern England this bit deep into Tory majorities. The results clearly disconcerted Ministers who launched a series of attacks on the Greens orchestrated by the Party Chairman, Peter Brooks, who denounced them as 'extreme socialists' (Conservative Research Department 1989). But the difficulties Ministers faced in pressing the attack while also asserting their own environmental credentials was well illustrated by Michael Howard, a Minister in the DoE, who claimed that: 'We are all Greens now. The only serious question is not about whether we protect the environment, but how to do so most effectively. The first and absolute requirement is a healthy economy. One of the saddest delusions of the Green Party is that negative growth would be good for the environment' (Guardian, 28 June 1989).

Nicholas Ridley, for his part, argued that the Greens' support would evaporate when their policies were known. Claiming that their views on the environment were 'unscientific rubbish' and that they were spreading 'grievous misinformation' about pollution (*Guardian*, 11 July 1989), he proposed the establishment of an official bureau of environmental information to disseminate facts about the state of the environment. But the ineptness of the government's response, pouring scorn on the Green Party rather than addressing the public's concern for the environment, proved counterproductive and drew calls from the press for Ridley to be replaced (see, for example, the *Independent* and the *Daily Telegraph*, 17 July 1989).

The appointment of Chris Patten as Secretary of State for the Environment in July 1989 signalled a significant switch in political direction and marked a new phase in the party politicisation of the environment. As a 'One Nation' Tory and former protégé of Edward Heath, he was seen as a prominent 'wet' and, though a very ambitious and able politician, he had previously been given only junior ministerial positions – most recently as Minister for Overseas Development, in which position, though, he had won acclaim for an aid agreement with the Brazilian government aimed at protecting the rainforests. Patten adopted a far more conciliatory tone towards environmental interests. One of his first moves – intended, no doubt, to quieten the party's own shire supporters too – was to overturn his predecessor's decision to allow the building of a private new town at Foxley Wood in North East Hampshire. In another reversal of the Ridley line, Patten also promised 'as open a dialogue as I can with constructive and well-meaning environmental groups ... They have much to contribute to our understanding and to the development of policy' (Speech to the Conservative Party Conference, 1989). Writing to environmental leaders he commented: 'I am tired of seeing the UK pilloried as "the dirty man of Europe". The tag is simply not accurate. I intend to nail the lie not by words but by actions' (Letter to the European Environmental Bureau UK, 21 November 1989). Central to this commitment was the preparation of a White Paper which, Patten had told the Conservative Party Conference, 'will set out our environmental agenda for the rest of the country' (Speech, 11 October 1989).

In that speech, Patten also set out his particular philosophical approach. Where Ridley had conjured up Adam Smith, Patten proclaimed Edmund Burke – 'the greatest of Tories' – as his mentor, as someone who 'reminded us of our duties as trustees for the nation, as good stewards of its traditions, its values and its riches. A nation, wrote Burke, is a partnership between the past, the present and the future'. In such high Tory and paternalistic tones, Patten identified 'an overwhelming ethical argument for prudent management of the environment' and this placed a duty on 'Government to regulate on behalf of the community, to set the standards and the environmental goals'. And to show that he meant business, he announced the withdrawal of his predecessor's proposals to relax rural planning controls.

In an editorial referring to Patten as 'the leading exponent in the Cabinet of a traditional Toryism owing nothing to Mrs Thatcher', the *Independent* interpreted the speech as a signal of the party's wider retreat from Thatcherism, adding that, 'The rise of public concern about the environment has done most to hasten a realisation among Conservatives that Thatcherism has its limitations' (12 October 1989).

With a number of commentators predicting that Patten's projected White Paper would provide a central element for the party's next manifesto (see, for example, the *Daily Telegraph* and the *Independent*, 12 October 1989), the growing sense that the future direction of the party was implicated in the environmental debate initiated another round of pamphleteering from the left and the right of the party. On the left, the arguments and, indeed, the author were already familiar. Tony Paterson of the Bow Group declared Thatcherism to be 'a spent force unless it can adapt itself to the electorate's new priority tasks for government: to improve the quality of life at home and to help save the planet' (Paterson 1989, p. 20). The need was for the government to fall 'back on basic Tory principles which are readily adaptable to environmentalism: efficiency, order, patriotism, tradition, thrift, self-help, individual responsibility and international leadership' (Paterson 1989, p. 1).

The distinctly new element in the debate was a sustained counterattack from the right in a string of publications (see, for example, Redwood 1989; Whelan 1989; Ehrman 1990). In a sense, as the right began to lose its grip on the leadership, so it sought to rally its ideological forces and, for the first time, to formulate a clear 'new right' perspective on the environment. The most radical, free-market approach came from Robert Whelan, UK Director of the Committee on Population and the Economy, who denounced contemporary 'Greenery' as a form of fanaticism that could turn affluent western society into an 'ecological hell'. He expressed concern that governments were losing their resolve to liberalise the economy in the face of this challenge, and without the resultant growth the resources would not be available to improve and protect the environment. Instead, the best way to provide for future generations was to exploit resources, not conserve them. Market forces and human ingenuity would always take care of shortages by providing solutions which left us better off than we were before (Whelan 1989, p. 29). As with other authors on the right, Whelan also argued that 'nothing encourages protection of the environment more effectively than private property rights and the profit motive. People look after that which is their own' (Whelan 1989, p. 37). But such views increasingly held less sway with government policy making which, in turn, was becoming more sensitive to outside opinion on these matters.

The Environment Secretary certainly consulted widely in preparing the

White Paper, and the process raised expectations amongst the environmental lobby. Patten had declared that the White Paper would 'bring together our whole strategy on the environment in a comprehensive document' which would 'confirm our place as a nation prepared to carry our share of the world's burdens in the next decade' (Speech to the Party Conference, 11 October 1989). In subsequent interviews he made it clear that he hoped radically to shift government thinking (see, for example, *Guardian*, 1 December 1989). But when the White Paper was published in September 1990, under the title *This Common Inheritance* (Cmnd 1200), there was considerable disappointment amongst environmentalists because, despite its considerable length (295 pages), it was thin on new and firm proposals for definitive action. This disappointment set the tone for the press reaction. The *Independent* characterised the White Paper 'as feeble as it is lengthy' (26 September 1990), the *Financial Times* as 'a compendium of muted declarations of hesitant intent' (26 September 1990), and the *Guardian* as 'not an action programme, but a discussion paper' (26 September 1990). It was apparent that Patten had been unable to extract from his ministerial colleagues, particularly those in Transport, Energy, Agriculture and the Treasury, tangible commitments to alter policy. Lying behind this failure to win ministerial support for a green strategy across government was identified as a lack of sustained commitment from the Prime Minister herself (*Guardian*, 27 September 1990; *Financial Times*, 28 September 1990; *Guardian*, 5 October 1990).

But though the White Paper did not amount to a green strategy and, given Margaret Thatcher's role in publicising atmospheric pollution, was lamentably weak in rising to that particular challenge, it did nevertheless represent a milestone. It was the first comprehensive statement of Britain's environmental policy. It also put forward a set of general principles on which government action in this field should be based.

These drew partly on an Environmental Charter issued by the DoE in 1988, in proposing that action should be based on the best scientific and economic information; that precautionary action should be taken where justified; that many environmental problems require international remedies; and that public access to environmental information is necessary to ensure that society makes informed choices on the environment. These principles, which owed little to party ideology but derived more from informed scientific, environmental and EC circles, were sandwiched between two others in the White Paper. First and foremost, indeed what was claimed to be the foundation of the government's approach, was 'the ethical imperative of stewardship' which meant that 'we have a moral duty to look after our planet and to hand it on in good order to future generations' (para. 1.14). The sentiments were fittingly those of paternalistic Toryism, but the White Paper suggested: 'That is what experts mean when they talk of "sustainable development"' (para. 1.14). Significantly, obeisance to market liberalism was left to the final principle which concerned the use of 'the best instruments' to safeguard the environment; and which, in a suitably pragmatic, if not ambivalent, posture, committed the government to 'look at ways of using the market further to encourage producers and consumers to act in ways that benefit the environment', but conceded that 'The regulatory approach has served Britain and other countries well in the past and will continue to be the foundation of pollution control' (Summary of the White Paper, p. 3).

While proponents specifically of a carbon tax and more generally of the use of market mechanisms to protect the environment were thus deeply disappointed (see, for example, *Independent*, 26 September 1990), the most important potential reform signalled by the White Paper was in the machinery of government (see also *Guardian*, 28 September 1990; *Financial Times*, 26 September 1990). In order to improve the integration of government policy as it affects the environment, it was announced that the standing Cabinet Committee that had scrutinised the draft contents of the White Paper would remain in being to co-ordinate the approach to environmental issues; that each government department would nominate its own 'green' minister; that annual departmental reports would describe action following up the White Paper; and that the government would regularly produce a state of the environment report. Without obvious irony, Ministers at the launch compared these procedures to those adopted just five years earlier to implement the White Paper *Lifting the Burden*, the deregulationists' gospel. No more poignant indication of the ebbing of Thatcherism was there than the possibility that similar machinery might now be used 'to put the regulation back in'. As well as the first comprehensive statement of environmental policy and the establishment of inter-departmental co-ordinating machinery, the other sense in which the White Paper was a milestone was in marking the maturation of the process of party politicisation of the environment in Britain. As Fiona Reynolds of the Council for the Protection of Rural England pointed out: 'Mr Patten's White Paper triggered similar exercises within the other political parties, and while they may not command the same media and public attention, they are undoubtedly much better placed to put Mr Patten and his team under pressure' (*Guardian*, 28 September 1990). Within a month of the publication of the White Paper, indeed, weighty policy statements were issued by the Liberal Democrats, *What Price our Planet?*, and the Labour Party, *An Earthly Chance*.

What is apparent from the three documents is that there is considerable overlap between the parties' environmental policies. They broadly agree on what the major problems are and there is a large degree of consensus as to policy targets, though the opposition parties call for tougher deadlines. Disagreement focuses on the precise measures to be taken, although all agree on the need to move away from an over-reliance on regulation and to experiment with economic instruments such as pollution taxes. Indeed, the simultaneous appearance of such detailed but convergent documents must be seen as part of a broader return to consensus politics in Britain at the end of the Thatcher era.

The Future

A month after the last of these documents appeared, the Parliamentary Conservative Party was plunged into a leadership campaign in which Mrs Thatcher was forced out of office. The issue which induced Michael Heseltine finally to challenge her was not the environment but that other cross-party issue which much more deeply divided the party, that of the pace and direction of European integration. The eventual winner of the contest, though, was Mrs Thatcher's favoured successor, John Major, the Chancellor of the Exchequer, but he quickly moved to bring Heseltine into the Cabinet again, specifically to rethink the local government poll tax whose introduction had cost the government considerable popular support. As a result, Heseltine moved back into his old department (Patten became party chairman), and just as the 1980s had begun, so did the 1990s, with this mercurial figure as Secretary of State for the Environment in a new Conservative administration, but within a completely transformed political landscape.

Notes

1. CEG, *Prospects of Success*, 4 May 1979.
2. CEG, *Looking at the 'Limits'*, undated.
3. CEG, *Ecological Constraints on Economic Expansion*, undated.
4. Margaret Thatcher, *A Message of Support to the Conservative Ecology Group*, undated, ca. 1978.
5. Ibid.

References*

Bracewell-Milnes, B. (1982). *Land and Heritage: The Public Interest in Personal Ownership* (London: Institute of Economic Affairs).

Carlisle, K. (1984). *Conserving the Countryside* (London: Conservative Political Centre).

Conservative Research Department (1982). 'The quality of the environment today', *Politics Today*, January.

Conservative Research Department (1989). *The Green Party and the Environment* (London: Conservative Research Department).

* Party publications are only listed here if they are quoted from in the main text. For a complete list of party publications, see Table 1.

Ehrman, R. (1990). *Nimbyism: The Disease and the Cure* (London: Centre for Policy Studies).

Hood, C. (1980) 'The politics of quangocide', *Policy and Politics*, Vol. 8, pp. 247–65.

Johnson, S. (1981). *Caring for the Environment* (London: Conservative Political Centre and European Democratic Group).

Lowe, P. and Flynn, A. (1989). 'Environmental politics and policy in the 1980s' in Mohan, J. (ed.), *The Political Geography of Contemporary Britain* (London: Macmillan).

Lowe, P. and Goyder, J. (1983). *Environmental Groups in Politics* (London: Allen and Unwin).

Paterson, T. (1984). *Conservation and the Conservatives* (London: Bow Group).

Paterson, T. (1989). *The Green Conservative* (London: Bow Group).

Redwood, J. (1989). *Rebuilding Britain: Can 'Greenery' and Growth be Reconciled?* (London: Conservative Political Centre).

Rose, C. (1990). *The Dirty Man of Europe: The Great British Pollution Scandal* (London: Simon and Schuster).

Rüdig, W. and Lowe, P. (1986). 'The withered greening of British politics: A study of the Ecology Party', *Political Studies*, Vol. 34, pp. 262–84.

Sullivan, A. (1985). *Greening the Tories: New Politics on the Environment* (London: Centre for Policy Studies).

Wilson, H. (1970). *New Society*, 5 February, p. 209.

2. Green Prospects: The Future of Green Parties in Britain, France and Germany*

WOLFGANG RÜDIG

Department of Government, University of Strathclyde, Glasgow, UK

and

MARK N. FRANKLIN

Department of Political Science, University of Houston, Houston, Texas, USA

Introduction

Green politics is coming of age. There are now green parties in every Western European country. Many of them have seats in national parliaments. Most green parties appear well established, and voters continue to support green parties in sufficient numbers to guarantee their continued existence. But what have they actually achieved? In no country has a green party ever been part of a national government. It is only in Germany that Greens have acquired a more substantial experience of governmental responsibility. At state level, Hesse, Berlin, and Lower Saxony have seen coalition governments involving Greens, and throughout Germany, Greens have played an important role in local government for many years.

It is perhaps somewhat premature to expect a new political force such as the Greens to play a major part in government formation after a relatively short period of time. Greens have just about managed to establish themselves and be taken seriously in some countries; but the question has to be asked whether the Greens have any long-term role to play in electoral politics. Political scientists have mainly seen the function of small parties as being to raise new issues (cf. Merkl 1980; Fisher 1974). Few would doubt that the Greens have made an impact here. But with so many existing parties now jumping on the green bandwagon, green parties appear to be in some danger of losing their momentum. With real power so far off and little to show for past electoral successes in terms of tangible policy achievements, are many voters not likely to be disillusioned about the Greens, turning their attention to mainstream parties which have been eager to green their image? Green parties that really want to make a policy impact have to win over a reliable, stable, and faithful electorate whose continued support does not depend on issue-related protest voting.

*We are grateful to T. T. Mackie for his helpful comments on an earlier version of this chapter.

In this chapter, we explore the future prospects of green parties by looking at the stability of green voting in three major European countries: France, Germany, and Britain. Explaining why people voted green in a particular election can be helpful in this endeavour. Even more important is to analyse the future voting intentions of people who are now green voters and the potential for the rest of the electorate to turn to the Greens in the future. Using data gathered by the European Elections Study[1] in the summer of 1989, we look at the voting intentions of 1989 greens and non-greens in future European and national elections. In the final part of the chapter, we look at the development of the three green parties since 1989 and assess how reliable our predictions about their future prospects have turned out to be so far.

Green Parties and the 1989 European Elections

The elections to the European Parliament in June 1989 were a major success for green parties across Europe. Almost everywhere, the Greens managed to increase their share of the vote (cf. Curtice 1989; Mackie 1990). These results represented rather different stages in the development of the green vote in individual countries, however. At the one extreme, we find Britain where the Greens came from nowhere to capture 14·9 per cent of the vote. Equally surprising was the result for the French Greens which, despite a long history, had never before managed to establish themselves in the national political system. At the other end of the spectrum, the well-established German Greens only managed to repeat their last national election result and could not make any gains (Table 1).

What do these results suggest about the status of green politics in these countries? Is the German result a sign of the beginning of a period of decline for Die Grünen? Is the very sudden rise of the Greens in France and Britain just an ephemeral phenomenon?

Looking at the specific conditions in each individual country, there would be reason to believe that the outcome of the European elections was determined by rather special circumstances. The German Greens appear to have been stagnating for some years. Their momentum seemed to have been broken by acrimonious internal conflicts, financial scandals, resignations of some prominent party members, and the experience of having to make painful compromises to enter state government (cf. Poguntke 1990). But while they appeared to have reached the limit of the electorate, their voters continued to turn out for them faithfully time after time, at least until the 1990 all-German elections. In France and Britain, the special circumstances of the European elections appeared to have favoured the Greens. France uses a proportional representation system for European elections (as opposed to their two-ballot majority voting system used for

Table 1 Green Party election results

Party	1989 European elections	1987–8 National elections	1984 European elections
Die Grünen (West Germany)	8·4	8·3	8·2
Les Verts (France)	10·6	0·4[1] 3·8[2]	3·4
The Green Party (Great Britain)	14·9	1·3	0·5

[1] National Assembly elections
[2] Presidential elections

national elections), providing the perfect opportunity for those disaffected by the socialist government to make a protest. The French Socialist government has pursued a relentlessly growth-oriented policy and has continued with its commitment to nuclear energy, giving rise to a potential for protest voting by ecologically-minded socialist supporters. In Britain, the protest vote explanation seems to hold even more currency. Environmental issues had played an unusually important role in the preceding year, the centre parties were in steep decline, and (more than any other EC country) European elections were not considered particularly important affairs: the political cost of voting green thus was very low (cf. Frankland 1990).

Two key questions arise from this very preliminary analysis: first, how stable is the green electorate? Will German green voters really continue to stick to the Greens? How committed are British and French voters in turning to the Greens in unprecedented numbers in 1989? And, second, what is the potential for green voting in the future? Can green parties sustain or even enlarge current levels of support by attracting more voters from the established parties or, indeed, from the ranks of non-voters?

Political scientists have previously given very different answers to these types of question. One attempt to evaluate the stability of green voting has argued that Greens are essentially the outcome of the frustrations of a new academic proletariat which finds that its way into positions of influence and power is blocked. Bürklin (1987) and Alber (1989) argue that the future chances of the Greens are thus quite limited: once the specific German conditions for the creation of an academic proletariat subside and present academic plebeians outgrow their rebellion from the margins of society, the basis for a green party will have disappeared.

A rival explanation of green politics predicts a more secure future for the Greens: as their rise is based on 'postmaterialist value change' with individuals remaining true to the values internalised in adolescent socialisation, the Greens could rely on the continued commitment of its constituency (cf. Müller-Rommel 1989). But the value-change theory also implies some reservations about the durability of green parties: as Greens represent the highly educated sector of the population who make up their mind independently about policy matters and who refuse to tie themselves to any particular party, the chances of the Greens relying on a group closely identifying with the party seems to remain slim. Inglehart (1989) sees green voters predominantly as cognitively mobilised non-partisans. As more of the electorate lose their commitment to one of the established parties, the chances of the Greens are enhanced but, at the same time, it is exactly this lack of party identification displayed by the potential green electorate which makes it difficult for the Greens to establish themselves permanently and durably. However, we feel that the theory of cognitive mobilised non-partisans relies heavily on notions prevalent in the early phase of green party development. It is hardly surprising that green voters rejected established party politics and had a low level of party identification in the early years of Green Party existence. But with green parties now being established within most national party systems, the key question is whether green voters remain non-partisans or develop a closer attachment to the Greens. It is thus of crucial importance whether green parties actually can develop a higher degree of identification with the party amongst its supporters and potential voters. The data we will analyse in this chapter will have a direct bearing on this question.

The Data

The data of the European Election Study allow us to answer these questions in a truly comparative context. There have been a number of previous analyses of the green vote in the three countries concerned (cf. Kellner 1989; Boy 1989; Müller-Rommel 1989; Poguntke 1990; Schmitt 1989), but all of these studies were national studies looking at individual green parties in isolation. We are now able to compare the response of green voters in all three countries to identical questions at the same time, giving us a unique opportunity to evaluate the real differences between these parties.

We will look at a number of variables which would give us an indication of the stability of the green vote in the three countries under consideration.

First, we can look at the actual green voters. Did they vote green in previous national elections? Do they intend to vote green at a national election? Do they feel close to the Green Party? Do they intend to vote green at the next national election?

Second, we can look at the potential to vote green. How big is the potential in each country? Which party have potential green voters supported so far? How do they intend to vote in future? And how attractive are the Greens to those voting for one of the other parties at the moment? Furthermore, we can explore the attractions of other parties to green voters. If they should vote for a different party, which ones are they most likely to be attracted to?

While the data of the European Election Study give us a unique opportunity to compare green voting in different countries, there are also limitations of which we have to be aware. First of all, we have to be very conservative in our interpretations of the data on actual green voters. With a total sample of around 1,000 in each country, the sub-sample of green voters is rather small: 86 in West Germany, 77 in France, and 81 in Britain. To distinguish between different types of green voters within such small groups is rather hazardous. However, as we have no other data which are truly comparative, we nevertheless feel it worthwhile to make as much of these data as we can. Bearing in mind that there will be a large margin of error, we are confident that we can at least identify some dominant features of green voting and its potential.

There are measures we can take to ensure that we are not totally led astray. First, we can check the consistency of the various findings. We have a number of indicators at our disposal which we can use to measure the durability of green voting. If we consistently find the same trend then the chances that it is the result of random error are significantly reduced. Second, wherever possible, we can compare our findings with those of national surveys. And third, the restrictions of the small size of the sub-sample of actual green voters do not apply to the data on potential green voters. By comparing and combining the data on actual and potential green voters, we can test our hypotheses on the basis of a random sample of sufficient size.

The 1989 Green Voters: Where Do They Come From, Where Are They Going?

Who voted green at the European elections in 1989? Green voters are predominantly young and highly educated. They are also far more concerned about the environment than other voters, they prefer libertarian values, and they generally place themselves rather more to the left of the political spectrum. This profile in many ways is as expected but, as analysed in more detail in a separate paper(Franklin and Rüdig 1991), we found that the influence of these variables is by no means as great as theories of green politics have suggested. Green voters are spread quite widely; they are not that

Table 2 Previous vote and future voting intentions of 1989 green voters

Party type	West Germany		France		Great Britain	
	Previous vote	Future vote	Previous vote	Future vote	Previous vote	Future vote
Far Right	–	–	1·3	–	–	–
Right	5·8	4·7	3·9	1·3	24·7	16·0
Centre	7·0	10·5	1·3	2·6	27·1	9·9
Left	11·6	8·1	49·4	22·1	18·5	23·5
Far Left	–	1·2	1·3	–	–	–
Greens	59·3	73·3	27·3	63·6	7·4	42·0
Abstention	10·5	–	6·5	2·6	14·8	1·2
Others/ Don't Know/ No Answer	5·8	–	9·1	5·2	7·4	7·4
Totals*	100·0	100·2	100·1	100·0	99·9	100·0

*Figures do not add up to exactly 100 per cent because of rounding

well defined in socio-demographic terms. Of all our socio-demographic variables, only youth was a a consistent predictor of green voting. Moreover, the socio-demographic profile together with left–right placement, post-materialism and pro-environmental and arms-limitation attitudes only explain 6·9 per cent (Britain), 13·5 per cent (France) and 16·8 per cent (West Germany) of the variance in green voting, the importance of the environment as a political issue emerging as the only attitude variable consistently related to green voting. The relatively low overall influence of these variables makes it very difficult to deduce anything from these results about the durability of the electoral commitment of these voters. The more precise definition of the green vote in Germany as compared with Britain could suggest that the green vote is more stable in Germany and rather more transient in Britain. But on its own, this is a very weak indicator and we would need far more evidence to support such a contention. In general, these results convince us that the use of socio-demographic variables is not a particularly useful way to assess the durability of green voting. Rather than tying the green vote to any particular social group, it may be more fruitful to see how closely green voters identify with the Greens and how faithfully they have maintained their support over a number of elections.

Green voters' previous party allegiance and future voting intentions may give us some first important indications. Looking at the parties they voted for in the previous national elections and intend to vote for at the next national elections, an interesting picture emerges (Table 2).

Looking first at the level of previous green voting, we find that a rather high share of European green voters in West Germany had already voted green in the previous national elections. For France and Britain, the picture is rather different. In France, the number of people recalling having voted green before is relatively high while it is predictably low in Britain. Where do most of the new green voters in France and Britain come from? The contrast between the three countries is very marked here. Almost half of the green vote in France has come from former supporters of the Socialists while virtually no support has come from the centre-right parties. In Britain, on the other hand, most of the new green voters had voted SDP/Liberal Alliance or Conservative before.[2]

Looking at future voting intentions, the first important result is that the retention rate of the British Greens is rather low. Only 42 per cent of those voting green in the European elections say they would vote green again if there was a general election tomorrow. By contrast, almost three-quarters of German green voters (73 per cent) and just under two-thirds of French green voters (64 per cent) indicate that they would stick with the Greens in a future national election.

These results confirm some, but not all, of the prior assessments of the prospects of green parties in these countries. First, the German case is one of stability and high commitment to green politics. The indication is that Die Grünen can draw on a core of supporters which is willing to support them at national and European level. In that sense, the interpretation of the German European election result as a confirmation of a stable green electorate appears to be justified, and there are no signs here that green support is seriously weakening.

The green vote in Britain looks very unstable in comparison. Quite a high share of voters turning to the Greens in the European elections seem to see this as a temporary diversion. Even right after the European elections, at the height of green political euphoria, about half of them declared their intention to go back to the established parties in a general election. A further slide in green support once that euphoria died away is thus almost predictable. This may not be entirely surprising given the nature of the electoral system in Britain. Indeed, the number of people who nevertheless expressed an intention to vote green in a general election is perhaps rather higher than one would expect. However, the contrast with France is illuminating. Despite the fact that national elections in France are conducted according to a majority voting system, the commitment to future green voting is remarkably high. Because respondents were asked about their voting intentions in the first round of parliamentary elections, the 'wasted vote' argument is not quite as convincing as in Britain because everybody gets a chance to choose again in the all-important second round. But as the end result is very likely to be the same (no representation), there must be other factors which account for the willingness of French green voters to vote green in National Assembly elections as well.

Another way of assessing the durability of green electoral support is to compare the green 'retention' rate with that of other parties: in West Germany, the Christian Democrats (92 per cent) and Social Democrats (95 per cent) enjoy rather higher retention rates than the Greens. Only the liberal FDP (70 per cent) and the right-wing Republikaner (71 per cent) have retention rates on a similar level to the Greens. Interestingly, these retention rates drop to 78 per cent for the Christian Democrats, 86 per cent for the Social Democrats and 56 per cent for the FDP if one compares the recalled vote at the last national election with the intended vote at the next one. For the Greens, however, an unchanged retention rate of 73 per cent provides a further indicator of relative stability.

Looking at Britain, the figures are rather less encouraging for the Greens. A comparison with the last national elections makes little sense because of the very small number who voted green on that occasion. A comparison with other parties' retention rates at the next national elections shows that the Greens' relatively low figure contrasts with very high rates for the established parties: 95 per cent for the Conservatives and 96 per cent for Labour. Even the Social and Liberal Democrats manage a retention rate of 79 per cent. In France, the established left wing parties also hold their electorate quite well: the Greens' 64 per cent retention rate compares to 88 per cent for the Communists and 90 per cent for the Socialists.[3]

There are other indications to suggest that the British green vote is much weaker than those in the continental countries. In Britain, only 28·4 per cent of 1989 green voters actually feel close to the Green Party, as opposed to 37·7 per cent in France and 62·8 per cent in West Germany. Comparing the share of green voters feeling close to their party with other parties, the Greens do not come out terribly well: in Britain, 60 per cent of Conservative, 55 per cent of Labour and 45 per cent of SLD voters feel 'close' to their party. In France, the figures are 92 per cent for the Communists and 80 per cent for Socialists, but only 58 per cent for the National Front. In Germany, on the other hand, the gap between the Greens and the established parties is rather smaller: only 72 per cent of CDU/CSU voters and 63 per cent of SPD voters feel 'close' to their party. The other small parties, the liberal FDP and the far-right Republikaner are behind the Greens with 57 per cent and 49 per cent of their voters feeling a closer attachment to them. Again, the evidence points towards firmly established German Greens, with the French fast catching up fast; but British Greens are much more fickle.

Looking at the overall proportion of the population feeling 'close' to these parties including those respondents who did not vote for them, these findings are reinforced: 4·8 per cent feel close to the Green Party in Britain, 7·0 per cent in France, and 7·1 per cent in Germany. A comparison with the other parties again shows the strength of the German Greens: only 2 per cent of our sample feels close to the FDP and 2·5 per cent feel close to the Republikaner. In France, the Greens have the edge over the Communists who only manage 4 per cent of close adherents and the National Front with 4·2 per cent. But even in Britain, the Greens compare well with the SLD which only command a closer attachment from 3·3 per cent of our sample. Remarkably, the pattern of party attachment is quite similar across all three countries: the big left and right parties command around 20 per cent and then are followed by the Greens, with centre parties and extreme left and right parties well behind.

To turn this feeling of attachment into more substantial electoral successes, the Greens have (a) to get their supporters out to vote and (b) to compete successfully for the votes of the unattached. But the Greens have been failing on both these counts so far: our data indicate that more than half of those feeling close to the Greens in France did not vote at all in the 1989 European elections. In Britain, only half of those who feel close to the Greens voted for them in the European elections. As expected, the German Greens did rather better, mobilising almost two-thirds of their 'close' followers. As to those not feeling attached to any particular party, the Greens are not very successful here either: in all three countries, the unattached were slightly less likely to vote green than the population as a whole.

In 1989, the Greens were thus not very successful in mobilising their own supporters and unattached voters. But how about the next national elections? Is there evidence that the good result for the Greens, particularly in Britain and France, mobilises new sections of the electorate to come out in support of green parties?

We can first look at the responses of our sample to the question on their voting intention in a coming general election. Remarkably, the share of our sample intending to vote green increases rather than decreases in all three countries (see Table 3), particularly in France. Where do all these potential new voters come from?

A look at Table 4 reveals that the overwhelming share of new green voters comes from previous abstainers. On the one hand, this is good news for the Greens: they may be seen to capture the hearts and minds of those previously alienated from party politics. On the other hand, however, the data in Table 4 do not bode well, particularly for the French and British Greens. First, abstention in previous elections may be a good predictor of abstentions in future elections. There must be some considerable doubt about the rate at which abstainers will actually make the effort and vote next time, particularly as the electoral systems of both countries make it very difficult for the Greens to gain representation.

Table 3 Recalled green votes in last general election and 1989 European elections; intended green vote at next general election; share of entire sample, including non-voters, don't knows, etc.

	Last national election	1989 European elections	Next national election
	%	%	%
West Germany	7·4	7·2	8·5
France	3·2	7·4	14·1
Britain	0·8	8·5	8·4

Second, and more worrying, is the fact that the Greens appear to be unable to attract any further support from current voters of the other parties. In Britain, for example, virtually nobody who voted for another party in the European elections is prepared to switch to the Greens – and that at a time of unprecedented green euphoria right after the European elections. Looking at the previous general election vote of the new green electorate, the proportion of votes coming from all three major parties is roughly equivalent to those of the green vote at the European elections. The British green vote continues to have a centre-right slant. Unlike in France, the electoral success of the British Greens has not uncovered a previously latent leftist vote for the Greens.

The problems are roughly the same for the French and German Greens: there is very little indication of further voters coming from the other parties. The increase in the French green vote is almost entirely due to the mobilisation of European non-voters. As in the case of the European election, most of the new green voters were previous Socialist voters. The Greens clearly fail to attract the traditional left and do not benefit from the declining Communist vote; and only about 10 per cent (as opposed to almost 40 per cent in the British case) come from former centre-right voters. There is even less indication of movement in the German case. Practically no votes stand to be gained from any supporters of the main parties. The only noticeable input come from former SPD voters, but this is limited to little more than 10 per cent, and, importantly, the gain from previous non-voters is substantially less, both in terms of European and previous national elections, than in France and Britain. Again, the same picture emerges: in Germany, we have a well-defined, stable green electorate but which is unable to mobilise any new parts of the electorate. The situation in France and Britain is more volatile. The French Greens in particular appear to be still on the move, attracting those disaffected with party politics and previous Socialist supporters.

Table 4 Previous voting behaviour of those intending to vote green at the next national elections

Party type	West Germany		France		Great Britain	
	Last national election	European election 1989	Last national election	European election 1989	Last national election	European election 1989
Far Right	–	1·0	2·0	0·7	–	–
Right	2·9	1·0	8·8	5·4[1]	20·0	2·5
Centre	0·0	0·0	1·4	2·0[2]	20·1	1·3
Left	11·8	2·0	28·6	2·7	16·3	0·0
Far Left	–	–	1·4	0·7	–	–
Others	–	–	2·0	–	–	–
Greens	63·7	61·8	19·0	33·3	7·5	42·2
Abstentions	11·8	27·5	26·5	45·6	32·5	52·5
Don't Know	9·8	5·0	12·3	9·6	3·8	1·3
Total*	100·0	100·3	100·0	100·0	100·2	99·8
N	102	102	147	147	80	80

[1] UDF-RPR
[2] Centre: Liste Simone Veil
* Figures do not add to exactly 100 per cent because of rounding.

The Future Potential of Green Voting

What are the chances that green parties will attract new voters from other parties or from non-voters in the longer run? We can expect that voters asked how they would vote in a general election shortly after having voted in a European election may be somewhat unlikely to indicate a different voting choice, and therefore our analysis of 'retention' rates with regard to future elections may underestimate the likely degree of volatility of these choices. But we have another indicator at our disposal which should give us a more balanced picture. In the European Election Study, respondents were asked about the probability of them ever voting for individual parties in future European elections. Their responses were recorded on a scale of 1 (not at all probable) to 10 (very probable). The results are presented in Table 5.

The first striking feature is the very high potential for green voting in France. There are rather few people who cannot imagine ever voting for the Greens, and a remarkably high number of people who consider it quite likely that they will vote green in the future. To some extent, this may be

Table 5 Potential green vote

Question: 'Some people always vote for the same party. Other people make up their mind each time. Please tell me for each of the following how probable it is that you will ever vote for this party in European elections?'
(*Scale:* 1=Not at all probable, to 10=Very probable, 0=Don't Know)

Scale	West Germany	France	Great Britain
0	8·3	7·7	4·1
1	33·1	15·8	31·3
2	7·2	4·3	7·2
3	7·7	5·7	7·2
4	7·3	5·4	6·1
5	6·1	14·0	12·2
6	6·7	8·8	6·4
7	7·2	8·6	7·8
8	6·0	10·2	7·1
9	4·2	9·2	5·9
10	6·3	10·3	4·7
Mean probability*	5·6	4·0	4·2

* excluding Don't Knows

a reflection of the different voting system employed in France for European elections (proportional representation with a 5 per cent hurdle),which is rather kinder to small parties such as the Greens than the system employed for National Assembly elections. But generally, there is the indication of a remarkably high potential green vote in France which cannot alone be explained with reference to electoral systems.

Germany is perhaps surprisingly placed at the lower end of the scale. A third of the electorate considers it extremely improbable that they ever would vote green, and relatively few people assign a high probability to a future green vote. In Britain, the mean probability is also high, but relatively few people (fewer than in any of the other countries) consider it highly likely that they would vote green in the future.

Where do these potential green voters come from? In terms of the sociodemographic profile, they are somewhat better defined than the actual green voters: highly educated, young, employed in the public sector, and concerned with environmental and left-libertarian matters. There is very little variance between the countries in those terms (Franklin and Rüdig 1991).

Table 6 Potential green vote according to 1989 vote (average probability to vote green at future European elections, scale 1–10; 1= Not at all probable, 10=Very probable)

Party Type	West Germany	France	Great Britain
Far Right	2·0	3·2	–
Right	2·1	4·1[1]	3·0
Centre	1·9	5·2[2]	5·0
Left	4·3	5·9	3·9
Far Left	–	4·3	–
Nationalists	–	–	4·7
Greens	8·4	9·1	7·5
Non-voters	4·5	5·8	4·2
Overall average	4·0	5·6	4·2

[1] UDF-RPR
[2] Centre: Liste Simone Veil

However, in terms of their previous voting behaviour and their intended future voting behaviour at national elections, they are very different. Let us first look at voters of different parties at the European elections and their respective probabilities of voting green in the future (Table 6).

All three green parties can take some comfort that their electorate does indicate a strong commitment to voting green again; but the average probability of green voters voting green again is lowest in Britain. French green voters indicate a very high probability, even more than the Germans.

From where could other future green voters come? In the German case, the centre-right is clearly very alienated from the Greens and it is virtually only SPD voters who indicate some willingness to vote green in the future. The picture is rather different in France where the centre-right is not quite as hostile to the idea of voting green and where Socialist voters display a very high probability of voting green. In Britain, it is SLD voters (and Scottish and Welsh nationalists) who are most inclined to consider voting green. Labour voters are clearly far less inclined to turn green than are left-wing voters in Germany or France. Conservative voters are least likely to consider voting green but their rejection is not quite as decisive as in the German case.

How about the dangers of 1989 green voters switching to another party? Table 7 shows that the reverse movements do not necessarily have the same strengths and directions. In West Germany, green voters overwhelmingly do not consider voting for the far-right or the Christian

Table 7 Average probability of 1989 green voters to vote for a particular party at future European elections (Scale 1–10; 1 = Not at all probable, 10 = Very probable)

Party type	West Germany		France		Great Britain	
	Green voters	All	Green voters	All	Green voters	All
Far Right	1·9	2·6	1·3	2·5	–	–
Right	3·0	5·2	2·6	4·3[1]	3·9	5·0
Centre	3·7	4·1	3·1	4·2[2]	3·8	3·4[9]
			2·7	3·9[3]	3·1	2·8[10]
			2·4	3·5[4]		
Left	6·5	6·4	6·4	5·4[5]	4·9	5·0
			3·9	3·2[6]		
Far Left	–	–	1·8	2·5[7]	–	–
			2·9	2·6[8]		
Greens	8·4	4·0	9·1	5·6	7·5	4·2

[1] RPR [2] PR-UDF [3] CDS-UDF [4] Radical-UDF [5] PS [6] MRG [7] PC [8] PSU [9] SLD [10] SDP

Democrats; the FDP is also not very popular. The SPD is clearly the main rival party. The pattern in France is very similar, matching the German green voter all along. Britain stands out again: Labour has the highest average probability, but for green voters it is actually lower than for the electorate at large. The Conservatives do remarkably well among Greens, far better than equivalent parties in France or West Germany and, in terms of the average probability, even better than the SLD. Green voters are more likely than the electorate as a whole to consider voting for centre parties, but only marginally so.

Finally, let us look at the relationship between voting potentials between the various parties. If we look at potential green voting and its relationship to potential votes for other parties, this should give us a fairly good impression of the green political landscape of the future. Table 8 highlights some important features, some of which we have not really come across in this form.

The first somewhat surprising result is that the negative correlation to potential voting for extreme right-wing parties such as the National Front in France and the Republicans in Germany is not that strong. In Germany in particular, a potential vote for the Republicans is far less strongly (negatively) correlated with green voting than a potential CDU/CSU vote. And also in France, the correlation is only marginally stronger for the National Front. What are we to make of this? Potential green voters are not very likely to vote for these parties, but they tend to give a lower probability to

Table 8 Correlations between the potential green vote and the potential votes for other parties (Scale: 1–10, Pearson's r)

Potential vote for other parties	Potential green vote		
	West Germany	France	Great Britain
Far Right	−·101***	−·142***	–
Right	−·428***	−·173***	−·208***
Centre	·032n.s.	−·059*[1]	·219***[8]
		−·014n.s.[2]	·208***[9]
		−·020n.s.[3]	
Left	·372***	·316***[4]	·097**
		·318***[5]	
Far Left	–	·090**[6]	–
		·278***[7]	
Nationalists	–	–	·117***

Significance levels: n.s. not significant * p≤0·05 ** p≤0·01 *** p≤0·001
[1] PR-UDF [2] CDS-UDF [3] Radical-UDF [4] PS [5] MRG [6] PC [7] PSU [8] SLD [9] SDP

voting for the mainstream right-wing parties than for voting for the extreme right. This is an indication that rejection of established parties appears to be an important feature of potential green voting, in other words that there is a 'protest vote' element which gives some probability to voting for these right-wing anti-establishment parties despite the fact that, ideologically, their policies are diametrically opposed to those of green parties.

The strong rejection of the CDU/CSU by potential German green voters is not matched in France and the UK where the relationship is rather less extreme. An even greater contrast arises as far as centre parties are concerned: we find clear evidence that there is no strong rejection of these parties in any country, and that Britain sticks out in providing a fairly strong positive correlation between potential centre party and Green Party voting. Britain again stands alone in producing an extremely low positive correlation between Green and Labour Party voting potentials. By contrast, in Germany the correlation is the most positive, and in France, only potential voters of the Movement of the Left Radicals (MRG) allied to the Socialists display a marginally higher correlation. The traditional Left in France in the guise of the Communist Party, on the other hand, does not appear to share any great enthusiasm for voting green, while potential voters of the New Left PSU are far more attracted to the Greens.

The size of the correlations gives us some indication of how well defined the potential green vote is in these three countries in terms of their relationship to other party potentials. In a world of absolute certainty about party choices, each individual vote would be completely explained by the *negative* relationships to potential votes for other parties. Positive relationships and zero-order correlations are slightly more difficult to explain: a predominance of positive correlations would indicate a high degree of competition but it would also indicate that the new party does not really represent a fundamentally new quality. A generally low level of negative and positive correlations could be seen as a sign of complete unpredictability and volatility, but it could equally be interpreted as an indication of a very broad-based appeal which tapped a new cleavage which has not been previously represented in the party system. Overall, the degree to which the potential to vote for one particular party can be explained by the potential to vote for other parties can be taken to be an indicator of the definition and stability of green voting.

A multiple regression analysis with potential green voting as the dependent variable and all other potential scores as independent variables produces an $r^2 = \cdot 226$ for Germany, $\cdot 093$ for Britain and $\cdot 170$ for France. Clearly, it is in Germany that a potential vote for the Greens is most closely defined by the voting preferences for or against other parties. In terms of the durability of green voting, however, the key question is the relative importance of positive and negative relationships: the higher the negative element, the better the chances for a durable existence; the higher the positive element, the stiffer the competition. Here, we do have an interesting difference: in both France and Britain, the individual variables showing up as most important in the multiple regression analysis are a potential vote for left and centre parties. In Germany, the very strong negative relationship to the CDU/CSU tops every other individual factor. The regression also confirms the rather unimportant role of the rejection of far-right parties. Rejection of the Republicans adds virtually nothing to the explanation once the potential for other parties is accounted for, and basically the same applies in France. As the figures presented in Table 7 and 8 show clearly, actual and potential green voters are overwhelmingly unattracted to extreme right-wing parties, but there is a fairly small group of people with an inclination to vote for anti-establishment parties and for whom both Greens and far-right parties therefore have some appeal.

The Future of Green Parties

What can our results tell us about the future development of green parties in France, Britain and Germany? Obviously, the data collected in 1989 only provided a snapshot of voters' preferences at that particular time. The prospects of any party are bound to be influenced by a variety of imponderables which cannot be captured in advance even by the most carefully designed survey.

There are, however, some quite clear indications from the 1989 data: the British green vote is identified as the most feeble and far more centre-right in comparison with France and Germany. Significantly, this less 'leftist' nature of the green vote in Britain is also evident in the potential green vote, suggesting that this is an intrinsic characteristic of green politics in Britain which is not limited to the 'protest vote' elements of the 1989 election. In Germany, on the other hand, the green vote looks stable, but it is also clear that it is limited. Among the electorate at large, the Greens are not particularly popular and there appears to be very little scope for growth. At the same time, the SPD is the clear competitor for the green vote. French green voters of 1989 are less committed to the party than in Germany, but the potential for green voting in France is much higher. The average potential is the highest of all three countries. For the French Greens, it is also the Socialists who are the main rivals. While there is a very low level of opposition to the Greens in the electorate at large and a high level of potential, the French Greens had major difficulties motivating those who feel close to it to come out and vote. Despite the high green potential in France, some question mark must be raised as to whether this can actually be transformed into real votes for the Greens in coming elections.

How reliable are these characterisations of the green vote in Britain, Germany and France for the prediction of their fortunes in the 1990s and beyond? A look at how green parties have fared since the 1989 European elections will give us some first indications. Figure 1 shows the development of the public opinion poll standing from 1989 to 1991. The main trends are very clear. In Britain, green support has gradually but steadily declined, and stands now at only 1–2 per cent. The immediate electoral prospects of the British Greens thus do not look too promising. The German Greens managed to remain fairly stable until December 1990 when they suffered a rather bad defeat in the first all-German elections. They did, however, recover fairly well in the polls, although their general level of support is down from the pre-election period. And finally, the French Greens look like the most successful ones, improving on their share of the vote in the European Elections and maintaining at least that level of support throughout the entire period.

The devolution of opinion poll standings confirm some of our predictions, particularly in the British and French cases. In the British case, the disintegration of the green vote was fairly predictable from the beginning. But, in interpreting this, we have to take account of the rather high level of volatility in British politics. The fairly low levels of attachment to the two main parties, and the very low level of attachment to the centre parties, indicate that a fairly large part of the British electorate appears to float between the parties, not having any special relationship to any of them. Given the right circumstances (as in 1989), the Greens may benefit from

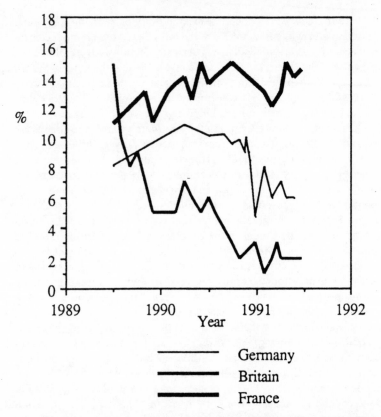

Figure 1 Opinion Poll Standing of Green Parties in France, Britain, and Germany, 1989-1991
Sources: *The Observer* (Britain), *Der Spiegel* (Germany), *Paris-Match* (France). The results for
June 1989 are actual election results in all three countries. In Germany, results up to December 1990 refer to West Germany only. The figure of December 1990 is the actual result in the all-German elections, subsequent figures refer to Germany as a whole. All poll
results refer to responses to a question about voting intentions if there were a parliamentary election next Sunday or next week. In France, the question refers to the first round
of elections to the National Assembly.

this situation, but if they do attract a large part of that vote as in 1989, they
are liable to lose it just as quickly. The dynamics of green voting thus seem
to match those of the Liberals in post-war Britain, constantly 'waiting for
something to turn up' (Clarke and Zuk 1989). It remains to be seen
whether this highly volatile situation would be changed if a Labour government should gain power again. The data on green potential voting
instil some caution: current and, even more importantly, potential Labour
voters are not attracted to the Greens in any great numbers. Despite the
highly volatile nature of its support, the political continuity of Green Party
activity does not appear to be threatened as Green Party activists are pur-

suing a medium- to long-term strategy and are unlikely to be discouraged from further activity should the Greens not do so well at the next general election (Rüdig et al. 1991).

In the German case, the situation is rather different. The SPD is the main rival for votes. Many SPD voters are attracted by the Greens, but equally, Green voters are attracted by the SPD. During eight years in opposition, the SPD has taken quite a lot of green policies on board. In 1990, both parties shared a very cautious attitude to unification against the main trends of public opinion. The circumstances for the German Greens in 1990 were thus very unpromising. Continuing internal problems did not help but in the face of their continuous existence in the past, they cannot really be blamed for the result. More important was that the motivation for green voters to turn out and vote for the Greens in December 1990 was probably at its lowest ever. The Greens appeared to do well enough in the polls immediately before the elections to be assured of a place in the new parliament; at the same time, the outcome of the election was seen as a foregone conclusion with the government coalition well ahead. There are thus reasons to believe that the 1990 result was the outcome of very special circumstances (cf. also Rüdig 1991), and that the existing fairly stable green electorate will return to the Greens in the coming years. Indications from Land elections in 1991 confirm this prediction as the Greens have been doing rather well.

Finally, the French Greens remain something of an enigma. Their standing in the national polls has been very stable since 1989. In the past, the French Greens were seen as unable to mobilise Socialists with 'left-libertarian' values, which was regarded as a major reason for their weakness (Kitschelt 1990). The 1989 result suggests that they are now appealing to Socialist voters, and our data confirm this. There appears to be a core of green supporters, many of them previous Socialist voters, who look determined to continue voting green. It remains to be seen whether the Greens can survive in between the two big blocs. Unlike the German Greens, Les Verts, under the leadership of Antoine Waechter have always stressed that they are not 'left wing'. This may have brought it some sympathies from the centre-right, but there is no indication in our data that the centre-right in France is an important source of votes as in the case of Britain. It is a different matter whether former Socialist voters have actually developed a closer identification with the Greens, or whether they just intend to vote green in the first stage of the elections to register their environmental protest because they know they can vote Socialist with the second vote and do not run a major risk of letting in the Right. As far as 'Greens' identifying with the party are concerned, the fact that half of them were abstainers in the European election demonstrates their level of alienation from the political system, and it remains doubtful whether they can form a stable basis for a green vote. While our data thus allows a prediction of a significant potential for the Greens in France, our analysis also reveals a number of problems to be overcome if that potential is going to be realised.

In our analysis, we find some evidence in Germany and France that an identification of the green electorate with the Greens is developing. The retention rate of green voters from election to election is approaching those of the major parties. While this is a sign of a higher durability of the Greens, the relatively small size of these parties still means that fairly minor fluctuations of votes in a downward direction could have dire consequences. The Greens' future clearly is more secure in the 1990s, with a base of supporters and a fairly promising potential. But although the Greens are clearly not short-term 'flash parties', the electoral performance of the Greens still depends heavily on both a favourable political agenda with new green issues coming up, and the failure of established parties, in particular socialist parties in power, to address their concerns adequately.

Notes

1. The European Elections Study 1989 (EES '89) is a joint effort of Western European social scientists to take advantage of the elections for the European Parliament, held simultaneously in all European Community countries in June 1989, in order to engage in cross-nationally comparative electoral research. The study was designed and organized by a core group of researchers consisting of Roland Cayrol (University of Paris), Cees van der Eijk (University of Amsterdam), Mark Franklin (formerly at the University of Strathclyde, now at the University of Houston), Manfred Kuechler (Hunter College, City University of New York), Renato Mannheimer (University of Genova) and Hermann Schmitt (University of Mannheim) who co-ordinated the efforts of this group. The study consisted of three independent cross-sectional surveys that were conducted in each member country of the European Community before and immediately after the elections for the European Parliament. The questionnaires, which were administered in the language of each country, constituted one part of the European Omnibus Surveys which also contained the regular Eurobarometre surveys of the Commission of the European Communities. With the kind permission of the director of Eurobarometre surveys, we have been able to derive from the Eurobarometre data a number of variables such as demographic and background characterisations to employ in conjunction with our own questions. The relevant Eurobarometre surveys were number 30 (autumn 1988), 31 (spring 1989) and 31A (summer 1989, immediately after the European elections). Each of these waves involved interviews with some 12,500 respondents divided into independent national samples of about 1,000 respondents each. In the present chapter, we focus on data collected in the third (post-election) wave of interviews.

   Funding to support the first two waves was obtained from a consortium made up of European mass media and other institutions; funding for the third wave was provided largely by a grant from the British Economic and Social Research Council. The data will be deposited at the ESRC Data Archive at the University of Essex, the ICPSR at the University of Michigan, and other data archives, and released into the public domain in January 1992.

2. An *Independent*/NOP poll of 190 green voters in England showed very similar results. According to this survey, 29 per cent had voted Conservative in 1987, 27 per cent SDP/Liberal Alliance, 18 per cent Labour, 6 per cent Green, and 15 per cent had abstained. This matches our own results almost exactly. The only slight difference concerns the higher number of previous Conservative voters in the NOP sample. This may be due to the fact that their sample excluded Wales and Scotland (Kellner 1989).

   In France, an IFOP/*Le Monde* exit poll of 3,835 voters asked about their vote in the first round of the 1988 presidential elections. The published results (Parodi 1989) present only the percentages of the presidential vote which have gone to various parties in the European elections but (using the official results of the Presidential elections and assuming the same level of abstentions and don't knows), we calculated the 1988 votes of 1989 European green voters to be as follows: Far Right (Le Pen) 2·7 per cent, Right (Chirac) 3·7 per cent, Centre-Right (Barre) 6·2 per cent, Left (Mitterrand) 44·5 per cent, Far Left (Boussell and Lajonie) 1·9 per cent, Green (Waechter) 25·3 per cent. A comparison with our results reveals a fairly close match, despite the fact that our data are based on a question about the previous vote at the National Assembly elections.

3. The figures for the centre-right in France are not really analysable in this context: the RPR formed an alliance with the UDF for the European elections, but one part of the UDF declined to join and formed its own list. For national elections, the survey asked for the support for the RPR and the three constituent parts of the UDF separately. This lack of continuity leads to rather low 'retention' figures which may, however, be entirely artificial due to the design of the survey.

References

Alber, J. (1989). 'Modernisation, cleavage structures, and the rise of green parties and lists in Europe', in Müller-Rommel, F. (ed.), *New Politics in Western Europe: The Rise and Success of Green Parties and Alternative Lists.* (Boulder, CO: Westview Press), pp. 195–210.

Boy, D. (1989). 'L'écologisme en France: Evolutions et structures'. Paper presented at the ECPR Joint Sessions, Paris, April 1989.

Bürklin, W. P. (1987). 'Governing left parties frustrating the radical non-established left: The rise and inevitable decline of the Greens', *European Sociological Review,* Vol. 3, pp. 109–26.

Clarke, H. D. and Zuk, G. (1989). 'The dynamics of third-party support: The British Liberals, 1951–79', *American Journal of Political Science,* Vol. 33, pp. 196–221.

Curtice, J. (1989). 'The 1989 European elections: Protest or green tide?', *Electoral Studies,* Vol. 8, pp. 217–30.

Fisher, S. L. (1974). *The Minor Parties of the Federal Republic of Germany: Towards a Comparative Theory of Minor Parties.* (The Hague: Martinus Nijhoff).

Frankland, E. G. (1990). 'Does green politics have a future in Britain? An American perspective', in Rüdig, W. (ed.), *Green Politics One 1990.* (Edinburgh: Edinburgh University Press), pp. 7–28.

Franklin, M. N. and Rüdig, W. (1991). *The Greening of Europe: Ecological Voting in the 1989 European Elections.* Strathclyde Papers in Government and Politics,

No. 82. (Glasgow: Department of Government, University of Strathclyde).

Inglehart, R. (1989). *Culture Shifts in Advanced Industrial Society*. (Princeton, N. J.: Princeton University Press).

Kellner, P. (1989). 'Decoding the Greens', *Independent*, 7 July.

Kitschelt, H. (1990). 'La gauche libertaire et les écologistes français', *Revue française de science politique*, Vol. 40, pp. 339–65.

Mackie, T. T. (ed.) (1990). *Europe Votes 3. European Parliamentary Election Results 1989*. (Aldershot: Dartmouth).

Merkl, P. H. (ed.) (1980). *Western European Party Systems: Trends and Prospects*. (New York, N.Y: The Free Press).

Müller-Rommel, F. (1989). 'The German Greens in the 1980s: Short-term cyclical protest or indicator of transformation?', *Political Studies*, Vol. 37, pp. 114–22.

Parodi, J.-L. (1989). 'L'éclatement de l'électorat de M. Mitterrand et le centrisme secret des Verts', *Le Monde*, 22 June.

Poguntke, T. (1990). 'Party activists versus voters: Are the German Greens losing touch with the electorate?', in Rüdig, W. (ed.), *Green Politics One 1990*. (Edinburgh: Edinburgh University Press), pp. 29–46.

Rüdig, W. (1991). 'Green party politics around the world', *Environment*, Vol. 33, No. 8, October, pp. 6–9, 25–31.

Rüdig, W.; Bennie, L. G.; Franklin, M. N. (1991). *Green Party Members: A Profile* (Glasgow: Delta Publications).

Rüdig, W. and Lowe, P. (forthcoming). *The Green Wave: A Comparative Analysis of Ecological Parties*. (Cambridge: Polity Press).

Schmitt, M. (1989). 'Was war "europäisch" am Europawahlverhalten der Deutschen?', *Aus Politik und Zeitgeschichte*, B43/89, 20 October, pp. 39–51,

3. Alliance Patterns of the European Environmental Movement*

RUSSELL J. DALTON

Politics and Society Department, University of California, Irvine, USA

In the past two decades the environmental movement has emerged as a contentious new actor in the political process of most western democracies – but they are not alone. Politics is a process of coalition building; allies must be courted and possible opponents must be counterbalanced. Often these allies have been other challenging political groups, such as the women's movement, peace groups, or the remnants of the 1960s student movement. The opponents of the environmental movement seem most prominent among representatives of the established political order – business interests, labour unions, and agents of the state.

Identifying these potential friends and allies is a crucial step in defining the identity of the environmental movement and in building the political coalitions that can produce the policy reforms advocated by environmentalists. But the significance of alliance patterns is a matter of contention among social movement scholars.

The organizational emphasis of resource mobilisation theory focused attention on how coalition processes form a crucial element of social movement organizations (SMOs). Curtis and Zurcher (1973) first introduced the concept of a 'multi-organizational field' to describe the complex organizational networks that can envelop SMOs, and this work has been expanded by others (McCarthy and Zald 1977; Tilly 1978; Klandermans 1989). At the individual level, participants in a social movement retain personal ties to other social and political groups; these multiple affiliations establish an exchange link between a social movement and other social groups. Personal linkages are an important part of the mobilisation process of social movements, as well as affecting the behaviour of individual SMO members (Klandermans et al. 1988). For instance, adherents of the environmental movement overlap considerably with supporters of other

*Support for this research was provided by a grant from the National Science Foundation (SES 85-10989) and the Council on Research and Creativity, Florida State University.

New Social Movements and are drawn disproportionately from communities with already high mobilisation levels for 'alternative' political groups (Kaase 1990; Kriesi 1988; Kitschelt 1989).

Research drawn from the resource mobilisation perspective also underscores the importance of networks at the organizational level: the ties linking SMOs to other social groups and political organizations within their multi-organizational field. A social movement is itself a network of supporters, and this network is then linked to other organizational networks through these alliance patterns. Here Charles Tilly's (1978) distinction between members of the polity and challenging groups (such as social movements) is relevant. Although not a formal part of the social movement itself, members of the polity can facilitate the development and maintenance of the movement. The contribution of funds, personnel and organizational expertise from established organizations – such as labour unions, churches, charitable foundations and political institutions can be crucial in assisting a movement to overcome the hurdles of creating a new organizational entity. Members of the polity may serve as a conduit for political influence, giving a challenging group at least indirect access to the political process and linking SMOs to potential supporters and advocates within the political establishment. The importance of alliance patterns is illustrated by research indicating that the number of organizational allies supporting an SMO is a significant predictor of success (Gamson 1975; Steedly and Foley 1979; Turk and Zucher 1984). Resource mobilisation theory thus sees social movements as embedded in a complex network of organizations – a 'network of networks' in Neidhart's (1985) terms – with overlapping political interests, personnel, resources, and bases of popular support.

In contrast to the resource mobilisation perspective, many of the initial writings on New Social Movements (NSMs), such as environmental groups or the women's movement, described these organizations in terms of their estrangement from members of the polity and other established social and political groups (Brand 1982; Brand et al. 1986; Offe 1984). Claus Offe, for example, attributes the isolation of New Social Movements to their dichotomous view of society – the world is a conflict between 'us' and 'them' and this viewpoint discourages political exchange or gradualist political tactics (1985, p. 830). Offe further maintains that NSMs distance themselves from established socio-political groups because the popular base of these movements is drawn from the new middle class and other 'decommodified' groups that consciously remain on the periphery of society (1985, pp. 851–2). Other scholars link the supposedly autonomous tendencies of NSMs to their lack of resources and hence their inability to engage in the bargaining exchanges of normal politics (Melucci 1980). The burgeoning empirical literature on New Social Movements yields mixed support for these contrasting images of the organizational networks of these movements (Walsh 1989; Diani 1990; Rucht 1989; Brand 1985; Diani and Lodi 1988).

This research evaluates these contrasting images of the environmental movement by examining how the European environmental groups relate to the established social and political interests of their respective nations. Our findings are based on a survey of sixty-nine major environmental interest groups in ten West European states. We are first concerned with the extent to which environmental groups are embedded in a network that helps to support and sustain the movement. If alliance patterns do exist, what is the composition of the support network for the movement – are environmental groups linked to established members of the polity or do they develop alternative allies and supporters? Rather than follow the course of past research, which has looked at the overlap in membership or leadership between various social sectors, this chapter taps environmentalists' perceptions of the major social and political groups that structure contemporary political competition. What social groups and political actors are perceived as sympathetic toward environmental reform, and thus may serve as potential allies, and what actors are viewed as the opponents of reform? This information enables us to determine how the environmental movement perceives the multi-organizational field in which it functions.

Research Base

The collection of detailed information from a wide cross-national spectrum of environmental groups is a major research undertaking. During the summer and fall of 1985, we contacted the leading five or ten national environmental groups in each of the ten member states of the European Community; the core of this list was drawn from the membership of the European Environmental Bureau in Brussels (Lowe and Goyder 1983, Chapter 10). From each group we requested copies of their newsletters, policy papers and annual reports. These materials provide background information on the structure of the groups and a chronicle of their activities over the prior year. In December 1985 our research team travelled to Europe to interview group representatives; interviewing was completed in spring 1986. The interviews lasted approximately 90 minutes, based on a common survey questionnaire adapted to the national context. The interviews focused on perceptions of environmental conditions, the policy activities of the group, the organizational structure of each group, and the political views of group representatives.

A total of sixty-nine environmental groups were surveyed, including most of the major environmental groups in Western Europe (see Table 1).

Table 1 European environmental groups

Belgium
*Les Amis de la Terre
Bond Beter Leefmilieu
*Greenpeace
+Inter-environment Wallonie
+National Union for Conservation
Raad Leefmilieu te Brussel
+Reserves Ornitologiques
+Stichting Leefmilieu
+World Wildlife Fund

Denmark
+Friluftradet
+GENDAN
*Greenpeace
+Naturfrednings Forening (DN)
*NOAH
+Ornitologisk Forening (DOF)

France
*Les Amis de la Terre
+COLINE
CREPAN
+FFSPN
*Greenpeace
+Inst. European Environmental Policy
+Journalists and the Environment
Nature and Progress
+Society for the Protection of Nature
+World Wildlife Fund

Great Britain
+Civic Trust
+Council for Environmental
   Conservation
*Conservation Society
+Council for the Protection of Rural
   England
+Fauna and Flora Society
*Friends of the Earth (FoE)
Green Alliance
*Greenpeace

+Royal Society for the Protection of
   Birds (RSPB)
+Town and Country Planning Association
+World Wildlife Fund

Greece
Ellinike Etairia
+EREYA
*Friends of the Earth
+Friends of the Trees
+Hellenic Society for Nature Protection
PAKOE

Ireland
+An Taisce
+Wildlife Federation

Italy
+Agriturist
*Amici della Terra
+Fondo per l'Ambiente Italiano
+Italia Nostra
*Lega per l'Ambiente
*Lega per l'Abolizione della Caccia
+Lega Italiana per la Protezione degli
   Uccelli (LIPU)
+World Wildlife Fund

Luxembourg
*Mouvement Ecologique
+Natura

Netherlands
*Greenpeace
+IVN
*Stichting Milieueducatie (SME)
*Stichting Mondiaal Alternatief
+Stichting Natuur en Milieu (SNM)
*Vereniging Milieudefensie (VMD)
+Nederlandse Vereniging tot Bescher-
   ming van Vogels
+Vereniging tot Behoud van de Waddenzee

West Germany
*BBU
BUND
+Bund für Vogelschutz
+Deutscher Naturschutzring
*Greenpeace
*Robin Wood
+Schutzgemeinschaft Deutscher Wald
+World Wildlife Fund

Conservation groups are marked by a + sign; ecologist groups by a *.

Our intent was to study ongoing, national, multi-issue groups that represent the diversity of the European environmental movement, ranging from the larger established organizations to student-run activist groups, from traditional wildlife protection groups to critics of advanced industrialism, from amenity societies to Alternativbewegungen. We feel the surveyed groups fulfil this objective. The sample includes 47 mass-membership groups, 13 national 'umbrella' organizations, 6 research or educational institutions, and 3 'by invitation only' groups of environmental elites.

These groups represent a permanent organization base for the environmental movement and boast broad popular support. The forty-seven mass-membership groups in our survey include over 1·5 million members, and the umbrella organizations represent several thousand national and local subgroups. The combined operating budgets of all sixty-nine groups was over $40 million in 1985.

Research on the environmental movement frequently focuses on the unconventional and anti-establishment groups: Greenpeace, Friends of the Earth and other New Left groups such as the BBU and Robin Wood in West Germany or NOAH in Denmark. We adopted a broader definition of the environmental movement because ecologists, conservationists, wildlife groups and other environmental groups often have common issue interests, as well as sharing a partially overlapping membership and financial base.

The diversity of the environmental groups in our survey enables us to examine the New Social Movement thesis in a more focused way by comparing the behaviour of the 'old' and 'new' components of the environmental movement. Drawing upon similar distinctions made by Lowe and Goyder (1983), Cotgrove (1982) and Rucht (1988), we distinguish between conservation and ecologist components of the environmental movement. The nature conservation component largely consists of traditional organizations that address the consensual issues of environmental policy such as protection of wildlife, nature conservation and amenity societies. Lowe and Goyder refer to these organizations as 'emphasis' groups, 'by which we mean groups whose aims do not conflict in any clear-cut way with widely held social goals or values' (1983, p. 35). These groups tend to be more conservative in their political philosophy and adopt conventional policy styles. Within this sector, for example, we include the national bird protection associations, the World Wildlife Fund, and other nature conservation groups. Of the organizations included in our survey, thirty-seven are traditional groups; they are marked in Table 1 by a plus (+) sign.

The focus of attention of NSM theory lies, however, in the views and actions of the ecologist groups. Ecologist groups are more likely to question the dominant social paradigm of industrial society and endorse what has been described as the 'new environmental paradigm' (Cotgrove 1982; Milbrath 1984). Many of these groups advocate significant reforms in the economic and/or political systems, such as the creation of a sustainable society or the restriction of capitalist market forces. These political orientations are often combined with an unconventional style based on protests and other direct-action techniques. Friends of the Earth, Greenpeace and student groups such as Robinwood and NOAH best illustrate the vanguard component of the movement. A total of twenty-one organizations are classified as having ecologist orientations; they are noted in Table 1 by an asterisk (*).

Elsewhere, we have introduced a model of ideological mobilisation that argues that the ideology or political identity of an SMO affects the potential resources, political perceptions and political opportunities of the organization (Dalton, forthcoming). For instance, this model asserts that even though the Royal Society for the Protection of Birds (RSPB) and Greenpeace are both concerned with wildlife protection issues, there are predictable differences between the potential resources and political opportunities available to these two groups because of their different political identities. A group with a non-challenging ideology, like the RSPB, is more likely to receive support and build alliances with interests that are part of the prevailing social order; a group such as Greenpeace that challenges the social order may have to find its allies among other movement groups or dissident factions of society. Non-challenging groups also might be granted ready access to the political process, while challenging groups must place greater reliance on unconventional methods of political influence.

A comparison of different environmental organizations illustrates the diversity that exists within the rainbow of green groups. More important, it provides a stronger reference point for testing the New Social Movement theory, by comparing traditional conservation groups to the ecologist vanguard of the environmental movement.

Alliances and the Creation of Environmental Organizations

If alliance patterns are important to social movements, their role may start with the first efforts to create an organizational base to the movement. Indeed, the resources required to create and institutionalise an SMO may be the greatest institutional hurdle that an organization faces during its existence. Just as a new business needs working capital to establish itself in operation, an SMO requires an initial resource base in order to mobilise further resources, sustain the organization, and support its activities. Thus before discussing the present alliance tendencies of environmental groups, we want briefly to review the role that support networks have played in the creation of environmental movement organizations.

Several of the conservation groups formed during the first mobilisation wave of environmentalism (1880–1910) aptly illustrate the importance of having allies who can provide initial assistance. For instance, the Royal Society for the Prevention of Cruelty to Animals, formed in 1824, provided financial assistance and administrative support to the RSPB and other fledgling British conservation groups during this period. The Danish Ladies' Society for the Protection of Animals similarly aided in the formation of the Danish Ornithological Society. In many other instances, the 'venture capital' for the new conservation group was provided by wealthy benefactors: the RSPB sustained itself through its early years with the financial support of Hannah Poland, a London property owner; the Fauna and Flora Society, the SPNR and the National Trust of Britain all began as the instruments of wealthy benefactors (Sheail 1976). Similar patterns are found among other conservation groups, such as Natuurmonumenten and Heemschut in Holland, or the SNPN in France (Tellegen 1983). Although it is possible for an organization to be self-sufficient from the outset, the backing of other groups or wealthy patrons certainly eases the problems of institutionalisation.

Ties with established social interests and the government have been a continuing feature of conservation groups. For example, the British government established the Nature Conservancy Council in 1949 to administer nature reserves and advise the government on conservation issues; this became a key institution in British conservation politics and the Nature Conservancy Council further strengthened the conservation network by forming the Council for Nature in 1958. Government planning requirements have legitimated and expanded the role of other conservation groups, such as the Town and Country Planning Association in Britain and the Danish Society for Nature Conservation. The establishment links of the conservation movement are perhaps best illustrated by the World Wildlife Fund. WWF was founded in 1961 as a popular arm of the international conservation movement, and among its early leaders were the royal families of Europe (Prince Philip headed WWF-Britain and Prince Bernhard of the Netherlands was the president of WWF international). Indeed, the ability of many conservation groups to court such strong allies may explain their considerable success in mobilising generous budgets and a large membership base (Dalton, forthcoming; Rucht 1988).

It might be argued that conservation groups were nurtured by the social elite and government because the interests of these groups did not threaten the established social order, and in fact represented the hobbies and leisure concerns of Europe's upper class. Ecologist groups, in contrast, cannot rely on such endorsements. In reviewing the factors surrounding the creation of ecologist groups during the second mobilisation wave (1965–85), we seldom found evidence of the same patterns of elite support that assisted conservation groups. But albeit in another form, organizational alliances were important to the formation of most ecologist groups. For many ecologist groups and their founders, their initial political training and organizational expertise came from involvement in conservation groups: Friends of the Earth began as a faction of the Sierra Club in the United States; Robin Wood is a splinter group from Greenpeace in Germany; Actiongroup Straw established the Stichting Milieu educatie in Holland; and the Öko-Institut evolved from the German ecology movement. In a few instances, the benefactor was another challenging political organization: the Lega per l'ambiente was formed by intellectuals within the Italian Communist party and initially received financial support from the PCI. Greenpeace during its initial Amchitka campaign was dependent on the support of other alternative groups, sympathetic individuals and organizations who held access to vital resources, such as a boat (Hunter 1979). Yet even when there was an example of an emerging ecologist group receiving assistance from a business or other established group, the basis of this assistance was generally a single act of support rather than the development of more structured ties between ecologist groups and other social interests. Instead of having established patrons, ecologist groups often depended on their ability to mobilise a mass of individual supporters, while drawing sustenance from other alternative social and political groups.

Another distinctive feature of the second mobilisation wave was the creation of multinational environmental groups; an organization formed in one nation provides the resources to establish affiliates in other nations. Friends of the Earth spread from the United States to Britain and France in the early 1970s, and from there to several other European states. Greenpeace began as a Canadian organization, then moved southward to San Francisco and then across the Atlantic to Europe. The World Wildlife Fund spread to almost two dozen nations within the period of a single decade. Once an international network is established, it provides a resource base to support the formation of other affiliates in other nations.

Certainly it is true that a new organization may begin as a purely spontaneous grassroots movement (though we are unsure whether any such 'pure case' exists among the organizations we studied), but it is clear that many of today's environmental groups surmounted the considerable hurdles of building a new organization by utilising a little help from their friends. It is also clear that these networks or friendship patterns vary across organizations. Thus the mere existence of alliance patterns may not be what distinguishes conservation and ecologist groups – they are differentiated by who helped them to build their organizations.

Perceptions of Alliance and Conflict Networks

If we shift our attention from the formative period of environmental groups to their ongoing activities, we may find that many of the action-oriented alliances between environmental groups and other political actors are fleeting affairs. Jeffrey Berry (1984, pp. 202–5), for instance, describes coalition-formation as a ubiquitous part of interest group politics, where kindred spirits are constantly working to form new coalitions as old ones dissolve. A specific issue, such as waste dumping at sea, may assemble a coalition of environmentalists, dockworkers and fishing interests that exists only for this issue and breaks apart once the issue is resolved. Similarly, a campaign to prevent the destruction of tropical rain forests might create a political coalition that is united on this campaign, but which cannot agree on actions aimed at the destruction of European forests caused by acid rain (see Dalton, forthcoming, Chapter 8 for a discussion of the political tactics and activities of environmental groups).

But beyond the short-term instrumental ties of a specific political campaign, there are recurring patterns in how other political actors generally respond to calls for environmental reform. These general patterns of response define the multi-organizational field in which the environmental movement functions. Bert Klandermans (1990) points out that this multi-organizational field contains both supporting and opposing sectors. The alliance system consists of groups and organizations that regularly support the general goals of the movement; the conflict system consists of those actors and groups which routinely oppose the movement, often including agencies of the state.

By defining the multi-organizational field of environmental groups we can gain a better understanding of how the movement is related to established social interests and governmental institutions – knowing the members of the alliance and conflict systems of the environmental movement tells us about the potential resources available to environmental groups and the forces that block their course. For instance, if the movement does distance itself from the government and established polity members, then its claim to represent a challenging ideology must be given more weight. The question of how the movement relates itself to the traditional left/right pattern of political cleavage can tell us a great deal about the movement's potential for restructuring or realigning the socio-political space of advanced industrial democracies.

In order to look beyond the short-term patterns of specific issue alliances, we assessed the multi-organizational field of the environmental movement by asking group representatives about their perceptions of other important social and political actors. That is, rather than constructing the field based on formal institutional ties (which are difficult to assess reliably because of the fluid nature of the environmental movement), we measured the field in perceptual or psychological terms. We asked the respondents in our survey to define their allies and opponents in terms of how well various social and political organizations were addressing their nation's environmental problems. We consciously focused on the potential alliance patterns between the environmental movement and what might be considered members of the polity – government agencies, socio-economic interest groups, and the major political parties – to determine how European environmentalists perceived these established political actors. Access to the organizational and political resources of these polity members would greatly contribute to the development of the environmental movement, and the pattern of these relationships is a key factor in theorising about the nature of the environmental movement. These data enable us to determine which members of the polity environmentalists perceive as sympathetic to their goals, and therefore may serve as potential allies to the movement, and which actors represent the opponents (or are at least are viewed as unsupportive) of environmental reform.

Figure 1 displays the environmental ratings of each political institution averaged across the combined European sample (responses are coded so that 4·0 represents an 'excellent' evaluation by all environmental groups and 1·0 represents a consistently 'poor' rating). The average evaluations are presented separately for conservation groups (marked by a darkened circle) and ecologist groups (marked by a clear circle); in every instance the European average lies between these two poles. These data enable us to see if there are systematic differences in the rating of political groups that transcend national borders, and provide a standard against which evaluations of specific actors in each nation can be judged.

Social movements organize in order to address an issue that is not recognised or accepted by the dominant forces in society, hence the need for the movement. Therefore it is not surprising to find that only two institutions – green parties and newspapers – are ranked above the good/bad midpoint of the scale. European environmental leaders give predominantly

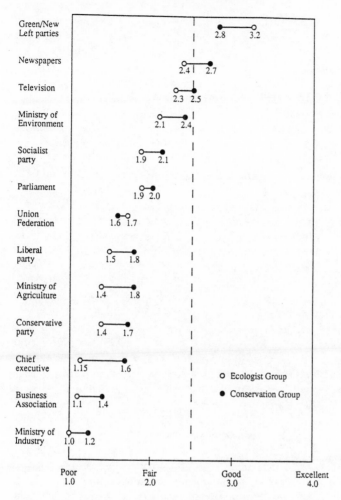

Figure 1 Environmental evaluations of social and political actors

negative environmental performance ratings to the wide range of other social and political institutions included on the list, and often these evaluations are sharply critical.

One of the more favourable ratings is given to the respective national Ministry of the Environment (MoE); it is ranked near the top of the list of institutions, but still below the midpoint of the scale. By comparison, nearly all European environmentalists are sharply critical of the actions of their Ministry of Industry (MoI) and the Ministry of Agriculture (or their equivalents). The MoI is ranked at the bottom of the scale, often with accompanying comments that even a 'poor' classification is too positive.

The relative rankings of the MoE and the MoI reflect the policy-making problems of the environmental movement. In the battle between a weak MoE and strong MoI, most of the environmental leaders (71 per cent) feel the Ministry of the Environment will lose.

A similar imbalance exists in evaluations of parliament and the chief executive. The respective national parliaments generally receive an environmental rating above the average of other institutions (mean=1·96). In contrast, the chief executive consistently garners negative evaluations (mean=1·43), regardless of whether the left or right controls the government. In an age in which the power of the executive is predominant, this pattern cannot be considered a positive sign for potential environmental reform.

When one scans the ranking of all the actors in Figure 1, and thus the perceptions of the alliance and conflict systems of the environmental movement, the shadow of a familiar pattern is seen. Although environmentalists often boastfully claim that they represent a new political movement that is neither left nor right, perceptions of the allies and opponents of environmental reform at least partially reflect a traditional left/right political alignment. Across all of Europe, environmentalists are consistently critical about the representatives of business, agriculture and industry in their nation. Nearly 90 per cent of our respondents assign their Ministry of Industry a 'poor' rating (mean=1·11); and over 75 per cent give similar scores to business associations (mean=1·27). Environmentalists apparently have little difficulty in identifying these foes. By comparison, labour unions are rated more positively than business or agricultural interests, though unions are still not seen as receptive to environmental reform. For instance, almost half of all environmentalists give labour union federations a 'poor' rating for their environmental performance (mean=1·70).

This modest left/right pattern in environmental perceptions also emerges for evaluations of party groups across Europe (also see Dalton, forthcoming, Chapter 9). Beyond the positive support for green and new left parties, most environmentalists give negative ratings to all of the established parties, but modest differences emerge between the major party groups. European Socialist parties (mean=2·02) are rated slightly better than Liberal parties (mean=1·66), and Conservative parties are rated a notch lower (mean=1·55). Averaged across ten separate party systems, the differences between these three established party groups follow a left/right pattern, but the largest gap still separates all the established parties from the green/new left parties. Certainly, a comparison of labour leaders or business executives would display far sharper differences in how these same parties are perceived for their economic policy positions.

The patterns in Figure 1 also illustrate how environmental ideology can affect perceptions of the multi-organizational field. The ranking of actors is relatively similar between conservation groups and ecologist groups, but the absolute ratings follow a systematic pattern. Conservation groups are almost always more positive in their evaluations of social and political actors, in part because established institutions are more receptive to conservation issues. The colouring of ideology is especially strong for institutions identified with the dominant industrial order: the Prime Minister $(r = \cdot 38)$, business associations $(r = \cdot 33)$, the Ministry of Industry $(r = .31)$, and the Conservative Party $(r = \cdot 28)$. There are two notable exceptions where these patterns are reversed and ecologist groups are more positive in their evaluations: green/new left parties $(r = -\cdot 25)$ and labour unions $(r = -\cdot 07)$. This first correlation suggests that ecologist groups are more likely to view green parties as the parliamentary arm of the movement. The second correlation hints at the potential for old left/new left alliances within Western Europe, though ecologists and conservationists are still rather critical of the unions' environmental stance.

These evaluations based on the total sample of environmental groups are useful for identifying regularities in political evaluations that transcend national boundaries. At the same time, we must be cautious about these data because they aggregate together evaluations of different institutions and actors. Environmentalists are not responding to the same stimulus, but to different objects in each nation. For instance, ratings of the chief executive intermix opinions about Papandreou, Mitterrand, Thatcher, Kohl and the other European heads of state; such forced commonality sometimes may be inappropriate. Therefore, we next want to go beyond these European-wide patterns and look more closely at the national patterns underlying these aggregate findings.

Governmental Institutions

As contenders for political influence, the relations between a social movement and government agencies strongly affects the political potential of the movement (Tilly 1978; Gamson 1975). Government agencies constitute some of the most important actors in the multi-organizational field of the environmental movement. If the movement is able to find allies within the government, this can facilitate the mobilisation of resources and access to the decision-making process. Strong opponents within the government – such as antagonist agencies or political parties – can drain the resources of the movement and restrict its opportunities for influence.

The cross-national pattern in the evaluation of three key government institutions – the Ministry of the Environment, the parliament, and the Prime Minister – is displayed in Figure 2. These data should be treated with some caution because the results are based on a small number of cases (Ireland and Luxembourg are not even included because only two organizations were contacted in both nations). At the same time, the groups we surveyed do represent the major environmental actors in each nation, and nearly the universe of major environmental groups in Europe; thus their responses are important evidence of the perceptual field of the movement.

Among government institutions, environmental groups generally give their highest ratings to their respective MoE. This is to be expected. The MoE is the supposed protector of the environment and the advocate for policy reform; if the movement is to find an ally within the government, it should be here. And yet the absolute rating of environmental ministries is quite modest; only three – Denmark, Holland, and France – receive ratings above the midpoint in the scale. As we heard throughout the interviews, relations between the movement and the MoE often have an adversarial tone, falling far short of the normal neo-corporatist arrangement that might be found between the transport industry and the ministry of transportation, or farmers and the agricultural ministry. One senior official of Britain's Department of the Environment observed that it was the only government department where the civil servants were expected to work together with a clientele that is being continually criticised by the leadership of the same department. Indeed, in most nations the MoE is cited by environmentalists for their inaction or poor relations with the movement. These relations were most strained in Germany, where environmental concerns were handled by the Ministry of the Interior. The tensions between environmental issues and the ministry's other concerns, and the conservative political orientation of Interior Minister Friedrich Zimmermann, may explain why the German government established a separate ministry for the environment and nuclear safety the following year.

Parliament is normally ranked second in each nation, with two notable exceptions: Belgium and West Germany. In both of these nations, and only in these nations, green parties held parliamentary seats at the time of our survey. The Belgian ECOLO/Agalev and the German Greens use this position to increase legislative action on environmental issues, making the parliament the most responsive agency of government in these two nations. The Danish Folketing receives the highest marks of any parliament, reflecting the progressive stance of its leftist government on recycling, conservation issues, opposition to nuclear power, and other environmental matters. Many Danish packaging and pollution standards are at the forefront of environmental reform in Europe, to the point where some other EC member states claim that these regulations (such as recycling requirements) are an indirect restriction on intra-EC trade. British groups also see the House of Lords (mean=2·44) as being slightly more responsive than the House of Commons (mean=2·11). In most nations, the 'fair' evaluations of national parliaments are regularly interlaced with positive

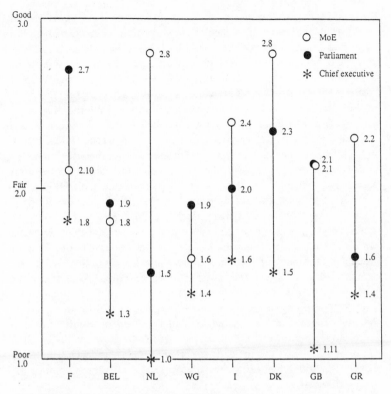

Figure 2 Environmental evaluations of political institutions

evaluations for certain parliamentary committees or specific MPs. Over-all, European environmentalists find pockets of support within the legis-lature, even if they view the entire institution as less supportive.

Many European heads of state have paid at least symbolic attention to environmental issues during the 1980s – Kohl's concern for acid rain and Papandreou's expressed sympathy for Athens' pollution problems – but all of these political figures receive low marks for their handling of environmental problems. In each nation the chief executive receives the lowest score from among these three governmental institutions (often rivalling the abysmal ratings of the Ministry of Industry). Among Europe's leaders, the worst performance ratings are earned by Ruud Lubbers in The Netherlands and Margaret Thatcher in Britain. Lubbers has been a foe of the environmental movement since the mid-1970s, when as Minister of Economics he spearheaded a drive to develop nuclear power in Holland (Hatch 1986). At least one respondent in our survey felt that even the lowest category was too positive for Lubbers' performance; in fact, all

Dutch groups give him a 'poor' mark for his environmental record (mean=1·00). Margaret Thatcher's ratings are almost equally bad; all but one group assign her a 'poor' score (mean=1·11). Under Thatcher's administration Britain earned the label of the 'dirty nation of Europe', a recognition that the Prime Minister sometimes seemed to bear with pride. Official governmental policy was often marked by a failure to recognise the existence of problems such as acid rain or even conform to international environmental standards. Faced by growing public concern for green issues, Thatcher tried to remake her environmental image in the late 1980s, but the legacy of her earlier image remains. For example, an *Economist* survey of British executives in 1990, certainly a group with values much different from our environmentalists, finds that over 60 per cent of executives who rate the environment as an important issue give Thatcher a fairly poor or very poor mark for her performance (*Economist*, 21 July 1990, p. 55).

The highest rated executive in our survey is President François Mitterrand of France. Mitterrand has had a tempestuous relationship with French environmentalists. After courting their support in the 1981 presidential elections, he reversed his position on the critical issue of nuclear power once in office, earning him disdain from many environmentalists. The 1985 bombing of the Greenpeace ship, *Rainbow Warrior*, by agents of the French government created a further feeling of enmity towards Mitterrand, who never fully distanced himself from the incident. Thus Mitterrand's positive rating relative to other European leaders is somewhat surprising, though in leading the pack Mitterrand still receives quite poor marks (mean=1·78).

The results of Figure 2 carry several lessons about the perceptual field of the European environmental movement. The majority of environmental groups are deeply involved in the policy-making process, which leads them to search for potential allies within the institutions of governance. As New Social Movement theorists claim, this search bears little fruit at an institutional level in most nations. Every European government now has a ministry or department devoted to environmental issues, but these agencies are seldom seen as strong allies of the movement. Similarly, a growing number of politicians are expressing a concern for environmental issues, especially around election time, but this is not translated into perceptions of a responsive parliament. Even more telling, the chief executive represents the culmination of political (and partisan) power within the government, and these office-holders receive consistently poor ratings from environmental groups. As we move up the ladder of interest aggregation and presumably political power (MoE, parliament, chief executive), the perceived responsiveness of governmental institutions decreases. Indeed, these patterns are what should be expected of a social movement that is challenging the goals and procedures of the established socio-political order.

Business and Labour

The still-dominant social interests in most contemporary societies are the economic interests represented by business and labour: the competition between these two forces is a major factor in structuring the nature of political competition in these societies; the issues raised by these two groups often dominate the political agenda; and the resources available to these groups overshadows most other interest groups. Thus the location of these economic interests in the perceptual field of the environmental movement is of fundamental importance in determining the political status (and possible partisan orientation) of the movement.

Labour unions often find themselves cross-pressured on matters of environmental reform. On the one hand, unions traditionally view economic growth as a prerequisite for improving the material standard of living for the working class and as a precondition for social progress. This orientation frequently has led unions to oppose environmental regulations which might restrict economic growth, especially large infrastructure projects such as nuclear power, highway construction and airport expansion. As representatives of the specific economic interests of their members, unions adopt a protective stance on these issues. The economic recessions of the past two decades often pushed the unions to emphasise their role as the guarantor of their members' economic interests over social issues such as environmental reform. For instance, in the tripartite negotiations between government, labour and business during the mid-1970s recession, the German trade unions took an even harsher stance against environmental protection than did the employers (Ewringmann and Zimmermann 1978). Employers have played on the unions' fears that industrial pollution regulations will lead to lay-offs and plant closures in order to build a business/labour alliance in opposition to environmental reform (Kazis and Grossman 1982; Siegmann 1985).

On the other hand, unions generally act as a progressive political force in contemporary society, and their members also benefit from measures that protect the environment and enhance the general quality of life. And in recent years, many individual unions have shown a greater reluctance to equate ecology with the loss of jobs. The ongoing dilemma for the unions is how to balance these two tendencies.

The values and orientations of the business community also contain a mix of motivations. Industry represents one of the strongest advocates of the dominant social paradigm; surveys of business leaders underscore their continuing commitment to the free market, the supremacy of private property, the acceptance of hierarchical authority patterns, and the creation of wealth as a near moral imperative (Cotgrove 1982, Chapter 2; Milbrath 1984). These values and the predictable opposition of most industrialists

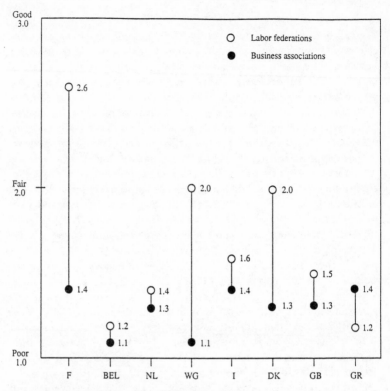

Figure 3 Environmental evaluations of social groups
Key: F = France; BEL = Belgium; NL = The Netherlands; WG = West Germany; I = Italy; DK = Denmark; GB = Great Britain; GR = Greece

to environmental regulation lead most scholars to locate the business community firmly within the conflict system of the environmental movement. Although the value contrasts between environmentalists and business leaders are indeed sharp, there are also instances when the interests of both overlap. There is a potential affinity between business interests and nature conservation groups regarding issues of wildlife protection and the preservation of nature (Offe 1985); such bonds have been a regular feature of the conservation movement. In addition, businesses are now realising that a display of environmental awareness can improve their corporate image and possibly boost sales: Cadbury wraps chocolate bars in wildlife prints with the seal of the World Wildlife Fund; magazine advertisers flock to buy space in special issues commemorating the anniversary of Earth Day; and one German manufacturer claims that buying its washing machine will protect newts. If it pays to be green, businesses will change colour.

Figure 3 portrays how environmentalists think national business and labour associations have acquitted themselves on environmental issues. Despite some attempts by business leaders to project a greater sensitivity toward green issues, European environmentalists are virtually united in identifying business associations as a major political opponent. The average evaluation of the major business association in each nation never exceeds 1·50 on a 1·00–4·00 scale. Individual businesses or business leaders may aid the environmental movement, but as a collective group, business interests are clearly part of the conflict system of the movement.

Evaluations of labour unions are more varied, reflecting the ambivalent relationship between the labour movement and the environmental movement. The French unions receive relatively positive scores because the object of evaluation is the Confédération Française Démocratique du Travail (CFDT). The CFDT has a long history of sympathy for the environmental movement and new left causes; it was one of the first established groups to criticise nuclear power in France and jointly worked with environmentalists in compiling the ecologist slate in the 1978 elections (Nelkin and Pollak 1981). In contrast, the Communist-leaning Confédération Générale du Travail (CGT) (which was not included in our survey) is more critical of the French environmental movement and more likely to approach environmental issues strictly in terms of the economic consequences for their members. The German Federation of Labour (DGB) and the Danish Labour Organization (LO) receive at least modest approval ratings for their environmental actions. The actions of the DGB perhaps illustrate the potential for coalition building between old left and new left constituencies. From its earlier position of hostility toward the environmental movement, the DGB has substantially changed its position in recent years, especially once the SPD had left government and the party had revised its position on green issues. A major DGB report in 1985 stresses the policy goal of 'qualitative growth' and acknowledges that 'only environmentally-sound jobs are secure jobs'. From a position that environmental reform threatens worker interests, the DGB now maintains that anti-pollution legislation is a method of job-creation. These views are still debated among the constituent unions of the DGB, but an expanding network of alliances is building between green organizations and the labour movement.

Beyond these positive examples, however, the remaining labour federations in Europe receive generally poor marks from environmentalists. The British TUC, for instance, has a mean environmental rating of 1·50, barely above that of the CBI. British environmentalists see more support coming from the rank-and-file union members and younger labour officials than from the present union leadership; thus the prospects for change in the future are brighter than the present situation. In Belgium, Holland, Italy and Greece, the perceptions of labour are virtually indistinguishable from those of business. The overall prospects for labour–environmental alliances across Europe still appear uncertain.

The Movement and the Media

The mass media are an especially important actor in the political space of a social movement (Schoenfeld et al. 1979; Rochon 1988). For the average citizen, the media provide a window for observing world affairs. In most instances, it is only through media coverage that individuals can experience the devastation wrought by an oil spill or see the threats to endangered species. The media can also be a potent source of popular education on political issues, especially in forming opinions on new topics, such as green issues.

But beyond these normal information functions, the views and actions of the media are of critical importance to a citizen-based movement. For a large, geographically dispersed popular movement such as environmentalism, the media's reporting of environmental topics provides a vital information link between the movement and its actual and potential members. Media coverage furnishes citizens with political cues from the movement, and provides some legitimacy for the movement itself. In addition, media coverage can be a key element in the mobilisation of popular support for the movement. The drama of Greenpeace zodiacs battling a whaling ship or FoE demonstrating against industrial pollution is directly experienced by only a few, but witnessed by many through the media.

Thus the quantity and quality of media coverage of green issues and the movement itself is an important factor in understanding the patterns of environmental action. A sympathetic and interested press can be a vital member of the movement's alliance system. A sceptical and distrusting press can isolate environmental groups and minimalise their popular appeal.

There is evidence that journalists are generally sympathetic towards the environmental movement; for instance, small environmental groups specifically for journalists exist in several nations (Journalists and the Environment in France, and a large journalistic contingent in Britain's Green Alliance). Media coverage of environmental issues has also grown dramatically in the last two decades (e.g., Schoenfeld et al. 1979).

Our survey finds that environmentalists normally perceive the media as supportive of their cause (Figure 4). Both newspapers and state television receive relatively positive environmental ratings in most nations. We often heard comments that television was the most important medium for the movement, but newspapers almost always receive more positive ratings for their environmental performance. Newspapers can cover a story in more depth than television reporting, and are free of the political

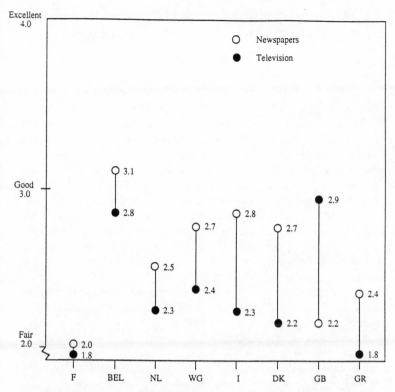

Figure 4 Environmental evaluations of the media
Key: F = France; BEL = Belgium; NL = The Netherlands; WG = West Germany; I =
Italy; DK = Denmark; GB = Great Britain; GR = Greece

constraints of state-run television stations. State television receives its best
marks in Belgium and Britain, two nations with an abundance of regularly
scheduled programmes dealing with environmental matters (Elkington *et
al.* 1988, p. 197). The poorest marks for television are scored in France and
Greece, where governmental resistance to the movement is seen as extending to television coverage. Britain is the only nation where television
receives higher marks than the print media. Several British environmentalists signalled out the positive coverage in 'elite' newspapers, such as the
Guardian and the *Observer*, and then contrasted that with the poor handling
of the same issues in the daily tabloids.

Although there are significant national variations and even variations
between specific newspapers and television networks, most environmentalists place the mass media within their alliance network. This support is
crucial because of the media's role as a communication and mobilisation
tool for the movement. Without the media, the movement might not

exist. Moreover, this is an active alliance, with media contacts representing one of the frequent activities of environmental groups (Dalton, forthcoming, Chapter 8).

The Implications of Perceptual Networks

The findings of this chapter illustrate how environmentalists view the
political world that surrounds them. Not surprisingly, environmentalists
are clearly aware that most members of the polity are not committed to
environmental reform. In some instances – such as the Ministries of
Industry and Agriculture, and business interests – environmentalists are
confronted by outright opposition. In many other cases, it appears that calls
for environmental reform are met by indifference or ambivalence. Even
some institutions that are seen as supportive of environmentalism – such
as the Ministry of the Environment or the media – receive only modest
evaluations. Only green/new left parties are viewed as clear political
allies of the environmental movement, but the radicalism of these parties
may actually mediate their value in building broader-based political
alliances. In short, the perceptual field of the environmental movement
includes many powerful opponents among the established members of the
polity and only tentative or uncertain allies.

The political distance between the environmental movement and
established interests is further illustrated by the variation in environmental ratings as a function of political aggregation. As interests (and political
influence) are aggregated to higher organizational levels, there is a drop-
off in support for environmental reform. For instance, among political
institutions the perceived support for environmental action systematically
decreases as the size of the political agent increases: some individual MPs
are more supportive of environmental legislation than their party overall;
some parties are more supportive than parliaments overall; and most
parliaments are more supportive than the head of government. The same
patterns apply for business interests and the labour movement: some
individual businesses may be sympathetic towards the movement, but the
national business association is a clear opponent; some unions are supportive of environmental legislation, but most national labour federations are
negative.

From one perspective, environmentalists' perceptions of the established
social and political actors in these nations supports the contention of New
Social Movement theorists that the environmental movement views itself
as challenging the prevailing socio-political order of advanced industrial
societies (Brand et al. 1986; Cotgrove 1982; Milbrath 1984). None of the
strong adherents of that order fall into the alliance network of the movement. The greatest alliance opportunities for environmentalists lie with

other social critics – such as the women's movement, peace groups, or anti-system parties – but these actors are also outside the circle of polity members and therefore lack the access to resources shared by groups such as labour business, and government agencies. The status of the environmental movement as a challenging force is further underscored by the tendency of ecologist groups to be systematically more critical of the environmental records of major business and political institutions.

These findings do not preclude the formation of alliances that resource mobilisation theorists would stress, but they do have implications for the types of alliances that might form most easily. Environmentalists' negative perceptions of most members of the polity apparently limit the potential for broad political alliances to form between the movement and the established interests of advanced industrial democracies. But we also find that environmental evaluations of social groups vary significantly by nation, which suggests that the political context can influence alliance potential beyond the limitations of ideology (Kitschelt 1989). In Denmark, for example, a pragmatic environmental movement has been able to build at least psychological ties to labour, parliament and the Ministry of the Environment. Moreover, the environmental movement is itself expanding the members of the polity to include green and new-left parties that can provide them access to government resources and decision-making processes. Furthermore, while ecologists are more critical of most established social and political interests, conservation groups are generally more positive in their evaluations of these same actors. Thus another chain of alliance possibilities exists: from ecologist group to conservation group, from conservation group to established interests. In other words, the environmental movement is not invariably isolated from the polity, but the linkages often will be weak and indirect rather than based on broad political alliances.

Our findings also carry several implications for the strategies and tactics for the environmental movement that follow from their negative perceptions of most polity members. If we accept the classification of the movement as political outsiders, environmentalists will frequently find themselves dependent on unconventional tactics to upset the prevailing political balance. This might entail dramatic actions meant to pressure public agencies, or spectacular events designed to capture media attention and mobilise political support for their cause. Indeed, the one important ally that was missing from these analyses is the broad popular support that environmental reform receives from European publics (Dalton, forthcoming, Chapter 3; Milbrath 1984). The populist base of environmentalism makes the relationship between the movement and the mass media especially important, because media coverage is vital to developing and mobilising public support in order to tilt the political balance. The perceptual field of the movement also suggests a firm basis for the motto, 'think globally, act locally'. Because political aggregation increases the influence of dominant social interests, a challenging group may be more successful in working with local government or individual businesses, than in dealing with Prime Ministers and national economic associations. Even if business (or labour) as a whole is unsupportive, allies can be found at the level of the individual firm (or union). At least on a small scale, environmental groups can develop (and have developed) allies that can strengthen the movement and expand its influence; or temporary alliances can be built on specific issues. Furthermore, with expanding influence from such efforts, other alliance possibilities may develop.

In sum, our findings illustrate the constraints that face the environmental movement when dealing with the established social and political interests in western industrial democracies. How environmentalists are able successfully to work within these constraints, or broaden the base of their alliance network, will have direct implications for the future success of the movement.

Notes

1. Ironically, in the later half of the same article, Offe discusses the potential coalitions that might link new social movements to established interests on either the Left or Right.

2. This classification is primarily based on the information gained from our personal interviews, supplemented by the published material obtained from each organization. In addition, we consulted other research publications that have categorised European environmental groups along a similar continuum (Cotgrove 1982; Lowe and Goyder 1983; Milbrath 1984; Rucht 1989; Diani and Lodi 1988).

3. The French Communist Party played a similar role in supporting peace groups during the early 1980s (Rochon 1988), as did leftist and other alternative groups for the German peace movement (Mushaben 1989).

4. The question reads: 'Now we'd like to get your ideas about how well various institutions are addressing the important environmental issues facing (your nation) today. Would you indicate whether you think each of the groups I list is doing an excellent, good, fair, or poor job on these issues?' For these analyses, the response categories are coded: 1. poor, 2. fair, 3. good, and 4. excellent.

5. This item measures evaluations of the Green parties in Belgium, France, and West Germany, as well as the following New Left parties: the Italian Radicals, Danish Radical Venstre, Dutch PSP, and Greek KKE-Interior.

6. The relevant agencies were the Ministry of Environment in France, Italy, Luxembourg, and Denmark; the Department of the Environment in Ireland and Britain; the Department of Public Health and Environment in Belgium; the Ministry of Housing, Physical Planning, and Environment in Holland; the Ministry of the Interior in Germany; and the Department of Physical Planning and Environment in Greece.

7. The House of Lords has taken an active role in focusing public attention on environmental issues and publicising the issue throughout the past two

decades (Lowe and Goyder 1983, Ch. 4). In addition, many members of the Lords, such as Lords Sanford, Beaumont, and Kennet, are strong advocates and participants in the conservation movement. However, one British environmentalist claimed that the House of Lords is sympathetic to conservation issues because the majority of the peerage live on estates where the land is owned by the National Trust.

8. The relevant offices were the Prime Minister in Belgium, the Netherlands, Italy, Luxembourg, Denmark, Britain and Greece; in France, the President; in Germany, the Chancellor; and in Ireland, the Taoesich.

9. The logic held that since the appliances used less water and electricity, they made less demands on natural resources and the disposal of waste water (Elkington et al. 1988).

10. The relevant organizations are: France, Conseil National du Patronat Français (CNPF); Belgium, Belgian Business Federation; Netherlands, Union of Dutch Enterprises (VNO); Germany, Federation of German Industry (BDI); Italy, Confidustria; Denmark, Employers Association; Britain, Confederation of British Industry (CBI); Greece, Confederation of Greek Industrialists.

11. The respective labour union federations were: France, CFDT; Belgium, Federation of Workers in Belgium (FGTB); Netherlands, Dutch Federation of Labour (FNV); Germany, Deutscher Gewerkschaftsbund (DGB); Italy, Sindicati; Denmark: Landsorganization (LO); Britain, Trade Union Congress (TUC); Greece, Confederation of Greek Workers.

12. In each nation, the questionnaire simply referred to newspapers as a general term. The television question had a varying reference: France, TF1/A2/FR3; Germany, ARD and ZDF; Italy, RAI; Britain, BBC; Greece ERT1, 2; and simply 'television' in the other nations.

13. In fact, we find that environmentalists hold very positive feelings toward other social movements (see Dalton, forthcoming). Other researchers find that there are strong political, personal and resource ties binding these new social movements together (Mushaben 1989; Kriesi 1988; Klandermans 1990).

References

Berry, J. (1984). The Interest Group Society. (Boston: Little Brown).

Brand, K.-W. (1982). Neue soziale Bewegungen: Entstehung, Funktion und Perspektive neuer Protestpotentiale. (Opladen: Westdeutscher Verlag).

Brand, K.-W. (ed.) (1985). Neue soziale Bewegungen in Westeuropa und den USA: Ein internationaler Vergleich. (Frankfurt: Campus Verlag).

Brand, K.-W., Büsser, D. and Rucht, D. (1986). Aufbruch in eine andere Gesellschaft: Neue soziale Bewegungen in der Bundesrepublik, revised ed. (Frankfurt: Campus Verlag).

Cotgrove, S. (1982). Catastrophe or Cornucopia: The Environment, Politics and the Future. (Chichester: Wiley).

Curtis, R. and Zurcher, L. (1973). 'Stable resources of protest movements', Social Forces, Vol. 52, pp. 53–61.

Dalton, R. (forthcoming). The Green Rainbow: Environmental Groups in Western Europe.

Diani, M. (1990). 'The network structure of the Italian ecology movement,' Social Science Information, Vol. 29, pp. 5–31.

Diani, M. and Lodi, G. (1988). 'Three in one: Currents in the Milan ecology movement,' in Bert Klandermans et al., From Structure to Action. (Greenwich, Conn.: JAI Press).

Elkington, J., Burke, T. and Hailes, J. (eds.) (1988). *Green Pages*. (London: Routledge).

Ewringmann, D. and Zimmermann, K. (1978). 'Umweltpolitische Interessenanalyse der Unternehmen, Gewerkschaften und Gemeinden,' in Jänicke, M. (ed.), *Umweltpolitik: Beiträge zur Politologie des Umweltschutzes*. (Opladen: Leske Verlag & Budrich GmbH).

Gamson, W. (1975). *The Strategy of Social Protest*. (Homewood, IL: Dorsey Press).

Hatch, M. (1986). *Politics and Nuclear Power: Energy Policy in Western Europe*. (Lexington: University of Kentucky Press).

Hunter, R. (1984). *Warriors of the Rainbow*. (New York: Holt and Rinehart).

Kaase, M. (1990). 'Social movements and political innovation,' in Dalton, R. and Kuechler, M. (eds.), *Challenging the Political Order*. (New York: Oxford University Press/Cambridge, UK: Polity Press).

Kazis, R. and Grossman, R.(1982). *Fear at Work: Job Blackmail, Labor and the Environment*. (New York: Pilgrim Press).

Kitschelt, H. (1989). *The Logics of Party Formation*. (Ithaca, NY: Cornell University Press).

Klandermans, B., (ed.) (1989). *Organizing for Change*. (Greenwich, CT: JAI Press).

Klandermans, B. (1990). 'Linking the "Old" and "New": Movement networks in the Netherlands', in Dalton, R. and Kuechler, M. (eds.), *Challenging the Political Order*. (New York: Oxford University Press/Cambridge, UK: Polity Press).

Klandermans, B., Kriesi, H. and Tarrow, S. (eds.) (1988). *From Structure to Action*. (Greenwich, CT: JAI Press).

Kriesi, H. (1988). 'Local mobilisation for the people's petition of the Dutch peace movement', in Klandermans, B., Kriesi, H. and Tarrow, S. (eds.). *From Structure to Action*. (Greenwich, CT: JAI Press).

Lowe, P. and Goyder, J. (1983). *Environmental Groups in Politics*. (London: Allen and Unwin).

McCarthy, J. and Zald, M. (1977). 'Resource mobilization and social movements,' *American Journal of Sociology*, Vol. 82, pp. 1212-41.

Melucci, A. (1980). 'The new social movements', *Social Science Information*, Vol. 19, pp. 199-226.

Milbrath, L. (1984). *Environmentalists: Vanguard for a New Society*. (Albany, NY: SUNY Press).

Mushaben, J. (1989). 'The struggle within', in Bert Klandermans et al. (eds.), *Organizing for Change*. (Greenwich, CT: JAI Press).

Neidhardt, F. (1985). 'Einige Ideen zu einer allgemeinen Theorie sozialer Bewegungen', in Hradil, S. (ed.), *Sozialstruktur im Umbruch*. (Opladen: Westdeutscher Verlag).

Nelkin, D. and Pollack, M. (1981). *The Atom Besieged*. (Cambridge, M : MIT Press).

Offe, C. (1984). *Cultural Contradictions of Capitalism*. (Cambridge, MA: MIT Press).

Offe, C. (1985). 'New social movements', *Social Research*, Vol. 52, pp. 817–68.

Rochon, T. (1988). *Mobilising for Peace*. (Princeton, NJ: Princeton University Press).

Rucht, D. (1989). 'Environmental movement organizations in West Germany and France', in B. Klandermans (ed.), *Organizing for Change*. (Greenwich, CT: JAI Press).

Sheail, J. (1976). *Nature in Trust: The History of Nature Conservation in Britain*. (London: Blackie).

Schoenfeld, C., Meier, R. and Griffin, R. (1979). 'Constructing a social problem,' *Social Problems*, Vol. 27, pp. 38–57.

Siegmann, H. (1985). *The Conflicts between Labor and Environmentalism in the Federal*

Republic of Germany and the United States. (Aldershot: Gower).

Steedly, H. R. and Foley, J. (1979). 'The success of protest groups', Social Science Research, Vol. 8, pp. 1–15.

Tellegen, E. (1983). Milieubeweging. (Utrecht: Aula).

Tilly, Charles (1978). From Mobilisation to Revolution. (Reading, MA: Addison-Wesley).

Turk, H., and Zucker, L. (1984). 'Majority and organization opposition', in Ratcliff, R. (ed.), Research in Social Movements. (Greenwich, CT: JAI Press).

Walsh, E. (1989). Democracy in the Shadows. (Boulder, CO: Greenwood Press).

4. Vandals at the Gate: The Tasmanian Greens and the Perils of Sharing Power

P. R. HAY

Centre for Environmental Studies, University of Tasmania, Hobart, Australia

Introduction

Tasmania, an island about the size of Ireland, and containing less than half a million people, lies off the southern Australian coast, and is the smallest state in the Australian federation. It has an economy based around primary production, tourism and resource extraction, and this economy is dominated by a small number of large industries in mining, ore processing, forest harvesting and paper-making. It also has large tracts of temperate wetland wilderness, and the ecological significance of these areas has been so recognised that now roughly 20 per cent of the island's land surface has received World Heritage listing.

The achievement of this listing was the culmination of two decades of bitter political conflict, and even today is resented and opposed by perhaps a majority of Tasmanians, and by the Liberal Party, which is the single largest political party in the Tasmanian Parliament. From the bald outline provided above it is plain that Tasmania contains the conditions for prolonged conflict over preservation and development. In fact, the vulnerable Tasmanian wilderness and its unique and threatened fauna long suffered from an *absence* of such conflict. Thus the unique dog-like marsupial, thylacine (colloquially called the 'Tasmanian tiger'), is probably extinct (though its smaller cousin, the 'Tasmanian devil' has made a strong comeback after seeming to be heading for the same fate), and other plant and animal species have quietly slipped into oblivion. Conflict over whether competing factors deserved to be weighed in the balance against development was not generated until the late 1960s, when the Hydro-Electric Commission unveiled plans to dam Lake Pedder, an extraordinary lake with a huge, fringing expanse of white quartzite beach in the heart of the southwest wilderness. This decision turned a constituency of hitherto politically passive nature romanticists and genteel bushwalkers into hardened environmentalists.

That battle was lost, but since then Tasmanian politics has been continuously dominated by environmental issues. The complete and continuous dominance of the political agenda by 'the environment' probably makes Tasmania unique in the world in this respect (Hay and Haward 1988, p. 435), and merits a close scrutiny of the unfolding of events there by those concerned to account for the growth of the green phenomenon generally, and even more so by those who wish to prosecute its agenda. From the overwhelming dominance of Tasmanian politics by environmental matters several things have flowed. For instance, Tasmania spawned the world's very first green party, the United Tasmania Group (Walker 1989). It has developed one of the world's most tactically, organizationally and philosophically advanced environment movements (Hay 1988; Easthope and Holloway 1989). And sustained disputation over wilderness preservation has had an extraordinary impact upon the customary political cleavages, both ideologically and sociologically (Hay 1987).

This is, of course, much less than a comprehensive 'greening' of the Tasmanian community. But no community anywhere in the world has had the exposure to green values and aspirations that Tasmanians have had. The ideological fulcrum around which Tasmanian politics has swung for two decades is thus exploitation versus preservation, and this amounts to something more than just a different slant on a familiar politics. Flanagan, in a spirited attack on the incapacity of interstate journalists to comprehend the uniqueness of Tasmanian politics, gets it absolutely right: 'What was, and what is happening in Tasmania requires a new language. It cannot be adequately described in terms of machine politics, numbers games, statistical swings and marketing polls; any more than the atom bomb dropped on Hiroshima could be adequately described (as it was) as simply, and only, the equivalent of so many tons of TNT' (1989, p. 36).

But global focus upon this Lilliput at the end of the earth has by and large overlooked the broader context provided by these factors in preference to attending to two isolated 'spectacular' events – the mass campaign to protect the Franklin 'Wild River' from damming for hydro-electric development, and the election to the balance of power in Tasmania's dinky little House of Assembly of five green independents in May 1989.

I believe that green political activity in Tasmania has proceeded further than anywhere else in the world along the path of political development. Nowhere else do green aspirations so entirely dominate political disputation and questions of policy formulation. Nowhere else does political debate so exclusively centre around the question of whether the world should turn 'green'. Nowhere else are the basic political battle-lines structured around the forces of development and the forces of preservation. Nowhere else is the status of the natural world the central political question.

But it is argued here that the outside world's concentration upon just two green 'good news' events has obscured the real lesson that a close attention to Tasmania's political unfolding provides – and that is less an inspirational 'this is what fearless dedication can achieve' lesson (though I believe that to be, in context, an important message), than 'heed well the problems that attend success when it comes'. Firstly, though, let us look at the terms in which international attention has focused upon green developments in Tasmania.

Under the Global Microscope

In the early 1980s, the spectacular fight occasioned by the plans of the Tasmanian state government of Robin Gray to dam, for hydro-electric development, the Franklin River in the heart of Tasmania's acclaimed southwest wilderness, catapulted Australia's small and apparently insignificant island state into international prominence. It was a spotlight neither anticipated nor locally welcomed in a community that had become content in isolation and increasingly xenophobic in its attitude to outsiders – a latent hostility that not only extended to, but perhaps especially encompassed, 'mainlanders'. Tasmanian political life had become ideologically moribund since the the hegemonic vision of a future based on mega-industry and underwritten by cheap hydro-electricity had won complete and unchallenged acceptance in the decades between the wars. With public policy driven by a bipartisan vision of the island at the end of the world as a sea-bound equivalent of the Ruhr Valley, politics in Tasmania was reduced to mere administration, parties appealing to the electorate in terms of rival claims to the administrative competence to make the great dream of super-industrialisation a reality:

> Politics were thoroughly devalued, and Tasmanians became unpractised in political debate and analysis. There was no 'ideas' component to Tasmanian politics. The ALP [Australian Labor Party], in other states the political focus of challenge to orthodoxy, became entirely technocratic in Tasmania, and principles of democratic socialism were rarely raised in party forums. In keeping with an ideology of centralised technocratic decision-making, the focus of state political power became a small coterie of skilled bureaucrats and ALP strongmen ... (Hay 1987, p. 5).

Though the old and basic ideological cleavage of capital and labour had failed to fire the political visions of the industrial classes (electoral evidence suggests nevertheless, in the generalised way of these things, that richer people still tended to support the party associated with individualism and enterprise, the Liberal Party, and poorer people the party associated with collectivism and the interests of the underdog, the Australian Labor Party (ALP)), the moribund character of Tasmanian political life changed dramatically and permanently with the emergence of modern environmentalism in the early 1970s. With the mobilisation of vigorous opposition to hydro-industrial hegemony in the form of the campaign to save the 'jewel in the wilderness crown', Lake Pedder, Tasmanians were suddenly faced with disputation about first principles and alternative visions. It was a painful experience, and remains so, for there is still fierce resistance to the notion that politics is something that can be discussed over the dinner table without offending good taste, and resentment of the 'ratbags' who have forced an end to the comfortable intellectual laziness of the past remains strong. Throughout the 1980s, Liberal Party hard man Robin Gray cashed in on this, proffering the promise of a strong leader who, once elected, could be left to get on with the business of government, not troubling the citizenry further until the next inconvenient election. In vain did those who aspired to contribute to those decisions to which they would subsequently be subject rail against the last vestiges of political godfatherism. But this was yesterday's politics, and a major effect of the advent of environmental politics has been that the old complacent tech-nocratic anti-politics will never again command the field unchallenged. The Franklin River victory saw to that.

With the tumultuous campaign to save the Franklin 'Wild River', international attention focused upon Tasmania for probably the first time since the island had ceased to be a penal colony. Never before had a single wilderness preservation campaign attained global stature. Thousands of Australians – and a smattering of international celebrities – flocked to Tasmania to join the massive resistance in the forests, and to add their persons to the human flotsam that clogged Tasmania's hopelessly under-resourced machinery of justice and incarceration. But, despite much ill-informed scuttlebutt to the contrary at the time, the blockade was largely controlled locally, its tactical motor the Tasmanian Wilderness Society, and its charismatic leader a local doctor of medicine, Bob Brown. The block-ade threw up its own principles of actionist organisation – novelist James McQueen (1983, pp. 57–8) likened it to the anarcho-syndicalism of pre-Franco Spain – and all participants on the blockade received a mandatory smattering of training in the non-violent action techniques of the Quaker-inspired Movement for a New Society before going out to resist trucks and bulldozers. Police and hardhats doing battle with colourful banner-wielding 'greenies' in one of the world's most breathtaking environments – the media loved it, the national and international exposure thus gener-ated transformed a local issue into one of much wider import, and the pro-dam forces raged impotently as the matter was taken from their hands. In 1983 the newly-elected federal Australian Labor Party government moved decisively to stop the dam, subsequently defending its position against a High Court challenge brought by the Liberal Government of Tasmania.

This was about as spectacular as an environmental controversy can get, and the strategic, organizational, political, legal and ethical issues involved (Green 1983; McQueen 1983; Thompson 1984; Tighe and Taplin 1985) were all such as to warrant broad scrutiny. Much that occurred on the Franklin was, for a burgeoning and rapidly changing global movement still groping for a praxis, of a pathfinding nature. But this 'moment of time' preoccupation with and upon the Franklin River obscured (and continues to obscure) the fact that the Franklin was not an issue without historical context, but simply the most dramatic instance in an unbroken series of environmental *causes célèbres* that have fine-honed an increasingly sophisticated and ideologically-informed debate. The Franklin would not have been saved had there not been in place, here at the end of the world, a movement skilled in theory and practice that had tempered its capacities in the United Tasmania Group's fierce struggle against the odds in the fight for Lake Pedder (Walker 1989; Flanagan 1990).

It is this broader ideological and tactical development that really merits international attention. From such a perspective it is possible to judge the Franklin campaign as less than totally successful. For instance, Martin (1984) has insisted that the great failing of the Franklin River campaign was the passing up of an outstanding opportunity to pursue more fundamental paradigm change, particularly within intransigent agencies of the Tasmanian state bureaucracy. Others have also taken up this theme; for instance, Wescombe (1990, p. 188) has recently defended Martin's position (successfully I think) against criticism of it made earlier by myself. Whatever the merits of this argument, it is certainly the case that the circumscribed nature of the international and even interstate attention that focused upon Tasmania at the time of the Franklin River Blockade meant that the facets of green politics in Tasmania with greatest general significance have been largely overlooked.

Tasmania again captured a share of the spotlight in May 1989, when five green independents were elected to the 35-member House of Assembly. This was an increase upon the two who had secured election in 1986, and the reward for capturing over 17 per cent of the statewide vote.

Despite its prominence (by comparison with other political systems), the green movement in Tasmania has resisted political formalisation, holding that bureaucratisation and the triumph of an unprincipled oligarchy is an inevitable consequence of such a development, and that the emergence of such organizational pathologies not only militates against the successful prosecution of a green political project, but constitutes an intrinsic betrayal of such a project, being the antithesis of ultra-democratic green social principles. That organizational experimentation is prominent within Tasmania's green groups has already been noted – the major green activist organization, the Wilderness Society, eschews formal structure and leadership roles (though it has been argued that, in avoiding an institu-tionalisation of organizational power, the society has not been willing or able to prevent power gravitating to a small, comparatively closed clique; Holloway 1986). At a parliamentary level the determination to avoid formalisation has struck an electorally productive chord – thus a small but possibly significant component of the green vote is an expression of disenchantment with the perceived cynicism of party politics, channelled instead towards 'principled independents'.

As green support grew, so too did pressure to formalise increase. The Greens have attempted to have their cake and eat it by building a network of supporter groups and holding occasional statewide supporter meetings. The quasi-messianic nature of the movement has made the mobilisation of masses of supporters comparatively easy (though this was more notice-able before the 1989 election than it has been since). The election campaign was structured around a series of large bandwaggoning meetings, and prominence was given to the personalities of Dr Bob Brown, a larger-than-life figure since the successful campaign to save the Franklin River (and already a Member of the House of Assembly), and Christine Milne, the forthright, dynamic leader of a more recently successful campaign to prevent the construction of a giant pulp mill in the north of the island. Though that issue had been resolved prior to the election, it is clear that the groundswell of opinion-change wrought during that protracted strug-gle was the major factor in the dynamic increase in the green vote in 1989.

When the electoral dust had settled, the ruling Liberal Party had won only seventeen seats and the green independents had secured the balance of power. The Premier refused to resign and negotiations commenced between the Greens and each party, though talks with the Liberals were perfunctory and the Premier, bowing to pressure from hard-line anti-green elements on his backbench, subsequently announced that he would no longer 'treat' with the greens. Negotiations with the ALP (which had secured only 35 per cent of the vote – its lowest vote ever) were tense and protracted, and looked to have broken down on several occasions. The key sticking-point was logging in forests that were on the register of the National Estate. Then, on 29 May, Labor and the Greens signed a historic pact, subsequently labelled the 'Labor–Green Accord', whereby the Greens agreed to maintain a Labor government in office in return for enactment of much of the green agenda as specified in the Accord. On the same day the Premier, Robin Gray, branded the deal as 'unprincipled' and destined to fall apart in any case, and he vowed to stay in office until defeated on the floor of the House.

A time of great stress and uncertainty followed, as the island commu-nity again split asunder over an environment-based crisis. Of the two outraged camps, it was the pro-development forces rallying around the Liberal Party that generated the most potent rage. A number of emotional anti-Accord (and specifically anti-green) rallies and public meetings were held, and huge pressure was brought to bear upon the Governor (the holder of vice-regal power in an Australian state) to send the various contenders back to the polls. Constitutional experts had a field day, each side trotting out impeccably-argued opinions over the Governor's options (or lack of same). Finally, almost a month and a half after the election, Parliament convened. A dramatic all-night session ended with the ALP comprehensively out-finessing the government and securing the passing of no-confidence in the government in such terms that the Premier was left without constitutional options other than to seek an audience with Sir Phillip Bennett (the Governor) to report that he could no longer command a House majority. The leader of the ALP, Michael Field, was also summoned to Government House, as were the Greens, from whom a commitment to deliver stable government was sought. The independents agreed to support ALP budgets for the life of the Parliament, and the Governor then commissioned Field to form a minority government with the support of, but not, it is important to note, in coalition with the Greens.

In September 1990 the Greens formally left the Accord over the government's determination to pursue 'Resource Security' legislation, aimed at giving the forest industry the same security of access to timber production 'zones' that national park status gave from exploitation. That legislation has still to be introduced, and there is a chance that when that happens the Greens will bring the government down. In the interim, however, the Greens have agreed to stick by their agreement to maintain the government in power, and remarkably little has changed in terms of day to day relationships between the erstwhile partners.

Tasmania 1989 is, of course, not the first occasion on which Greens have achieved a sufficient measure of electoral success to hold the balance of legislative power. That occurred when the Green Alternative List won 8·2 per cent of the vote in the German state of Hamburg and, with it, the balance of power. But on that occasion negotiations with the SPD came to nothing, no alliance was made, and in the resultant election the Greens suffered a considerable voter backlash. With this lesson weighing heavily upon them (Parkin 1989, p. 122), the Greens in the heavily industrialised state of Hesse consented to enter into a post-election alliance with the SPD in 1984, and this provides the most obvious reference point for comparison with the Tasmanian experiment. There are those within the Tasmanian Greens who believe that the ALP drove too hard a bargain during the Accord negotiations, has been needlessly confrontational ever since, and has shown little interest in tapping the brimming reservoir of ideas that the Greens undoubtedly have. Whether or not there is justice to these perceptions, it has been sweetness and light compared to what happened in Hesse (Simons 1988, pp. 21–2) where, in three turbulent years prior to the election, SPD Prime Minister Holger Boerner referred to the Greens as 'fascists', destroyed a green village of wooden huts (including the church), and turned upon peaceful green protesters in a fury of tear gas, water cannon and waves of baton charges. Following the 1984 election the Hesse Greens maintained Boerner's SPD in power in accordance with an agreement not unlike Tasmania's Accord, but within a year that had become a formal coalition, and the Greens accepted a small number of ministries. Boerner treated his coalition partners with about the same degree of contempt that had characterised his pre-1983 stance, and in 1986 he brought the coalition to an end by summarily dismissing Green leader Fischer from the ministry. For the Greens internally the experiment was just as traumatic. The Hesse Greens split fiercely over the question of whether to deal or not to deal.

A similar division was apparent within Tasmania's greens in the wake of the 1989 election result, but the differences of opinion were nowhere near as bitter, nor the schism as long-lasting.

It is also worth noting that the Tasmanian experience adds considerable weight to Rüdig and Lowe's contention (1986) that as apparently 'green-neutral' a factor as the nature of the electoral system is one of the key factors in determining the extent to which green concerns obtrude into public life. Tasmania, like the states of West Germany, has a legislature based on multi-member electoral units, and this is an important factor in accounting for the greater impact of green values and projects in Tasmanian politics than has been the case in other Australian states, where electoral systems are based on single-member electorates, and where green politics, being of minor electoral relevance, has not reconstituted the issue agenda as it has in Tasmania.

But there are also points of contrast, and these should be of as much general interest as the points of similarity. Wescombe has argued that:

> Green ethics challenge the notion of a world in which all worth and meaning attaches to species homo sapiens, arguing instead for an ethic that fundamentally re-orients the ethical meaning of 'exploitation'. Instead of condemning exploitation in the manner of most other ethical systems, that is, on the ground that the moral standing of the victim of exploitation is such that the victim does not merit exploitation, green ethics have focussed upon the act of exploitation itself as meriting moral condemnation. Rich should not exploit the poor, strong the weak, male the female, white the black – and homo sapiens should not exploit other nature. Thus 'otherness' is to be respected in terms of its own essentiality, and non-human life forms are to be accorded the space in which to follow their own evolutionary destinies. This is not an injunction to human non-engagement (and hence that scornfully trumpeted 'return to the caves'). But our rights to impinge upon the species interests of others extend only

as far as our own vital species needs extend. Such a radical re-interpretation of our relationship with other nature requires a revolutionary shift in our accustomed ways of knowing nature. Since the Enlightenment 'nature' has had the status of mere resource at the disposal of the unbridled human project. There are thus no 'in principle' limitations upon our behaviour towards other species in any of the political/religious/economic value systems that were set in train by the Enlightenment.

If the revolutionary kernel of the green ethic resides in its attempted reformulation of the relationship between species Homo sapiens and other nature, then those places where the focus of green political activity is not primarily on the quality of human life (but is rather on attempts to ensure that other species are afforded the opportunity to unfold according to their own evolutionary destinies) are likely to exhibit a more sharpened sense of just what is at stake in the green challenge than is to be found in places where the focus of concern is more diffuse. This is most likely to be the case where the overriding green issue is habitat protection, an imperative that is most predominant in campaigns for wilderness preservation.

I have elsewhere argued that the political manifestations of 'green' in places where such issues have been at the forefront are characterised by a heightened sense of desperation and of struggle over absolutes (on the part of protagonist and antagonist alike), and that this is in contrast to dominant green themes in European countries where, as Rüdig and Lowe note, the anti-nuclear movement has provided the binding tissue for 'bringing the various local and single-issue environmental groups on one platform' (1986, p. 273). But 'an anti-nuclear politics ... can be readily accommodated within socialist and liberal streams of thought', whereas

> the assumption that the natural world is to be reacted to primarily as a human 'resource' is an essential and hitherto unquestioned axiom of western history and the economic and technological systems woven into that history. The impulse to defend the existential rights of wilderness in precedence over human-use rights has led to a spirited challenge to the most fundamental tenet of western civilization, the belief that ... no countervailing principle exists to bar humanity from behaving in any way it deems fit towards the non-human world. (Hay and Haward 1988, p. 437)

Tasmania provides the only instance to date of a green movement that is primarily and overtly dedicated to a politics based upon the proposition that other species are have vital interests that will conflict with those of Homo sapiens and that we are not entitled to use 'interests of humankind' justifications for the transgression of those interests. The effect of such a principle on the body politic is the stuff of the final segments of this chapter.

First, though, one final facet of the broader reaction to Tasmania's electoral experiment needs to be noted. As with the Franklin Dam dispute, the rest of the world (including the rest of Australia) has tended to see the 1989 election and the attainment by the Greens of a share of power as void of historical context. There is no appreciation of doubt, opportunities lost, or of limitation: the prevailing view among those who wish success to the Greens is uncomplicated and sunny – the Accord was seen as an inevitable step on the evolutionary path of social progress. Australian radicalism is undergoing the same fundamental reassessment that characterises western dissent generally. Amid this uncertainty, progressive forces within Australian society had high hopes that the Tasmanian Accord would supply decisive signposts to the future. In a sense the achievement of electoral success is the natural outcome of that recent history of intense political preoccupation with the values and aspirations of environmental-ism. Since the early 1980s green forces have fought Robin Gray's Liberals over plans to dam the Franklin River, over plans to log wilderness forests (these were resisted in a series of spectacular confrontations in the forests themselves), and over plans to build a giant chlorine-bleaching paper mill in the north of the state. In each instance the government lost; the resistance movements won – it seems a natural culmination then that Robin Gray's Liberals should suffer a final and emphatic blow from the Greens at the polls.

But it needs to be noted that in each of these confrontations except the election itself, the environmentalist cause carried the day because of the decisive intervention of the federal ALP government of Bob Hawke, and in particular of his high-profile environment minister, Senator Graeme Richardson. The decisive factor in each instance was centralised power and the structures of Australian federalism. Left to its own devices, the state and the people of Tasmania would not have opted for the green way. The factors and forces that serve to mute Tasmania's green achievement – and that stand ready to roll it back under changed circumstances – merit much greater consideration, for here are important lessons to be learned that have application beyond the shores of a little island and its miniature political system at the world's nether reaches.

Assessing The Accord: The Green Positives

The ALP-Accord lasted less than eighteen turbulent and unpredictable months. Despite the early scepticism and periodic crises, however, the Accord should be judged a success. From the Greens' viewpoint much was achieved. A World Heritage Area nomination far in excess of that which would otherwise have been possible (and which is actually in excess of that specified in the Accord) was lodged in Paris, and granted national park designation. An additional area of pristine dry sclerophyll forest, which caps a substantial but low-grade coal deposit, and which the Liberals had steadfastly refused to reserve, has also been accorded national park status. An energy efficiency programme has been announced, and traditional secrecy surrounding the electricity tariffs of bulk power-users has been ended. The government is moving to end the exemptions from compliance with the Environment Protection Act that had been granted wholesale to industry and municipal governments by previous administrations. A series of marine reserves are in the pipeline. The Greens had hoped further successes could be achieved in the conciliatory climate in which environmentalists had sat down with the forest industries to draft a forest industry strategy – something that was unthinkable in the old regime which thrived on confrontation. These hopes were dashed, however, when the forest industry 'peace plan' collapsed leading to the disintegration of the accord in late 1990.

Though the analysis of negatives (below) has been accorded much more space than I have here given the positives, and though the tone of this chapter is in essence pessimistic, the importance of these achievements can hardly be overestimated. They certainly justify the Greens' decision, questioned by many at the time, to enter into the Accord. But progress towards implementation of a green agenda was pretty much confined to the strict terms of the Accord. By and large the government did struggle to meet the Accord's specific policy undertakings, even though many of these commitments have major resource implications. But the 'fiscal crisis' that the Treasury successfully urged the government to recognise put on long-term hold the reform aspirations of both the Greens and the more progressive forces within the ALP. It has become a tight-fisted government of hard economic management, and undertakings given at the time the Accord was signed oblige the Greens to maintain it in power, with little hope of an ongoing green agenda, despite the Accord's formal collapse. And here we slip emphatically from the positive to the negative.

Assessing the Accord: The Green Negatives

It is doubtful whether the Greens really had any option than to enter into alliance with the ALP. Ritual overtures were received from the Liberals, but the ideological gulf between the two groups was always going to be unbridgeable. But the decision to bargain for a share of power nevertheless threw the Greens into deep crisis. This crisis stemmed not from possibly making the wrong decision, but from having a decision to make at all. Attainment of the long-sought goal of a share of formal political power brings the brave, clean phase of the movement's development to an end and, paradoxically, ushers in a phase which has a considerable down-side. From this point the exultant, crusading character of the movement suffers dilution. This new phase contains an uncertainty over identity that was never apparent in the early days. The price of electoral success, the German experience suggests, is to accept the likelihood of a halt (perhaps temporary) to the rate of community greening, whatever choice is made concerning the use of that electoral leverage. To have refused to 'treat' would have been to return power to the hated Gray government, which, presumably, would have survived for only a short period of time before being forced back to the polls. Under such circumstances the Greens would almost certainly have suffered an electoral setback far worse than that suffered by Hamburg's Alternative List in 1982. On the other hand, the very act of accepting a share of power is also likely to lead, initially, to a loss of support.

That the Greens lost support seems, in fact, to be the case. Opinion polls suggested that the ALP gained support at the Greens' expense after the election. The most important Accord commitments were implemented in the first months of government, and the pace at which other parts of the green agenda were being put in place slowed to a crawl. There was, among the Greens' most ardent supporters, disillusion with the rate of change. The same people were also disenchanted by the Greens' apparent incapacity to prevent the government from arriving at decisions that were decidedly antagonistic to green aspirations, or to implement those policies that did not coincide with the ALP's own policy agenda. Among such 'hard core' greens there may be a long-term turning away from the accommodatory politics of parliament. More significant, however, was the apparent loss of support from (presumably) the 'debutante' green voter of 1989. It seems likely that many of these voters have reassessed their stance on the 'environment-versus-development' debate and, faced with an effectively orchestrated scuttlebutt to the effect that the state's economy is in decay and that this is all the fault of the Greens, reverted to old allegiances.

The evidence for this – though capable of rival interpretation – is to be found in Tasmanian voting patterns in the 24 March 1990 federal elections, and the 7 April municipal elections of the same year. In the former, Tasmanian voters turned emphatically away from green candidates, and this at a time when Greens were scoring unprecedented triumphs elsewhere in Australia. For the first time, Tasmania was not Australia's green flagship, as Western Australia and much of New South Wales chalked up a higher green vote. In the electorate of Denison, a green vote in excess of 20 per cent in the 1989 state election fell in the 1990 federal election to just over 8·5 per cent. Even more emphatic was the result of the 7 April municipal elections, in which, with small exceptions, environmentalist candidates polled poorly throughout the state, and especially in Hobart, where the development-versus-conservation battlelines were starkly drawn. Here, in Tasmania's heartland of green support, the pro-development forces waged an inspired campaign with crusading elements reminiscent of popular environmentalist campaigns of the past, and won a staggering 74 per cent of the vote, compared to the progressives' 23 per cent. The tentative conclusion must be that the green vote is not settled but volatile, and if it is volatile, we must question the extent to which green values have laid lasting hold upon Tasmanian hearts and minds. Possible consequences of this are considered below.

There are sound reasons why Tasmania is not a suitable place for an experiment in green power-sharing. There are formidable centres of countervailing conservative power within Tasmania. The Upper House, one of the world's most powerful in that it has a capacity to force a government to the polls without itself having to face the electors, is dominated, courtesy of a powerful gerrymander, by hard-line rural conservatives, ostensibly sitting as 'independents'. Their antipathy to the Greens in the Lower House (and the wider movement) is deep and uncompromising. Municipal government is a similar bastion of local conservatism, the reforms in local government franchise and functions that have taken place in most Australian states during the last decade or so having largely passed Tasmania by. The legacy of decades of reliance upon resource-extractive industries is a network of powerful public sector resource agencies, and these partake of a bureaucratic culture that is also deeply antipathetic to green aspirations. In addition, Tasmania's economy is dominated by a small number of large industries whose individual strategic importance to the local economy far exceeds the importance of similar enterprises within larger political systems, and this provides these industries with an influence upon government which exceeds that customarily pertaining elsewhere: again, there are points of divergence between the economic interests of Tasmania's major employers and the aspirations of the Greens (an excellent analysis of these factors is provided by Crowley 1989).

Yet another reason why Tasmania is a less than ideal setting for an experiment in green power-sharing has to do with scale. And here is a dilemma. Since Schumacher (1974) gave us 'Buddhist Economics' and declared that 'small is beautiful', scale has been a key green social variable (though the more flexible notion of 'human scale' tends now to prevail). Tasmania is certainly small enough and, this given, might be deemed ideal for the implementation of a green agenda. In fact, diseconomies of scale make it rather more difficult to implement. With its small tax base and its reliance on annually shrinking Commonwealth funds, much of the infrastructure of environmental protection that is now taken for granted elsewhere is simply beyond Tasmania's means. Thus, state-of-the-art sewage schemes that avoid inflexible engineering technologies are not to be found. There are no native vegetation clearance controls, no incentive schemes for preservation of the built environment, no coastal zone management. The Environment Protection Act has not been overhauled for fifteen years and the penalties it imposes are laughable, as is the case with other Acts with an environmental protection component. Planning controls are few, flawed and ineffective. There is no heritage legislation, no hazardous waste management strategy, no trade waste policy, and no annual environmental audit. The government has conducted a review of aerial agricultural spraying that identifies procedural inadequacies and recommends remedial strategies, but the funding implications of the recommendations have caused the report to be shelved. Little or no contribution is made to national strategies on ozone depleting and green-house gases (there is an Act to regulate the use of chlorofluorocarbons – the first in the world – but its effectiveness is seriously limited). There is no capacity to purchase tracts of ecologically sensitive private land, even when the owners are keen for the government to buy. And the list goes on. Action on some of these matters is promised, but will still have to run the formidable gauntlet of the unsympathetic Legislative Council.

Tasmania's funding problems manifest in two ways – an absence of money to fund programmes up front (and the government's economic 'hard men' have shown no inclination to respect the policy priorities apparent at the time the Accord was being forged by generously funding the agencies charged with meeting those priorities) – and a bureaucracy too small (by mainland comparison) to undertake the policy-generating tasks that are elsewhere possible. For example, the Division of Environmental Management in the Department of Environment and Planning is so poorly resourced that, until recently, it has never had the capacity to work up (or on) policy initiatives. Nor can the market be relied upon to fill the void under these circumstances. The environmental issue that seems to have most comprehensively won public support is waste minimisation. There is an impressive popular desire to recycle. But, at a time when there is an unprecedented will to recycle, there is no capacity to do so. The Tasmanian recycling industry is at the mercy of plummeting interstate per-tonne purchase prices and crippling freight costs, and the smallness of the local market makes any downstream processing of recycled waste apparently uneconomic. It could almost serve as a metaphor for Tasmania's diseconomies of scale.

To this the green reaction has been more than a little dismaying. The Labor government has defined its most urgent task – one taking precedence over all else – as the resolution of the fiscal crisis, at the heart of which is the state's debt-servicing capacity. To say that it is running a tight ship is an understatement. But most of the green programme requires a considerable funding commitment, and this the government, having met the key demands of the Accord, is increasingly loath to provide. Not only was this a source of much tension between the Accord partners, and a major contributor to the growing disenchantment of much of the green rank-and-file with the Accord experiment, but it also revealed significant weaknesses in the green approach to matters economic, and here, I think, is the lesson of surpassing importance for the green movement generally to take from the Tasmanian experiment, for what has happened in Tasmania is likely to be repeated wherever Greens similarly attain an involvement in government.

The Greens have economic ideas. Many of them have a fully-fledged economic philosophy. The movement is familiar with the ideas of Daly, Cobb, Ekins, Schumacher, Sale, Max-Neuf et al. It envisions the commonwealth of small, comparatively self-contained economic communities, employing environmentally benign and de-scaled 'soft' technologies, that figures, with variations, in most of the green social literature. There are periodic workshops on green economics. For the Greens in Parliament this translates into a fierce advocacy of a small-business-based economy, and an e mployment-creating strategy of community recovery via government-sponsored local employment initiatives. And they have taken a drubbing. They have incurred the wrath of most of those unionists whose livelihood is bound up in existing economic institutions, particularly within the resource-based industries (in both sectors). They have attracted similar antipathy from those industries themselves. This much is to be expected. But they have not endeared themselves to the spokespersons for small business either; these latter have been much more impressed with the counter-claim that a small-business-based economy is a nonsense, and the only way in which small business can flourish is in a satellite relationship with big business, the latter providing the requisite demand for a range of industrial services and ancillary goods provision.

Any programme for change will encounter stiff opposition from those with a vested interest in the maintenance of what is. But what we have here is an absence of any programme, or even of any counter to the small business-as-spinoff argument noted above. What there is amounts to a vision of how things will (or should) be in an ecologically-based society, with no guidance of how we get from here to there – and if one searches the literature of green economics one will find it equally lacking in a specific programme for change. There are trenchant analyses of the fallacies and absurdities of received economic wisdom. There are edifying descriptions of the de-scaled mechanisms and principles of green economics in action, much of it based on 'real' experiment. But there is no programme to translate this enlightenment into the living economic orthodoxy of tomorrow, the waste and destruction of non-sustainable growth-fuelled industrialisation being, in the process, swept away. There is, in short, no political economy.

This failure is of incalculable political damage. Others have argued that green support is heavily drawn from a narrow sociological base – educated public sector professionals who are not charged with provision of the production infrastructure (Offe 1985; Gouldner 1987; Eckersley 1989) – and the evidence suggests a similar base of support in Tasmania (Hay 1987). This is hardly surprising considering that the key social sectors of capital and labour have an abiding interest in the continuance of existing economic conditions, and are thus likely to provide an opposition to green aspirations that is not only politically formidable but numerically dominant, and thus, beyond a certain point, further green recruitment becomes extremely difficult.

If any progress is to be made at all, it will be necessary to break the popular equation of development/jobs *versus* environment, for the Tasmanian experience suggests that this is the most difficult perception barrier to be dismantled. And this requires the addition of a dimension to green thought that has hitherto been lacking. To its philosophy, its economics, and its advanced organizational and tactical thought the Greens urgently need to add *strategy* – a capacity to think in terms of the intermediate; the 'how do we get from here to there'. I have no doubt that green economic prescriptions have a greater capacity to deliver full and stable employment than the labour-shedding imperatives of applied classical economics. But the road from here to there is likely to be paved with the victims of a massive economic reorientation, and it is cold comfort to such people – to those who have sunk their life savings into long-distance log haulage rigs, or to those builders' labourers who depend for their mortgage on the income supplied by construction of the alienating towers that are obliterating the human-ness of most of the world's large cities – that *ultimately* it will all have been worth it. Enough, then, of high principle. Enough of tactical thinking. The movement has made vast strides in both areas over the last two decades. Now, though, it is time to supply the linkages; to think in terms of *transitional strategies*.

There should be no embarrassment about this. After all, the dominant thrust of contemporary technological change is to displace labour with machinery, for labour de-intensification is the fast and easy route to shoring the profit margin. Thus the growth and consumption policies pursued by governments of all familiar complexions are destined to increase unemployment (and environmental devastation). In Tasmania it should not be impossible, the mammoth perceptual barrier notwithstanding, for the Greens to seize the high ground on the key index of work; the intermediate future of the Greens, indeed, would seem to be dependent upon its doing so.

But any strategy for change must find a mechanism to make inroads against the fierce hatred held for the Greens within the traditional industrial sectors of capital and labour. It is difficult to convey in an academic paper the strength of this antipathy. Mention has already been made of the anger unleashed by the signing of the Accord during the interregnum between the 1989 election and the fall of the Gray government. At that time the backlash was overtly led by spokespersons from small business and workers in the resource-based industries, but the sense that doom and devastation was the inevitable outcome of the election of green independents to the balance of power extended even to the man popularly described as the most powerful in Tasmania, media boss Edmund Rouse, who has since been convicted of attempting to bribe a newly elected Labor backbencher to cross the floor on the resumption of Parliament and to thereby restore to the Liberals a House majority.

More recently, 'ordinary Tasmanian' hostility to the Greens has manifested in a large coalition of groups representing traditional users of the wilderness – fishermen, shooters, 'mountain cattlemen', off-road vehicle enthusiasts, 'shack' owners, part-time wood cutters – who fear that the success of the Greens is freezing them out of their traditional pursuits. The truth that the Greens wince away from is that this represents a more broadly based and organic expression of the essential Tasmania than do the Greens themselves. During the Accord period I was involved in a series of public meetings aimed at selling the government's proposal to establish a small number of modestly-sized marine reserves in Tasmania. These meetings were tumultuous affairs, attended by large numbers of fishermen, humble folk who often struggled with cramping emotions to articulate their fury. They were convinced that these small reserved areas were the 'thin end of the wedge' that would lead to most of Tasmania's off-shore being 'locked up' in 'World Heritage Areas' from which they would be excluded, and though the marine reserves were largely an ALP initiative (though in the Accord), and though the Greens made only a minimal input privately and had little public involvement, for the outraged citizenry in attendance it was all a Green plot, and the (absent) Greens were subjected to a tirade of invective. Nor should it be assumed that this antagonism was engendered – as opposed to 'stoked up' – by the signing of the Accord. I earlier identified 'a barely suppressed fury against "greenies"', wherein 'violence seems perpetually near – very near – the surface. Environmental activists frequently express relief that no one died during confrontations over the Franklin River ... Bushwalkers express fear of danger-fraught chance meetings with timber workers in the forests' (Hay 1987, p. 6). In fact it goes all the way back to the Lake Pedder campaign, and many believe that in that struggle the assassination of a prominent wilderness campaigner did occur.

Though it is likely that the Green Movement draws heavily upon public sector employees for its electoral support, the bureaucracy must nevertheless be accounted another major impediment to the successful prosecution of a green agenda in Tasmania. The strategic influence of the resource agencies has already been noted. But the bureaucracy as a whole constitutes an impediment to furtherance of the green agenda. If a fundamental goal of the green project is de-bureaucratisation, there is more than a little irony in the fact that to pursue a programme through the official structures of government is to pursue one's aims via bureaucracy. Elsewhere in Australia environmental groups have solved this problem by jettisoning experiments in organizational radicalism for the alienating efficiencies of formalised hierarchies. Tasmanian groups, as we have seen, are among the most theoretically sophisticated in the world and, alive to the inner logic of the green paradigm, have resisted capitulation to organizational modes that are thought to be part of the problem rather than the solution. The Tasmanian bureaucracy itself has a complex relationship with the Greens which seems to be largely determined by the particular bureaucratic culture of individual agencies. Some proceed from assumptions that are fundamentally at odds with the aspirations of the Greens. But even where this is not the case, there is a tendency within senior management to see the Greens and their agenda as 'not quite legitimate', despite the strong degree of personal support for the Greens among state employees.

Finally, we must consider the Labor Party for, of all the obstacles that must be negotiated, the most important and obvious is that of the Labor government itself. In a general sense the emergence of the Greens constitutes a significant threat to the ALP. It is clear that most of the green constituency has been won from Labor, biting deeply into the party's comparatively new professional constituency, the winning of which has, Australia-wide, been the single most important factor in dramatically restoring the party's electoral fortunes from the early 1970s. But the more it attempts to compete for this constituency by 'greening up', the more it risks losing much of its traditional blue-collar vote, the latter being, on the whole, hostile to green values. In Tasmania, the Franklin Dam debate provides compelling evidence of what can happen. In the 'Franklin election' of 1982 the isolated mining communities on Tasmania's West Coast, hitherto Labor strongholds, swung spectacularly to the unreservedly pro-dam Liberal Party: 'The Liberals successfully portrayed the ALP as suspect to "green" infiltration ... the workers turned their backs on decades of voting tradition and threw in their lot with "the party of the bosses"' (Hay 1987, p. 10). In two elections since, the vote has stayed with the uncompromising party of development.

This is much resented by the ALP power-brokers, and the naive hope of driving the Greens into oblivion is still openly entertained and actively pursued. The Accord partners resented each other's enforced company, and for its part the ALP has, as a major electoral aim, the gleeful interment of the upstart and irritant Greens at the next election. Though the relationship between the Accord partners was probably more accommodating than that between the SPD and the Greens in Hesse, it has nevertheless been a tense and often stormy one, and this pattern is not likely to change. Some of the problems are personal. Though the Greens have established good relationships with individual ministers, the government's key advisers are stoutly anti-Green, particularly those employed in the offices of the Premier and Deputy Premier. Many of the Greens' antagonists among the government's support staff have shown little interest in coming to grips with the unique terms upon which the ALP has come to power. For them it is just Labor business as usual.

The communication problems are thus formidable, and the scope for misunderstanding is vast. But there is more to the tension than that. It is clear that the ALP is interested in no part of the green agenda that does not match its own, and there is growing uncertainty within the government over the extent to which it should be associated in the public mind with an environmentalist programme. There is no doubt that the government has been spooked by the powerful popular impression that the state's economy has ground to a halt. It assiduously woos business and industry, assuring them that their fears concerning the green-maintained ALP government are groundless. Certainly the government has never sought so dedicatedly to reassure the environment movement – and this despite the fact that business backed the Liberals in the 1989 election, and will back the Liberals in the next election, and has not, and will not, deliver votes to the ALP. But it has the capacity to create just such an electorally 'unhelpful' climate as that which pertained for much of the first year in office, and it is this that makes the ALP so sensitive to its public utterances. There are great dangers here for the Greens, particularly in so far as the key environmental agenda is concerned. The likelihood is that the government will seek to retreat from, or soft-pedal on environmental matters to avoid 'sending wrong signals' to a community thought to be judging the government harshly on its development record.

But what is there in all this to occasion surprise? It is only to be expected when one considers the incompatible pedigrees of the two Accord partners. The ALP is an umbrella party, containing within its fold a wide diversity of outlook and interest, including affiliated unions whose interests are embedded in the economic and technological arrangements that are identified by green analysis as impediments to human and natural emancipation. The party will naturally be sensitive to the demands of such groups, as well as those in the wider community that it must gather unto itself if it is to assemble the broad base of support necessary to win elections. In the 1980s the ALP has moved even more surely in this direction, abandoning its socialist ideological heritage in favour of the apparently more robust liberal ideological tradition of its opponents. Thus the ALP no longer seeks a communal shaping of human destiny via use of governmental mechanisms to establish mastery over impersonal natural and economic forces. Now, like the other major parties, the ALP is willing to put the future of individual and community at the mercy of the impersonal forces of the capitalist market and, like the other major parties, seeks merely to optimise the conditions of market 'efficiency'.

The ALP's 'road to Damascus' conversion to marketism, in defiance of its long and, at times, vigorously-held pedigree, astounded many of the party faithful. The green challenge provides a perspective for explanation. From the viewpoint of this radically new paradigm, it becomes clear that the differences between the great partisan traditions have always been more apparent than real. Both Liberal and Labor accept the fundamental tenets of the intellectual revolution of the Enlightenment, their differences being at the margins rather than the centre. Both subscribe to a view of human progress based upon materialism and the progressive imperialisation of 'other nature', the latter perceived as mere 'resource' for the greater good and glory of species *Homo sapiens*. Both view science in instrumental and atomistic terms, its purpose being to provide the technological means for more efficient exploitation of other species in the name of human progress. Both see 'economy' and 'environment' as rival claims upon government attention, with the perceived requirements of 'the economy' taking precedence – even in the face of growing evidence that massive global catastrophe is a looming consequence of such a ranking – because the 'normalcy' and 'naturalness' of 'growth' and 'progress' are the central articles of faith in the sunny Enlightenment view of historical unfolding.

For the ALP then, the key green concern with ecological well-being has the status of 'issue', neatly compartmentalised and contained within boundaries, to ensure its separation from 'economic', 'welfare' and other issues. For an ALP government, 'environment' is bound to remain a circumscribed area of policy formulation, confined within the walls of a portfolio and a department, not a touchstone to inform and guide the entire gamut of policy formulation.

The central index of wilderness best demonstrates this. Though more progress has been made towards meeting the central need for wilderness preservation than is the case in any other area of the green project, Labor and green perceptions of the justification for wilderness preservation are dramatically at odds. Given its endemic anthropocentricism, the ALP can only justify wilderness preservation in terms of its value to humans. It is seen primarily as an economic resource, the cornerstone of the state's growing tourist industry, and this conception will always bring it into conflict (over management prescriptions, for example) with the Greens' ecocentric justification for wilderness preservation. Given the Enlightenment assumptions deeply and fundamentally lodged within the essential tissues of the ALP (lodged much more firmly and fundamentally than its vanishing legacy of democratic socialist values), the ALP will never seek wilderness preservation as an end in itself, as primarily justified by the requirement to respect the vital species needs of 'other nature'. An instance: early in 1990 the Wilderness Society, responding to a call for public submissions on management of the enlarged World Heritage Area, called for the removal of dams and roads, and introduced fish, an end to track construction, and an end to detailed map production (and more). The society was publically upbraided by the Premier as surrendering all credibility and being thoroughly out of touch with the Tasmanian people. But, of course, it is not primarily the interests of the Tasmanian people that the Wilderness Society was here seeking to promote, and whatever defects the submission may have in terms of short-term politics, it is an unequivocal affirmation of the ecocentric principles central to any long term 'greening'.

Undoubtedly, in terms of issue-based tactics the submission was disastrous, and the Greens in Parliament, interestingly, promptly distanced themselves from it. And here is another problem for the Greens. To focus on a parliamentary path to change is to inevitably shape one's politics to a politics of issues, not a politics aimed at a fundamental break from the assumptions of the Enlightenment paradigm. This is perhaps the key dilemma of green strategy — the line must be held, and issues must be contested, but there is a real danger that, in the process, sight is lost of the larger game, or even that, in attaining a legitimacy at one level of debate, the primary goal of thoroughgoing change takes on an appearance of utter outlandishness.

It may be that to fight and win on issues is all that is possible. As the Tasmanian experience shows, green success engenders an increasingly sophisticated and toughminded opposition, which greatly circumscribes the movement's capacity to make further headway, and as green values do not elevate to a transcendent status the specific interests of a segment of humanity, it cannot look to an identifiable (and, more importantly, self-identifiable) historical subject to prosecute the green agenda. The broader goal of fundamental value change must nevertheless be assayed, for the alternative is to accept the boxing of 'environment' within close bounds, whilst governments continue to make decisions in policy areas that are ostensibly 'non-environmental' but which, nevertheless, increase the human-use pressures upon global ecosystems so that the great and unsurpassed tragedy of our age – biological impoverishment – continues apace. Such decisions more firmly bind humankind to the imperatives of an alienating technology and the chains of a remote and inaccessible international economy, and they bring the planet ever closer to eco-catastrophe.

Conclusions

The international environment movement is wise to keep a keen interest in events as they develop in Tasmania. The small insular Australian state that provided the world's prototype green party and the first environmental single issue of global scope has one of the world's most theoretically, tactically and organizationally advanced environment movements, though this is more to be attributed to the constant preoccupation with environmental disputation than to the particular cataclysmic events surrounding the battle for the Franklin, or the election to the balance of power in the state Parliament of five green members. Continuously for two decades, Tasmanian political debate has, uniquely, focused upon green values and aspirations. What has happened, and is still happening in Tasmania, may well presage the pattern of political unfolding that can be expected if and when green aspirations are as successfully pushed to centre stage as they have been in Tasmania.

Now that environmental values are popularly seen to have the sanction of government, it is the assumptions that (rightly or wrongly) are seen by the community to have been officially displaced – in this case those coalescing around the development/growth/jobs nexus – that claim the moral high ground and have the greatest capability to engender an evangelical fervour. The very outrage of outsidedness provides a potent 'feet in the street' capacity. And in the middle is the voter who now feels perhaps that his/her daring vote for the Greens in the state election has consigned away too much of the economic agenda – who now feels less compassion for the trees than for the mortgage problems of builders' labourers and trucking contractors, and who now wishes to rectify matters.

But it is perhaps less the fact of power-sharing than the terms of that sharing that are the greatest contributor to the current malaise. As a sharer of power, though a sharer with considerably less power than the junior partner in a formal coalition could expect to enjoy, the Greens are in an invidious position. It is easy for the government to take credit for all the 'goodies' that emerge from the governmental sausage machine, because there is no formal and visible way in which the Greens can be seen to have made a major contribution to the creation of those 'goodies' (except in so far as they were to be found in the Accord document). In addition, the obvious means whereby the Greens could score some 'wins' – by taking prime carriage in the House of Assembly of legislation to which government and Greens are mutually committed – has been effectively closed off by the great hatred of the Greens held by the powerful ultra-conservative rump in the Legislative Council, which virtually dooms in advance any Green-sponsored legislation coming up from the Lower House.

Thus the Greens are effectively excluded from a share in the 'positives'. On the other hand, the powerful perception of economic malaise that has settled upon the state (and which is justified by some of the conventional economic indicators, but flatly contradicted by others), can be entirely blamed upon the 'dead economic hand' of the Greens on the shoulder of government, and this fiction, so convenient for the ALP, does not even require any Macchiavellian intervention on the part of its plotters and schemers. It seems likely, then, that the Greens will not maintain their vote at the next state election, and the power-sharing experiments that have occurred in Germany suggest, perhaps, that this is to be expected.

But, by virtue of the peculiar evolutionary circumstances of green politics within Tasmania, the small island at the end of the earth has achieved a more sustained and concentrated level of conflict and debate over the political implications of 'green' than has yet occurred in other political systems, and this justifies international attention, though not only for the 'good news' to be learned from scrutiny of one of the world's most successful and advanced environment movements.

The unremitting focus on things and ideas green make Tasmania a political system unique in the world. One of the most important lessons it teaches is the strength of the fierce antagonism to the green critique that will arise if and when it comes to control the political centre-stage, particularly when a focus on the existential rights of 'other nature' sharpens popular perceptions of just how fundamental and revolutionary is the green challenge. Its success engenders a reaction by those whose specific interests are threatened by the implementation of a green agenda, and this reaction is likely to be fierce (possibly violent) and broadly-based. National survey data has shown that there is much more positive support for the actions of environmental activists in Tasmania than anywhere in Australia – but the strength of deep-seated hostility to such activists is also greater in Tasmania, and by a greater margin(Williams 1989).

It is unlikely that this hostility will be defused unless and until the green movement effectively scuttles the potent myth that environmental well-being is fundamentally incompatible with economic well-being, and unless and until it devises workable practical strategies for the peaceful (but effective) replacement of prevailing economic practice with the environmentally benign processes advocated by green economics. There is a pronounced and unfortunate tendency within much green social theory complacently to assume that the manifest wisdom of the green message will, once it gains some impetus, sweep the world. The Tasmanian experience sounds a warning to such blitheness. The vandals can be evicted from the citadel, but they will mass around the gates with renewed vigour.

References

Crowley, K. (1989). 'Accommodating Industry in Tasmania: Eco-political factors behind the Electrona silicon smelter dispute', in P. R. Hay, P. R. Eckersley and G. Holloway (eds.), *Environmental Politics in Australia and New Zealand*. (Hobart (Aust.): Centre for Environmental Studies, University of Tasmania), pp. 45–58.

Easthope, G. and Holloway, G. (1989). 'Wilderness as the sacred: The Franklin River campaign', in P. R. Hay, R. Eckersley and G. Holloway (eds.), *Environmental Politics in Australia and New Zealand*. (Hobart: Centre for Environmental Studies, University of Tasmania, pp. 189–99).

Eckersley, R. (1989). 'Green politics and the new clas)s: Selfishness or virtue?', *Political Studies*, Vol. 37, pp. 205–23.

Flanagan, R. (1989). 'Masters of History: Tasmania, Tasmanians, Greens', *Island Magazine*, Vol. 41, pp. 35–40.

Flanagan, R. (1990), 'Return the People's Pedder!', in C. Pybus, and R. Flanagan (eds.), *The Whole World Is Watching: The Greens in Tasmania*. (Melbourne: Sun Books).

Gouldner, A. (1987). *The Future of Intellectuals and the Rise of the New Middle Class*. (London: Macmillan).

Green, R. (comp.) (1983). *Battle for the Franklin: Conversations with the Combatants in the Struggle for South West Tasmania*. (Melbourne: Fontana/Australian Conservation Foundation).

Hay, P. R. (1987). 'Will the "Tasmanian Disease" spread to the mainland?: The politics of land-use conflict', *Current Affairs Bulletin*, Vol. 64 (3), pp. 4–12.

Hay, P. R. (1988). 'The contemporary environment movement as neo-romanticism: A re-appraisal from Tasmania', *Environmental Review*, Vol. 12 (4), pp. 39–60.

Hay, P. R. and Haward, M. G. (1988). 'Comparative green politics: Beyond the European context?', *Political Studies*, Vol. 36, pp. 433–48.

Holloway, G. (1986). *The Wilderness Society: The Transformation of a Social Movement*. (Hobart (Aust.): Occasional Paper No. 4, Department of Sociology, University of Tasmania).

McQueen, J. (1983). *The Franklin – Not Just a River*. (Ringwood (Aust.): Penguin).

Martin, B. (1984). 'Environmentalism and electoralism', *The Ecologist*, Vol. 14, pp. 110–18.

Offe, C. (1985), 'New Social Movements: Challenging the boundaries of institutional politics', *Social Research*, Vol. 52, pp. 817–68.

Parkin, S. (1989). *Green Parties: An International Guide*. (London: Heretic).

Rüdig, W. and Lowe, P. (1986). 'The "Withered Greening" of British politics: A study of the Ecology Party', *Political Studies*, Vol. 34, pp. 262–84.

Schumacher, F. (1974). *Small is Beautiful: A Study of Economics as if People Mattered*. (London: Abacus).

Simon, M. (1988). 'Greens in power in den Bundestag', *Green Line*, Vol. 65, pp. 21–2.

Thompson, P. (1984). *Bob Brown of the Franklin River*. (Sydney: Allen & Unwin).

Tighe, P., and Taplin, R. (1985), 'Lessons from recent environmental decisions: The Franklin Dam case and rain forests in Queensland'. Paper presented to the Annual Conference of the Australasian Political Studies Association.

Walker, P. (1989). 'The United Tasmania Group: An analysis of the world's first green party', in P. R. Hay, R. Eckersley and G. Holloway (eds.), *Environmental Politics in Australia and New Zealand*. (Hobart (Aust.): Centre for Environmental Studies, University of Tasmania), pp. 161–74.

Wescombe, M. (1990). 'From world's end the greening starts: Assessing Tasmania's global mission', in Pybus, P. and Flanagan, R. (eds.), *The Whole World Is Watching: The Greens in Tasmania*. (Melbourne: Sun Books), pp. 170–93.

Williams, A. (1988). 'Environmentalists: Who cares?'. (Hobart (Aust.): Department of Sociology, University of Tasmania, mimeo).

5. The New Zealand Values Party: Challenging the Poverty of Progress 1972–1989

STEPHEN RAINBOW

Department of Politics, Victoria University of Wellington, Wellington, New Zealand

Introduction

New Zealand's Values Party was the first national green party in the world. It made an impact beyond its size or electoral support, because it brought a fresh approach to a stale political environment and appealed to a particular set of values on the political spectrum which was hitherto unrepresented. Its influence extended beyond the borders of New Zealand, with German Greens such as Petra Kelly identifying the importance of Values as a model of what could be done with green ideas in the political arena. Values' success was relatively short-lived, however, for a variety of reasons, not least of which was New Zealand's first-past-the-post electoral system. Other parties were quick to adopt the quality of life and environmental rhetoric of Values, proving that if nothing else, Values changed the political vocabulary of the time. Importantly in the longer term, however, Values helped to create a climate where issues such as a nuclear-free defence policy were much more politically palatable in New Zealand.

This chapter presents a brief history of the world's first national green party before examining the extent to which the Values Party was influenced by its national setting and the salience of environmental and lifestyle issues in New Zealand at the end of the 1960s.[1] There was an often explicit desire on the part of Values members to maintain New Zealand in its relatively 'untouched' – and privileged – state, giving the party an interesting tinge of conservatism and nationalism. The chapter then evaluates the party's changing outlook from an idealistic to a materialist analysis of society, and consider this along with other reasons for its decline. For whereas in the party's early days it had been part of a non-doctrinaire movement looking for imaginative solutions to contemporary problems, between 1976 and 1978 it came to embrace a more concrete analysis which led it in a direction barely distinguishable from existing minority socialist groups. Rather than being reflective of a mood, as it had been in its early years, the party came to appear to be handing out a pre-packaged solution from above which alienated many of its own members as well as the voting public.

A Brief Party History, 1972–89 [2]

The Values Party was formed in 1972, the brainchild of a former journalist turned political science student. Tony Brunt was one of a generation of people who had experienced the turmoil of the 1960s and was frustrated at the degree to which existing parties had failed to respond to the changing mood among a significant minority of young people. By 1972 New Zealand had experienced twelve uninterrupted years of National (conservative) Government, during which time, among other things, New Zealand had become directly involved in the Vietnam conflict. The main alternative, the New Zealand Labour Party, was still dominated by morally-conservative working people and showed a singular lack of understanding of the new generation of young people who had benefited from the universal education provisions of earlier Labour governments. After losing the 1969 election due to industrial action at the time, Labour did all it could to project a moderate image to the voting public. This included taking up anti-bikie and other hard-line policies which alienated liberals even within Labour's own ranks and provided the last push necessary for those who wanted to form a new party (Evening Post, 8 November 1972). Labour, Brunt claimed, was only a 'poor man's National Party' (Evening Post, 21 October 1972), and both parties in the two-party system were so wedded to a materially driven economic system that there was no real political alternative in New Zealand.

Brunt discussed the paucity of political options with flatmates and friends, and called a meeting at Victoria University in Wellington on 31 May 1972. About sixty people attended the inaugural meeting, but the big break for the fledgling party came when a television documentary covering the minor parties contesting the 1972 election ended up devoting its entire duration to Values, so impressed was the producer with Brunt and the party's ideas. This nationally broadcast programme saw the party inundated with enquiries and interest, so that by election time one month later, Values had forty-three candidates standing.

The party's first manifesto, Blueprint for New Zealand, borrowed its title from A Blueprint for Survival published in Britain in 1972. The British Blueprint was part of a wider genre of literature at that time based on the fear that the earth was using up all its non-renewable resources and that the human population was growing beyond the ability of the earth to sustain it. The Club of Rome used computer models to create its own doomsday predictions, published as The Limits to Growth. Many of those initially involved in the Values Party had travelled in Europe where this kind of literature was the frequent focus of discussion among intellectually-inclined circles. An early leader of the figure who joined the Values Party on returning from Britain stated unequivocally that: 'The New Zealand Values Party has given political expression in this country to a new ideological current flowing throughout the world' (Evening Post, 24 August 1974). The party's Blueprint concluded unashamedly with a reading list of books about stable state economics, the counter-culture and the control of technology.

The Blueprint spoke of the party's desire to meet the needs of the people rather than the system, and to provide a quality of life 'wherein there is the widest possible scope for human development and happiness' (Values Party 1972, p. 5). Values, it claimed, was concerned with the environment in its widest possible sense, and sought to give political expression to 'the new values' (Values Party 1972, p. 2). New Zealand, it claimed, was suffering from spiritual poverty and a depression of human values and national spirit. Politics was governed by expediency, and in the endless pursuit of affluence, people's non-material needs were ignored. The party's unashamedly utopian message touched an idealistic streak which had been unexploited in New Zealand politics for some time. Values spoke of the evil of short-sighted policy-making and the deficiencies of the election-oriented policy cycle. It proclaimed its concern about the future, and the need to redefine progress away from simple standard-of-living measurements. The party's message clearly touched a chord, for during the election campaign the party leader was able to attract more people to a pre-election rally in the Wellington Town Hall than the National Prime Minister had done some evenings earlier. Individuals ranging from a radical student leader to the Mayor of New Zealand's largest city, publicly endorsed the fledgling party which went on to win a credible 2·7 per cent of the total national vote in the November 1972 election. The same election also saw the Labour Party elected to government for the first time since 1957.

Environmental issues entered the 1972 election in the form of the battle to save a large southern lake, Manapouri, from hydro-electric development. But the environment was not a major issue in other respects and it was hard to pinpoint specific local environmental issues in New Zealand other than Manapouri. While Values had central policy planks of zero economic growth and zero population growth, publicly the party tended to focus on quality-of-life issues. The party's second leader, Reg Clough, spoke of the fundamental base of the party as the humanist ideal: 'the right of every person to complete fulfilment as an individual, spiritually and materially' (Evening Post, 26 August 1974). At local branch level, activities in the party's formative years tended to centre around local environmental clean-ups, collecting re-usable materials, and making submissions on issues such as the 1974 World Population Conference.

The question of party structure was problematic from an early stage. The party's first conference was held in 1973 and it considered a paper from a prominent environmentalist which recommended that not having leadership and structures was most in keeping with the party's stated principles of decentralisation and spontaneity. The adoption of this strategy meant that Values had effectively ceased to exist as a national party within six months. The 1974 Party Conference rectified this situation by adopting a more formal structure, as well as electing a new leader and deputy leaders. One new deputy leader, Cathy Wilson, became the first woman to hold such a high office in a political party in New Zealand. Wilson's election set the precedent for Values consistently to raise the visibility of women in New Zealand politics. A parliamentary by-election and local government elections during 1974 helped to raise the party's profile, and as disillusionment with the Labour government set in, the media, in particular, played an important role in enhancing Values' visibility.

Values capitalised on disillusionment with the performance of the Labour government, particularly attacking its immigration and energy policies, and its conservative stances on 'moral' issues such as abortion and homosexual law reform. Values' critique also focused on what it described as Labour's continuing commitment to a 'prehistoric obsession with development – with economic and population growth' (*Sunday Herald*, 24 March 1974). It is unlikely that Values would have attracted as much support as it consequently did were it not for the fact that there was a great deal of disappointment, among liberal people in particular, with the Labour government. The Values Party's prospects for the 1975 election were also raised by the fact that it was the first time that eighteen-year-olds were able to vote. The oil crisis after 1973 also served to legitimise in the public mind Values' claims about the depletion of nonrenewable resources. Values suggested that alternative soft energy paths provided a clear departure from the oil-based emphasis of the major parties' policies.

Values went into the 1975 election knowing it could not win, but hoping for a good vote so as to strengthen the party's hand as a catalyst for change. The party also saw the electoral platform as an opportunity to educate the public about the 'nightmarish consumer society'(*Evening Post*, 28 November 1975). Values went on to win 5·2 per cent of the total vote, with a Values candidate standing in every constituency. This result, followed by the winning of 9 per cent of the total vote in the Nelson by-election in January 1976, represented the high-point in Values' fortunes. The 1975 election also began a period of intense soul-searching for the Labour Party, who lost power after only one term in government. Polls during 1975 show that Labour lost a lot of its idealistic support to Values in the election (*Evening Post*, 6 November 1975) and Labour set about addressing that problem once it found itself in opposition again, fearing that the Values Party's long-term existence could permanently deprive Labour of electoral victory. Labour leader Bill Rowling met informally with the Values' leadership early in 1976, a meeting which led to the subsequent chastisement of the leadership by the Christchurch faction of the Values Party who were unhappy that such a meeting took place without membership knowledge or approval. Labour's new leadership attempted to shed the party's cloth-cap image, and this, combined with the polarising effect of the new National Prime Minister, Robert Muldoon, worked to threaten the loyalty of Values voters. For with New Zealand's first-past-the-post electoral system, a vote for other than Labour was seen to work to National's advantage. A widespread revulsion against Muldoon by liberals, in particular, and a worsening economic situation served to draw Values voters into the Labour camp. This process was assisted by the establishment of a Labour Womens' Council and the increasing visibility of young and liberal people in Labour's ranks.

Paralleling developments in the Labour Party, Values was also involved in its own process of change. The effects of a real stop to economic growth due to the economic downturn following the oil shock in 1973, had made Values' central policy plank of zero economic growth seem increasingly irrelevant. Even under the more populist approach of the new leader, Tony Kunowski — himself an economist — , the party was unable to shed the impression that it had no real understanding of economics, let alone solutions to the downturn. Values candidates had also complained about a lack of detailed policies during the 1975 election campaign and so the party set about formulating a more precise range of policies for achieving its stable-state society. Policy-making thereafter became Values' major focus, to the detriment of its more publicly-oriented activities such as membership recruitment. Policy working groups were established at the 1976 Conference with the brief of producing policy recommendations for the full Party Conference. As a result of their efforts, as well as those of a Policy Conference in January 1977, the Party Conference that year had to consider more than 500 remits.

The movement from broad ideals to specific policies and programmes exacerbated existing divisions within the party, especially over attitudes to the control and ownership of land and capital. The Christchurch-based Values Party was more socialistic than other parts of the party and it tended to use traditional leftist tactics to get its policies accepted by the party, much to the distaste of less doctrinaire sections. Sections of the party were also concerned at the compilation of all existing party policy into a sizeable Policy Manual (Values Party 1978a), which was seen by some to represent the increasing bureaucratisation of Values. Copious head office mail-outs, and the employment of both a full-time secretary and an organizer, were also seen to represent the decline of Values into a conventional political party. By the time of the 1978 election, however, Values had a comprehensive programme of alternative policies couched in the same language as the major parties in an attempt to convince the public that Values understood bread and butter issues as well as abstract ideals. Many of the central policy planks were the products of the Christchurch-based group who had used the Policy Working Groups to present policies to party conferences almost as a *fait accompli*. The Christchurch party was also responsible for the publication of *Critical Issues '78* (Values Party 1978b) which portrayed a protester on its cover carrying a placard reading 'Make Our Dollar Last'. It stood in marked contrast to the 1975 manifesto called *Beyond Tomorrow* which featured a cover photograph of two children sitting on a rock by the sea, with one of them peering off into the distance.

Policy disagreements hurt Values from 1976 onwards, as did diverse views about the party's aims and purpose. Several by-elections in 1977 and 1978 presented the opportunity for great soul-searching as Values revisited the perennial issue of whether it was primarily a political party or a social movement. At the 1978 Rangitikei by-election another minor party, Social Credit, was relaunched as a credible alternative for voters when it won the seat from the governing National Party. The negative effect on Values of its poor by-election showings were made worse by the media's focusing on party splits and by the announcement by a prominent party activist that voters in the 1978 general election should vote for any candidate – regardless of their party – where it would help to replace an anti-abortion Member of Parliament with a more liberal one. The party's honeymoon with the media was also over by now, with editorials often criticising Values for taking on a wide range of policies, therefore diluting the party's former unique concern with quality-of-life and environmental issues.

Values provided a national network for the promotion of two important petitions in 1976 and 1977. The Campaign Half Million petition against nuclear power, and the 'Repeal' petition against repressive abortion laws both relied for their success to a significant degree upon the legwork of Values Party personnel. Values was particularly active on the question of nuclear power and helped to create a climate of opinion which saw both Labour and National governments question the seemingly inevitable introduction of nuclear power into New Zealand. But the assistance which the Values Party gave to pressure groups on this and other issues was seldom reciprocated, as pressure groups strove to endear themselves to the major parties by pursuing political neutrality. In spite of efforts to forge links with pressure groups and other social movements – such as the Maori group, Te Matakite, who were invited to address the party's 1978 Conference – Values was singularly unsuccessful in establishing links with other movements which had the potential to provide Values with an ongoing power base and constituency.

The Party went into the 1978 election with the best-developed organization and policies it had ever had, which only served to increase the disappointment with the election result. Winning only 2·8 per cent of the total vote went against the perception of many Values leaders and activists that their percentage of the vote would increase at every election until Values was in Parliament, if not in government. The party never recovered from that electoral setback, and the Easter 1979 Conference provided the occasion for a great deal of acrimony and the withdrawal from the party of some of the diverse groups which had been brought together under its auspices as long as there was the potential for some political influence. The same conference also elected the first woman to head a New Zealand political party, when Margaret Crozier narrowly defeated the incumbent, Tony Kunowski, after the latter alienated many members by presenting an ultimatum demanding that the party professionalise its approach and organization if he were to stay on. Kunowski and his Christchurch followers withdrew from Values after his defeat and later regrouped in a Socialist Network, but they were never to return to the Values fold. The withdrawal of this group saw Values lose many of its most hard-working activists as well as the majority of those who saw Values' role as a radical political force courting public credibility and support. After this time Values' emphasis changed much more in the direction of its being a social movement with local political activity, rather than a national political party.

Many subsequent debates in the party centred around whether or not to contest elections at all, and when Values failed to contest the Christchurch Central by-election in 1979 it was the first time it had not contested an election since the party's formation in 1972. Rumours persisted in the media during 1979 that prominent Values activists were pursuing the possibility of amalgamating with the Labour Party. By 1980 newspaper editorials were stating unequivocally that Values was no longer a credible political force (Christchurch Star, 10 April 1980), and at the end of 1980 the Values Party in New Zealand's fourth-largest city, Dunedin, disbanded. During 1980 there were moves made inside Values to ensure that the party did not contest the 1981 general election at all, because of fears that this could assist the return of the National government by taking potential Labour votes in marginal seats. But the pro-electoral forces won out and Values stood seventeen candidates (out of a total of ninety-two) winning 0·2 per cent of the total vote.

The leadership troika which led Values into the 1981 election attempted to capitalise on well-publicised German Green gains, but to no avail. The floating of a proposal to form an alliance with a small Maori party, Mana Motuhake, did nothing to stem the flow of members from the party. Party conferences attracted less and less people and party activity increasingly became centred around the leadership figures in two provincial towns.

Party leaders put a brave face on the fact that twenty-nine candidates in the 1984 election managed to gain only 0·2 per cent of the total vote, but no amount of exhorting about the bright future in store for Values could disguise the obvious decline of the party. In 1986 the party changed its name, to 'Values, the Green Party of Aotearoa', but remained unable to capitalise on green developments elsewhere because of its association with the now discredited Values label. Values members continued to meet regularly because of long-term personal ties and a lack of alternative avenues for green political activity, but a 'Green Gathering' organized by Values in 1988 did nothing to revive or bring new personnel into the party.

At the party's 1989 Conference a paper was presented proposing that new green groups unassociated with the Values Party should be established to contest the impending local elections. With the adoption of this strategy in some regions and the consequent election of green members to local authorities in Wellington and Taranaki, the Values Party Council recommended in November 1989 that the party be disbanded. Lack of accurate membership records and the willingness of a minority of party activists to carry on, however, saw Values committing itself to carry on under the name of 'The Green Party of Aotearoa'. Members of this group met on several occasions with the emerging new green groups in late 1989 and early 1990 and finally agreed to the formation of a new unified group – The Greens – in March 1990.

The Greens went on to contest seventy-one of the ninety-five constituencies in the 1990 general elections, gaining a credible 6·6 per cent of the total vote, and an average 8·9 per cent of the vote in those electorates they contested. This was a significant showing for a party less than a year old, especially as both major parties, and particularly the Labour government, had made a major play of their respective environmental policies. Because of New Zealand's electoral system the Greens were constantly plagued with the accusation that they would help the National Party – whose environmental policies were far less developed than Labour's – into power. The Greens were also ridiculed by the media for their lack of detailed policies and their lack of conventional leadership structures. Nevertheless, they maintained a consistent 7–9 per cent in public opinion polls during the weeks immediately prior to the election, clearly establishing themselves as the most significant third party in New Zealand.

In their best electorates the Greens gained up to 20 per cent of the total vote, and came close to beating the Labour Party into second place in some National-held seats. They scored well in both rural and urban constituencies, with a crucial variable in their vote appearing to be how marginal the constituency was. In many cases people – not surprisingly – appeared more willing to vote Green where the outcome in the seat was perceived to be a foregone conclusion. Reform of the electoral system must therefore become the major focus of green energies in New Zealand over the next two years, as the incoming National government has promised a referendum on the issue in 1992. Without some form of proportional representation, there is no reason to believe that the Greens will not simply repeat the history of the Values Party (cf. Rainbow 1991).

The Values Party in Retrospect: The Politics of Happiness

While the Values Party was motivated by the immediacy of environmental destruction, it also embraced a general social critique of New Zealand society. It was a reaction against the lack of intellectualism in politics and in society more generally, and a response to the substitution of morality and ethics by commercial values alone. In its broadest sense it was an emotional reaction against the values of material and economic security of the older generations and the politics they dominated. Social critics like McLauchlan expressed articulately the anguish of a new generation appalled at the dominance of the philistinism of the dominant lower middle class in New Zealand:

> At last unhappiness has become such an epidemic that our smugness, once unassailable, is wearing thin. The time has come now to see ourselves as we really are – a racially and culturally homogeneous group of people who have nurtured in isolation from the rest of the world a Victorian, lower-middle class, Calvinist, village mentality, and brought it right through into the 1970s. We have established a society in which we have been spared the disgusting sight of the poor and the sick, the dirty and, particularly, the different. Materialism has been the coarse fabric of our dreams which we have overrun, dreams on which we have found (to our subconscious dismay), that we have expended ourselves. There was nothing else – just materialism. There is no passion to give us a dream of the good life, a vision of love and beauty, a sense of a variety of lifestyles, of alternative viewpoints and philosophies through which we may fulfil ourselves in different ways. (McLauchlan, 1980)

Acknowledging social problems and improving the quality of life in New Zealand was the Values Party's major concern. The 1973 Values Party Conference was addressed by an anthropologist, an economist and a psychologist on the subject of the organization of happiness. Journalist W. P. Reeves wrote after reading *Beyond Tomorrow* prior to the 1975 election campaign: 'Values promises escape from corrupting worship of the material to a nirvana where such non-material needs as "friendship, play, self-expression, a sense of individual identity, social approval, self-esteem and peace of mind" are satisfied' (*Sunday Times*, October 1975). The rise of the German Greens has been attributed to similar factors: to the need for imagination, spontaneity and affection in small groups – needs which industrial society has gravitated against (Deutsch 1985, p. 8). Values represented the desire of its educated constituency to take control of their own lives, and to avoid the seemingly inevitable progression in their life cycles to a forty-hour-week job and to married life in the suburbs.

Domesticity was a recurring theme in New Zealand art and culture of the 1970s, a decade when intimate issues such as abortion were to the fore and when there was a deepening concern for the condition of personal and intimate relationships (Oliver 1981, p. 457). The reaction against the seemingly inevitable suburban lifestyle was typified by New Zealand's most famous poet, James K. Baxter, whose alternative lifestyle made as much impact as his poetry. He wrote of the concern with lifestyle which Values alone gave political expression to:

> On Calvary St are trellises
> Where bright as blood the roses bloom
> And gnomes like pagan fetishes
> Hang their hats on an empty tomb
> Where two old souls go slowly mad
> National Mum and Labour Dad.
> (O'Sullivan 1976, p. 33)

The question of lifestyle became a central one for the new social movements which emerged during the late 1960s and early 1970s. There was a sense that technology should be harnessed for human needs and that society itself could be reshaped in the image of those who sought personal growth and new experiences instead of the entrapment of traditional adult routines (Oakes 1986, p. 114). It was inevitable that such social developments would be reflected in the political sphere, and given the inability of the existing parties to address non-material issues it was not surprising that a movement such as Values arose to articulate the concerns of the new social developments.

For New Zealand this was a time of urbanisation, and of an increasingly well educated population. The 1976 census showed for the first time a majority of the labour force in white-collar occupations, among whom workplace militancy grew throughout the seventies. It was a time of anti-Vietnam protests, a rising women's movement, a cultural flowering, and of new attention to economic, social and environmental planning. New Zealand society was changing, maturing, cultivating a diversity which had previously been quashed by the remarkable degree of unanimity about the validity of economic growth, prosperity and security. In a more affluent age people started to look more critically at certain aspects of New Zealand life, now that a high degree of economic security had been achieved. In some ways the Values Party was a direct result of the concerns with lifestyle and relationships. The major parties showed little awareness of these personal issues, and their concern remained with pocket-book issues. Growing demands for equality for women and for legally-available abortions were not represented in the major four parties' programmes, which were still dominated by the material and economic concerns of the 'old politics' agenda (Kolinsky 1984, pp. 187–9). Addressing concerns about lifestyle was just one of the ways in which Values embraced the dictum that 'the personal is political'. Values argued that the way in which individuals live, play and consume affects the general direction of society. Changes at the personal level affect the larger society, and people have a responsibility in their personal lives to live out the kind of society they want to see. Most of the major thrusts of Values policy depended on changing the behaviour of people in their daily lives, as Values deputy-leader stated unequivocally in 1975: 'Our message backed by our policies is simple and based on commonsense – people must exploit less, consume less, pollute less, plan more, share more and conserve more if their children are to have a country worth living in' (Evening Post, 14 August 1975).

Puritan tendencies underlay much of what Values advocated, reflecting the need for self-control in a society of limited resources. Levine wrote that Values' 'monastic neo-Puritan tendencies may be associated with revulsion towards the visible fruits of material wealth, suggesting the party as a fit subject for the political psychoanalyst' (Levine 1975, p. 121). Values' philosophy, he went on to suggest, 'deprecates indulgence and bases its economic policies on a willingness to forgo consumption of goods allegedly bearing little relation to basic human needs'. Jones likened the lifestyle which Values would wish upon us to that of the Trappist monks – 'the ultimate social order of an absolute totalitarian mentality and self-disdain'. He continued: 'Each with our own plot of land cultivating our own food, spinning our wool in the evening by candelight (electricity is sinful too, as its generation by any means other than windmills mucks up the landscape), turning our pots, giving birth on a pile of hay and collecting our bodily wastes as natural fertiliser' (Jones 1978, p. 63).

Similar criticisms are often directed at European green parties today. Values responded by asserting the need for pleasure based not on the consumption of goods, but on activities which are endlessly available such as friendship, conversation, creativity and contact with nature. Its 1975 manifesto quoted Rattray Taylor:

> In a natural society man gets exercise by swimming or dancing or in the course of his work; today he needs a car and a bag of golf clubs or a yacht. In a natural society, he gets status from his skills; today he needs to purchase status-symbols. Once, his fantasies were supplied by a human story-teller; now they need the elaborate machinery of television. Where he made his music by singing or playing he now depends on radio and gramophone. But is the satisfaction

they yield as great? We need to establish a need-oriented society in place of our present goods-oriented society. (Values Party 1975, p. 33)

It could thus be argued that the Values Party represented a continuity of the Romantic tradition which inspired the early ethical socialists. Such movements emphasise the importance of authentic human relationships, the need for personal happiness and a sense of community, as well as for beauty and aesthetic sensitivity. One political scientist wrote of the Save Manapouri Campaign's significance that for the first time it 'presented government with the necessity of weaving a strand of aesthetic consideration into its public policy-making' (Cleveland 1972). Values was part of a much broader movement challenging the purely material view of the world and asserting the need for the political system to address people's non-material needs. One political commentator comparing the Labour Party and the Values Party wrote that the 'Labour Party is principally a party of economics, Values of the spirit' (James 1978). The Values Party put back on New Zealand's political agenda some of the questions about the purpose of politics and the nature of the good society which had been ignored by the materially-driven consensus of the post-war years.

New Zealand as a South Pacific Paradise

Values was the first New Zealand political party to put the environment at the centre of the political agenda. While there were not a large number of pressing environmental issues at the time, Values was able to capitalise on the environment as a symbol of all that was threatened in the name of progress. The Save Manapouri Campaign had already shown how successful such symbolism could be: 'It is significant that the Save Manapouri Campaign generated a good deal of collectivist symbolism about the aesthetic value of the lake and the conservation of "natural assets" and the "natural heritage" ... Pressure groups' statements emphasised that the lake had become a symbol of nature despoiled in the name of progress' (Cleveland 1972, p. 39). The Save Manapouri Campaign brought together for the first time the combination of youthful protesters and middle-class liberals constituting a post-materialist constituency (Cleveland 1972). The Campaign also served to give local saliency to the increasing coverage given to international environmental issues by the media. A disproportionate number of people involved in the Values Party were foreigners who had chosen New Zealand as their home because of its image as a land relatively untouched by the worst excesses of northern-hemisphere industrialism:

This slender remnant of the Gondwanaland continent, an eloquent sculpture lying deep in oceanic space, has long been believed to be a natural paradise; an Eden for the spiritually emaciated Europeans flocking to its coasts in a great escape bid from an original sin whose workings they suffered in their industrialising homelands. (Trussell 1982, p. 32)

Even though it is a highly urbanised country, most New Zealanders have some ties with the land, which serve an important role in defining what it means to be a New Zealander. Values realised the importance of the fact that 'the natural character of the landscape plays a role in giving New Zealanders their national, regional and local identities' (Park 1988, p. 95). Values was initially able to appeal to this important component of New Zealand nationalism, as the following anecdote from political commentator Bob Jones revealed:

Shortly before the last election I chartered a small plane to make a hurried visit to another city for a speech engagement. I sat alongside the pilot who was a young man shortly to cast his first vote. I inquired who would receive it and he looked out of the window at the distant and therefore always beautiful landscape and said 'That's the way I want New Zealand – I'm voting Values.' (Jones 1978, p. 66).

Preserving New Zealand in a relatively unspoiled state extended to Values' strong opposition to large-scale immigration into New Zealand. Adopting a neo-Malthusian concern about population growth, a recurring theme in the party's 1972 and 1975 manifestos was the need to stabilise New Zealand's population. Population stabilisation was to be combined with zero economic growth to create a 'stable state society'. This amounted, according to the 1975 *Beyond Tomorrow*, to offering New Zealand a survival kit: 'The world today has two cancer-like problems – population growth and industrial growth. Neither is critical yet in New Zealand, but the dimension of these problems overseas constitutes a warning we must heed' (Values Party 1975, p. 13). Many party activists had lived abroad, and their focus was very much on ensuring that the negative consequences of industrialism observed abroad were not imported to New Zealand.

As well as protecting New Zealand against the excesses of industrialism, there was also a sense in party publications that New Zealand could provide a model for the rest of the world, as it had done in the 1930s by establishing the first comprehensive welfare state. Economic self-sufficiency was to be a part of this model, leading Values to be described in some quarters as 'fervent nationalists' to the extent of exhibiting a fascist element (Jones 1978, p. 64). Specific environmental policies were few and far between, with the 1972 *Blueprint* referring readers to the section on population growth after affirming its commitment to the conservation of New Zealand's natural and scenic resources. Urban environmental matters received greater detailed attention, with opposition to motorways and large building developments.

Values' approach changed as the party matured, but during its most active years (1972–8) its approach can only be described as nationalistic, especially where economics and immigration were concerned. Given that Values also claimed to embrace global concerns and an internationalist perspective, it is hard to reconcile this with the quasi-autarchic policies they advocated for New Zealand.

Values' Changing Outlook 1972–8

The Values Party was a particularly New Zealand expression of a broader quest in most parts of the developed industrial world at the end of the 1960s for a rediscovery of meaning and a re-evaluation of social and political priorities by a relatively youthful and well-educated minority. The Values Party was consequently founded on idealism, but ideals alone were not sufficient to sustain the party, especially as New Zealand's economic situation declined and material concerns once again began to dominate politics. The consequent movement from broad ideals to specific programmes and policies proved to be a destructive process for the Values Party. The development of detailed policies meant that the openness and creativity which had marked the early days of the party was replaced by a more doctrinaire approach which eventually came to be promoted by a small cadre of activists. An increasingly neo-marxist approach saw the party focus more on the economic and material aspects of life, and less on the broad questions and ideals which had initially given Values its unique appeal.

Values' message may have been implicitly socialistic from the outset, as one newspaper editor suggested after reading *Beyond Tomorrow*: 'We are now invited by a middle-class party owing nothing to working-class origins to admit that the profit motive not only fails to serve the common interest but also sweeps us headlong into disaster, and therefore to contemplate capitalism's overthrow. I can read no other message in the the manifesto' (*Sunday Times*, 19 October 1975). But during its heyday the   socialist message was never made explicit, and it would not have reflected the wishes or desires of most of the membership had it done so. A broad range of people were brought together in Values initially, ranging from former National Party members to Marxists. Their mutual concerns were for the quality of life and for the environment, along with a rejection of unthinking commitment to a progress seemingly beyond human control. During the creation of more detailed policies, particularly after the successful 1975 election, those committed to a vision of Values as a radical left party used their superior political skills and experience deliberately to steer the party away from its vague idealism and informal operating methods.

Most of the socialistically-inclined group emanated from the southern city of Christchurch, and were from trade union or Labour Party backgrounds. This faction of the party was politically experienced and more hard-nosed than the less ideological groups – often referred to as the 'love and peace brigade' because of the way they signed their letters – who dominated most party branches. One unionist in Christchurch told his colleagues that if they controlled the finances and the organ of the party, then they controlled the party.[3] Against a commitment to such traditional political tactics, the less organized and experienced party members had little chance. In any event the Christchurch group – sometimes referred to as the 'Christchurch Cabal' – offered themselves for positions of responsibility for which there were often no other candidates. After 1976 the party leader, the party's paid organizer, and the party publications secretary were all from Christchurch, while the party's newspaper editor could write shortly before the 1978 election that Values was now 'the natural party of the New Zealand working class' (Vibes, November 1978). The party's 1978 election strategy and publications emanated from Christchurch, and the policy working groups and 1977 policy-dominated Conference were the focus of concerted efforts to direct the outcomes in an explicitly leftist direction. This led to claims in the media by some branches of the party that Values was being pushed unwillingly in the direction of marxist economic and land policies.

There was a division in the party between those whose main focus was on gaining political influence through political and electoral activities, and those who attempted to live out their values through the pursuit of alternative life-styles. The group in the party more concerned with addressing existing power arrangements not only differed in their emphasis and on policy matters but also in their view of how the party ought to be organized. They preferred a more conventionally organized party with a clear hierarchy of responsibility to the 'egalitarian, feminine way of working' (Evening Post, 26 April 1979) which had been the modus operandi of the early party. They were often accused of being authoritarian and over-intellectual. Among their members was party leader Tony Kunowski, whose assertions that the party should learn from established principles of management drew accusations that he was now leading Values to ape other parties in the drive for power (Evening Post, 3 December 1978). Kunowski, in turn, felt that the lack of commitment and organization from members effectively sabotaged his efforts to present Values as a credible political alternative. In an impassioned speech to the party's 1979 Conference he spoke of Values' need to 'discard its alternative lifestyle image, stop being middle class wankers, and accept the label "socialist" and a powerful and disciplined central party organisation' (Evening Post, 12 May 1979). On

Kunowski's defeat, those who saw Values as a catalyst for radical social and political change left the party, claiming that the Values Party was 'no longer the political party through which working class people can confront capitalism'.[4]

What happened after 1976 was that the radical restructuring of existing society implicit in the early party publications was made explicit and carried to its logical conclusion by a programme designed fundamentally to alter the control and ownership of land and capital in New Zealand. This process was guided by a hard-nosed and politically experienced minority in the party who believed that Values needed to face up to being a party of the left, and to be outspoken in its opposition to capitalism. These members manipulated party processes to ensure eventual victory for their desire to see Values address those issues of concern to ordinary New Zealanders. They achieved success for their policies through tactics such as dominating policy working group proceedings – including circumventing those who did not agree with their approach[5] – by organizing bloc votes at conferences and by taking responsibility for party publications. In the process they alienated many members and gave the party a programme and a socialist taint which many of its own supporters, as well as the voting public, was less than enthusiastic about.

Explanations for Party Decline

Values has at last, it would appear, been superseded by recent green developments in New Zealand. But there remains much interest in Values from around the world, particularly in the reasons for the party's decline. Because Values was the first national green party in the world, it is also possible that its experience may be relevant to other, more recent, green parties.[6]

Values had a relatively short life-span in terms of its political effectiveness, which had subsided substantially, along with its public support, by 1979–80. There are a variety of reasons for this relating to external factors such as the political and economic environment, as well as to internal factors such as party processes and organization. On the external front, Values was born at a time of relative economic prosperity and security. By 1977 economic concerns, and particularly fear about unemployment, were back at the top of the list as New Zealanders' main worries (Evening Post, 1 September 1977). In an economically unstable situation, Values' appeal to quality-of-life issues embracing notions such as zero economic growth seemed to be a luxury, and even the most earnest attempts by Kunowski and his followers failed to convince the public that Values could develop more timely and sophisticated economic policies than its initial advocacy of zero economic and population growth. At the same time as the economy was deteriorating, Labour was becoming more attractive to the potential Values voter, and was indeed seen as the only alternative to the the Muldoon National government so despised by most of the liberals who made up the potential Values constituency. Labour's illiberal image on 'moral' issues such as abortion changed with an influx of new, younger members after 1975, and this reduced Values' ability to capitalise on the energy such issues had previously generated. For those who wished to cast a vote against either of the major parties, Social Credit grew rapidly in popularity from the end of 1977 (Evening Post, 27 February 1978).

New Zealand's first-past-the-post electoral system inevitably worked against the Values Party, and Labour devoted specific publicity in the 1978 election campaign to reminding voters that a vote for anyone other than Labour worked to National's advantage. Where a protest vote was to be cast for someone other than the major parties, there was an increasing likelihood that it would go to Social Credit, who had proven their appeal and viability by winning a seat in the 1978 Rangitikei by-election. Values had put minimal resources and effort into that by-election campaign, partly because the party could never fully decide whether or not to make the commitment to contest it. Values members were constantly confronted by the fact that the electoral system provided few political opportunities for a minor party, and this understandably reduced membership motivation to fight electoral battles.

Values' efforts to respond to these external events were hampered by the fact that they were always under-resourced in terms of money and personnel. By 1978 the party had a national organizer and a general secretary, with an office, on its payroll, but this could not disguise the limited membership base. The party never had a paid-up membership of more than 1,500 and its members were often involved in other forms of political activism, such as pressure groups. This was particularly the case in the larger cities, where there was a variety of pressure group activity, in contrast to smaller provincial centres where Values was often the only focus of alternative political activism. Values never did well in Auckland, which is politically most important in New Zealand because of its size. The Auckland Values Party also appears to have had more than its share of eccentrics and cranks; letters were reaching the national office as early as 1973 expressing concern about the number of 'crackpots' involved.[7]

Organizing Auckland was made difficult by the sheer size of the city, and the Auckland party incurred the wrath of party leader Tony Kunowski more than once because of their lack of coherent organization and the dominance of 'trendy limousine liberals' (Evening Post, 14 June 1979).

The party generally suffered from structures which failed to achieve continuity in decisions and personnel. Disillusionment among members was frequent as their efforts – with policy working groups, for example –

were ignored, overturned or duplicated. Party structures failed to capitalise on the human resources within the party or to reward people for their efforts. Values tended to attract strong-minded and individualistic people, but there were no mechanisms for dealing with the not infrequent personal disputes which occurred in party branches. With a maximum number of activists at any one time of 250–300, Values could not afford the disillusionment and conflict which its structures too often facilitated because of a desire to overcome traditional hierarchical methods of operating. Frustration and disillusionment among members was further encouraged by the fact that the party never truly reached any consensus on whether or not its prime object was as a political party, or as a social movement. Those devoted to electioneering and political activity were frequently frustrated by the lack of commitment and the political naivety of many members. The question of party structures and organization have contemporary relevance, because the desire not to repeat the hierarchical structures or the overriding of members' desires as the established parties do is very strong among current green parties. The challenge for Greens is to provide accountable structures which facilitate members' participation and responsibility without lapsing into a tyranny of structurelessness which fails to acknowledge where power and responsibility actually lie.

Values harboured unrealistic expectations about its own potential, with many activists believing that Values would constantly improve its electoral showing until it became the government, or at least entered Parliament. Consequently, the reduced vote from 1975 to 1978 was an extreme disappointment to many activists who, because of their largely middle-class backgrounds, had been used to achieving what they wanted. Class differences existed in the party, underlying the division between the more hardheaded Christchurch-based group and those they referred to in less than enthusiastic tones as 'middle-class environmentalists and alternative lifestylers' (Stewart 1989). Values never managed to bring together the diverse elements of which it was composed, nor was it able to establish any kind of reliable constituency among pressure groups or social movements. An electoral system which gave Values some degree of political representation might have provided the *raison d'être* to bind together the Values coalition on a more permanent basis, but without the prospect of political influence there was little incentive for many of the members to remain in the Values Party.

Finally, Values was unable to make a successful transition from an idealistic party short on specific measures, to a sophisticated political organization with a coherent world-view and a comprehensive programme and policies. Green movements develop through particular stages, as Pepper has observed (Pepper 1985). Like other green movements from the 1970s, Values was initially dominated by 'neo-Malthusianism and the lifeboat ethic, romantic anti-urbanism and rural escapism' (Pepper 1985). The limits-to-growth genre of literature was a powerful influence on Values in its nascent stages, as reflected by its dominant concern about population growth. The associated rural Romanticism and an aesthetic anti-materialism were of limited appeal and of dubious relevance to highly urbanised societies, such as New Zealand. Pepper contrasts the green embracing of Romantic ideals with its emphasis on personal fulfilment and the power of ideas, with the materialist approach of socialism with its focus on the mode of production as the primary force in social evolution. In fact the Values Party moved from its initial Romantic appeals to a much more materialistic approach to society, as reflected in the changing contents of its election manifestos. Whereas early manifestos were dominated by the theme of a world of beauty (Levine 1975) and riddled with quotes from prophets and musicians, by 1978 the party had published *Critical Issues*, which focused on issues such as 'the disappearing dollar' and 'the disposable worker'. Its emphasis was unashamedly on the material concerns of New Zealanders, in marked contrast to preceding publications.

This changing approach was deliberately designed to increase the party's appeal to the voting public by addressing 'bread-and-butter issues', but in fact it diminished the party's uniqueness and tempered the idealism which gave the party its initial appeal. Values moved along Pepper's continuum from the idealistic to the materialistic, but in the process it lost its exclusiveness and failed to compete with the major parties on their terms. Values appeared more like a traditional socialist minority group focusing on the maldistribution of power and resources, than a party whose initial manifesto had spoken of the problems of affluence and New Zealanders' spiritual poverty. This raises important questions about how green parties founded on broad ideals can make the inevitable transition to specific policies and programmes without losing their uniqueness or adopting traditional socialist rhetoric. It is inevitable that any political movement with concerns about resource depletion and the environment will have to consider issues of ownership and control. If green parties are unable to create imaginative solutions to these issues without mimicking existing socialist analyses, the New Zealand experience would suggest that their ability to appeal to a broad constituency from across the political spectrum will be severely reduced. The transition from general ideals to specific policies (and the associated issue of how best to work within existing power institutions once Greens are elected to them) is a major challenge for Greens today which was foreshadowed by the Values Party's experience before most of its contemporary counterparts were even founded. If Greens are to enjoy ongoing electoral support, then contemporary green parties will need to find more satisfactory solutions to this dilemma than the Values Party was able to.

Conclusion

The Values Party achieved limited success in the political arena, but – not unimportantly – for many of its members party involvement was an extraordinary personal experience, particularly in terms of intellectual stimulation. This occurred in part because Values coincided with the growth of the feminist and personal development movements in New Zealand. In many ways Values anticipated the personal and political questions which New Zealand and New Zealanders are dealing with in the 1980s, whether it be nuclear-free defence policies or race relations issues. Values advocated nuclear-free policies and more enlightened multiracial policies long before they were politically popular, and its lasting contribution was to extend the political vocabulary beyond the dominant 'hippocket' agenda of the established parties.

At the time of its inception, Values represented a radical break with traditional New Zealand party politics. Values gained an unexpected degree of support from the voting public, and it provided a valuable alternative source of feedback for the political system. Questions of the 'quality of life' and about the environment, which Values initiated, began to be addressed by all the other political parties, even if more in their rhetoric than in any substantive ways. Values made a particular contribution to the energy debate which raged after the 1973 oil shock, advocating a 'soft' energy path which was a distinct departure from the prevailing wisdom. Values also made a particular contribution to increasing the visibility of women in politics and to addressing issues of concern to women, such as abortion, which were formerly ignored by the major parties. Areas of personal life now began to be addressed more by conventional politics as a result of Values raising these issues.

Values raised important questions about the direction of development in New Zealand and, as with its more modern European counterparts, raised basic issues about the purposes and goals of politics, challenging prevailing views that standard-of-living criteria were the only significant measurements of the well-being of society. Values asserted that people's non-material needs also need to be recognised and valued by politics, and they did not hesitate to address concepts such as spirituality and happiness. In a political and cultural environment which always prided itself on its practical orientation, Values was unashamedly intellectual and idealistic. Thus Values represented the fact that New Zealand society was developing and maturing, and that by the 1970s increasing numbers of its citizens were tertiary-educated and had travelled abroad. New Zealand, like all developed nations, was experiencing an increased diversity of values. Values played a valuable representative function by providing a political voice for a growing minority on the values spectrum. In the process of doing this Values changed the shape of political publicity, employing the talents of some of its supporters to create a level of sophistication in television promotion and manifesto presentation not seen beforehand in New Zealand. The impact of the 1975 manifesto, in particular, was also felt abroad, where its message was devoured by large numbers of North Americans and Germans.

But in spite of these achievements, Values' existence as an effective political force was short-lived. This was largely as a result of a first-past-the-post electoral system which few other countries now employ. This essentially meant that at a time of economic downturn in New Zealand, it appeared to be a 'luxury' to vote for a party concerned largely with non-material issues. In contrast to the current situation, there was not an immediacy in the mid-1970s regarding environmental destruction to sustain the Values Party once its idealism lost its impact due to a deteriorating economic climate. The fact that European green parties have achieved electoral success at a time of economic uncertainty and mass unemployment shows that Values' experiences do not apply universally. Indeed, the creation of a permanent large group of people without access to the usual rewards of work may serve to enhance green fortunes. Contemporary green party experience in Europe suggests that at least some of the problems which the Values Party faced in terms of its ability to overcome its idealistic image and to address material realities, may have been overcome by the Green Movement in the 1980s. Less difficult to overcome, however, is the question of whether or not green parties are ginger-groups on the fringes of social-democratic parties, or whether they are a unique and permanent part of the political system in advanced industrial nations. The Values Party's fortunes were inextricably linked with those of the New Zealand Labour Party, and had the Labour Party proved more responsive and adaptable in the early 1970s, a new party catering for a post-materialist constituency, such as the Values Party, may never have arisen (Mackwell 1977).

While the Green Movement has now moved beyond the simplistic notion of zero economic and population growth, the more sophisticated concept of 'sustainability', which is currently in vogue, still has many implications for the current emphasis in liberal democratic societies on individual property rights. Values' attempts to address this issue impaired its effectiveness by alienating certain party factions as well as voters. A radical change of existing political and economic institutions is implicit in most green programmes, but debates about how to implement and make explicit such changes underlines divisions in green parties today as much as it did in the Values Party in the 1970s. Until such time as there are imaginative solutions created to the problem of how to pursue green goals such as the protection of common resources – like the environment – in societies based on the principle of private ownership, certain of the problems which New Zealand's Values Party attempted to grapple with will continue to plague its more recent counterparts.

Notes

1. Because public polling and other statistical surveys were not well developed in New Zealand at the time of the Values Party's major contribution, it is harder to gain the same kind of empirical data about the Values Party than it is about contemporary green parties. This problem is exacerbated by the lack of scholarly attention which the party attracted. This history, however, is based on the in-depth study of Values Party records deposited with the Turnbull Library, New Zealand National Library, and my own personal Values Party archive which is second in size only to the Turnbull's collection, to the best of my knowledge.
2. This section of the chapter is a significantly revised version of the part entitled 'The Values Party heyday 1972–78' in my article, 'New Zealand's Values Party: the rise and fall of the first national green party' (Rainbow 1989).
3. Interview with party activist, 1987.
4. National Library of New Zealand, Values Party Records, Acc 85/11, Box 11, File 112.
5. National Library of New Zealand, Values Party Records, Acc 85/11, Box 4, File iii.
6. I have recently completed a doctoral thesis examining the relevance of the Values Party's experience for contemporary green parties, and comparing it to the Finnish, German and Swedish Green Parties.
7. National Library of New Zealand, Values Party Records, 1430: 2.2.

References

Cleveland, L. (1972). The Anatomy of Influence. (Wellington: Hicks Smith).

Deutsch, K. (1985). 'The systems theory approach as a basis for comparative research', International Social Science Journal, Vol. 37, pp. 5–18.

Goldsmith, E., Allen, R., Allaby, M., Davull, J., & Lawrence, S. (1972). A Blueprint for Survival. (London: Tom Stacey).

James, C. (1978). In National Business Review, 24 May.

Jones, R. (1978). New Zealand the Way I Want It. (Christchurch: Whitcoulls).

Kolinsky, E. (1984). Parties, Opposition and Society in West Germany. (London: Croom Helm).

Levine, S. (1975). New Zealand Politics: A Reader. (Melbourne: Cheshire).

Mackwell, S. (1977). 'Radical politics and ideology in the coming of post-industrial society: the Values Party in perspective'. (Unpublished MA thesis, University of Canterbury).

McLauchlan, G. (1980). 'The passionless people', in Hill, D. & Smith, E. (eds.), The Seventies Connection. (Dunedin: John McIndoe).

Oliver, W. H. (1981). 'The awakening imagination', in Oliver, W. H. (ed.), The Oxford History of New Zealand. (Wellington: Oxford University Press).

O'Sullivan, V. (1976). James K. Baxter. (Wellington: Oxford University Press).

Oakes, L. (1986). Inside Centrepoint. (Auckland: Benton Ross).

Park, G. (1988). 'Understanding and conserving the natural landscape', in Phillips, J. (ed.), Te Whenua, Te Iwi: The Land, The People. (Wellington: Stout Research Centre, Victoria University of Wellington, Wellington).

Pepper, D. (1985). 'Determinism, idealism and the politics of environmentalism: A viewpoint', *International Journal of Environmental Studies*, Vol. 26, pp. 11–19.

Rainbow, S. (1989). 'New Zealand's Values Party: The rise and fall of the first national green party', in Hay, P., Eckersley, R., and Holloway, G. (eds.), *Environmental Politics in Australia and New Zealand*. (Hobart: Centre for Environmental Studies, University of Tasmania, Hobart).

Rainbow, S. (1991). 'The Greens and the 1990 New Zealand general election', *Sites* (a journal for radical perspectives on culture), No. 22, Autumn, pp. 87–94.

Stewart, J. (1989). Personal correspondence with author.

Trussell, D. (1982). 'History in an Antipodean garden', *The Ecologist*, Vol. 12, No. 1, pp. 32–42.

Values Party (1972). *Blueprint for New Zealand*. (Wellington: Values Party).

Values Party (1975). *Beyond Tomorrow*. (Wellington: Values Party).

Values Party (1978a). *Policy Manual*. (Wellington: Values Party).

Values Party (1978b). *Critical Issues '78*. (Wellington: Values Party).

6. The Birth of Green Politics in Brazil: Exogenous and Endogenous Factors*

JOSÉ AUGUSTO PÁDUA

Brazilian Institute for Social and Economic Analysis, Rio de Janeiro, Brazil

I

For political scientists, green politics is an extremely recent phenomenon. The first political party explicitly identified with ecology, the British Ecology Party, which in 1985 changed its name to Green Party (Rüdig and Lowe 1986) was formed in 1973. Most green parties emerged during the 1980s. In France, for example, where ecologists have participated in elections since March 1973, a unified green party was not formed until January 1984.

The recent nature of this phenomenon has two theoretical and epistemological consequences. First, we have to recognise that its scientific analysis is still in a primordial stage. This is due not only to the need for better empirical data and methods of investigation, but also, more fundamentally, to the rapid historical expansion of the object of study itself. Green politics is still a growing phenomenon, and can take surprising directions, forcing us constantly to reformulate our theoretical frameworks. Secondly, the possibility this presents to study an internationally relevant political current *pari passu* with its birth and historical evolution is a fairly rare theoretical experience. Robert Dahl noted this problem in the following manner: 'The most powerful ideologies of our age suffer from having acquired their shape and substance in the XVIIIth and XIXth centuries, or very much earlier, before the world in which we now live had come fully into view. They are like medieval maps of the world, charming but dangerous for navigating unfamiliar seas' (Dahl 1982).

Green politics is an exception to this rule. Of the internationally relevant political currents, it is by far the most recent (or perhaps more accurately, it is the only really recent one). This means that it carries within its very constitution some of the dilemmas and realities typical of contemporary life (as

*Translated from the Portuguese by Professor Margaret E. Keck, Department of Political Science, Yale University, USA.

is obviously the case with the ecological dilemma itself). Other currents with roots in prior historical contexts, such as liberalism (seventeenth century), conservatism (eighteenth), social democracy (nineteenth), and communism (beginning of twentieth), in spite of recurring efforts to recycle them theoretically, often encounter difficulties in reconciling their basic premises with the qualitatively new problems which have arisen at the end of the twentieth century. For this reason, I believe that green politics is a historical phenomenon which is likely to continue and to grow.

In recent years, at least, green politics has tended to become universalised, expanding well beyond its original birthplace in Western Europe. Today, for example, we can see signs of it in Eastern Europe, in North and South America, in Australia, in India, in Japan, etc. This development was not only geographical, but also qualitative, as green politics has shown itself to possess, with greater or lesser success according to the country, a set of political capacities which go well beyond the modest predictions made by some analysts at the beginning of the 1970s. These analysts essentially argued that the appearance of politics identified with ecology would be merely a tactical extension of the action of the environmentalist civic organizations which were multiplying during the previous decade, and that such political actions would therefore be sectoral and localised. Imprisoned by the specificity of the 'environmental question', green politics would be unable to produce a broader political identity necessary to elaborate a global party proposal for society. Its successes, in this view, would be merely topical, depending on the existence of a concrete external motivation (a nuclear plant, a polluting factory, etc.). By the end of the 1980s it was clear that these predictions were shortsighted. The green current, as it developed, demonstrated a capacity to formulate national political programmes, to become organized into stable parties, to influence the positions of other parties and the elaboration of the political agenda (helping to include new issues), to mobilise public opinion, and to win a significant coefficient of the electorate.

Especially important, in my view, was its capacity to formulate national political programmes which, as Pizzorno (1976) demonstrated, is a condition for modern party life. This is what demonstrates that the green current is not a simple extension, in the political arena, of environmental demands *per se*. The Greens have succeeded in establishing, in spite of some theoretical weakness, a set of more or less coherent transformative proposals for diverse aspects of social life, including platforms on the economy, culture, international relations, etc. These proposals are obviously not restricted to problems formally defined as 'environmental'. Of the fifty pages of the national programme of the German Green Party, only six deal exclusively with the latter. The Greens argue that the environmental question is not a 'specificity', but a dimension inherent in a global reflection on society. The model of society which is emerging from green programmes would in fact be an interesting subject for analysis, in so far as in it are combined elements which, in the history of political thought, are identified with traditions as different as conservatism, liberalism, anarchism and Marxism. The genealogy of the green project is thus quite complex.

This chapter does not go into depth on the problem of the birth, consolidation, and theoretical status of green politics. The question before us is the place of Brazil in the process of rapid international expansion of this current. This expansion in itself raises important questions. The first of these is the degree of identity or difference among the programmes and forms of action of greens in different countries. An initial comparative look allows us to affirm a fairly strong identity, to the point that we can speak of a substantively international phenomenon. Greens in different countries tend to share issues, proposals, styles, and even words. A more detailed analysis, however, reveals differences among the different green experiences. These differences are likely to become stronger in so far as the green current appears outside of its initial sociological universe in western polyarchies with a high level of socio-economic development. At this point it will be important to study its appearance in countries which are not polyarchies, such as those of Eastern Europe, or in countries which are polyarchies but are characterised by unequal development and a high level of mass poverty, as is the case in Brazil and Mexico. This is not to downplay the differences which exist in green politics in the affluent West. Some argue, for example, that Europeans place more emphasis on the anti-nuclear and pacifist struggles, and in the United States and Australia more stress is placed on the preservation of the natural environment and the rights of the non-human world (biocentric ethics) (Hay and Haward 1988). In macro-historical terms, however, this difference in emphasis does not represent a rupture, if only because the anti-nuclear struggle is important outside of Europe, and European Greens are also concerned with a biocentric sensibility. Nonetheless, continued historical expansion may yet produce more radical theoretical ruptures.

A second fundamental question concerns the way in which green politics expands to different countries. Here there are two theoretical possibilities, which can perhaps be discussed in reference to a not very recent article by Collier and Messik. Discussing the phenomenon of the adoption of social security, which is quite distinct from green politics but shares with the latter the fact that it expanded to different countries and continents, the authors point to two explanatory matrices: *prerequisites*, looking at the causes of the rise of social security policy within the context of each country (primarily the level of economic development); and *diffusion*, focusing on the imitation of welfare programmes from one country to another

(Collier and Messik 1975). These alternatives appear valid for a theoretical discussion of the expansion of the green phenomenon, together with the authors' warning regarding the possibility of combining the two matrices, and, particularly, on the need to pay sufficient attention to the diffusion factor.

Among the authors who examine the expansion of green politics from the point of view of prerequisites, most seek to delimit a sociological universe within which the existence of this kind of politics is possible. It tends to arise, in this view, in countries which are part of this universe which have a high level of economic development, urbanisation, and industrialisation, and where ecological problems gain visibility through counterproductive effects and through the impact of heavy technologies. This visibility is not simply objective (there are obviously very grave environmental and quality-of-life problems in less industrialised countries), but is also due to the impact of affluence on the subjectivity of citizens. Here we have the variations on the idea of an 'acquisitive agenda', the most influential of which is the theory of Ronald Inglehart on post-materialism. This political scientist, taking off from Abraham Maslow's theory of a 'hierarchy of needs', posits that the hyper-development of western societies after the war provoked a political refinement. Society, and especially the generation socialised during that historical period, was freed from concern with urgent material needs, allowing new kinds of more sophisticated qualitative demands to arise which he called 'post-materialist' (such as the search for spiritual realisation, peace, and environmental quality) (Inglehart 1977). The latter have little relevance in poorer societies, where the struggle for survival makes them a luxury.

There are elements of truth in the establishment of this relationship between the birth of green politics and the new political demands arising in affluent societies. One might argue, in fact, that it is valid even for the appearance of green politics in Third World countries like Brazil and Mexico. In the social fabric of these countries, side by side with mass misery we find a large and complex middle class. The latter will be the most immediate clientele for green parties. Thus the affluent spaces of newly industrialising countries fall within the universe described.

The possibilities of the real, however, are a great deal more complex; otherwise we would have a rigid historical materialist determinism in which ideological–political currents would automatically derive from economic stages. Brazil, in this respect, is an interesting laboratory. Green discourse in general, or at least elements thereof, has gained an influence in some important popular sectors. The brutality of the socio-environmental problems provoked by an accelerated process of urban industrialisation, which weighs most heavily on the poor, has opened up space for this kind of contact. The symbol of the possible emergence of an ecological discourse of the poor in Brazil was, beyond any doubt, the rubber tappers' leader Chico Mendes, who in fact had an excellent relationship with the Brazilian Green Party and assisted in its creation in Acre. This and other examples relativise the automatic linkage between green politics and affluence, in spite of the fact that the green electorate is still basically middle class in various countries.

The incorporation of the green question in the politics of popular sectors, especially in rural areas, is not limited to Brazil; it has also been observed in India and in Africa (Durning 1989). What is important to note is that certain political proposals, upon coming into contact with universes different from those in which they were formulated, can take on new dimensions and undergo important reinterpretations, which does not nullify their initial meaning but instead opens up new possibilities. Ecological agriculture projects, for example, which in the context of an affluent society are often motivated exclusively by concern for the health of the soil and of food products, can come to represent for poor peasants, without the means to buy industrial fertilizers, a form of economic emancipation. This same peasant might also be deeply concerned with the health of the soil and of food products, not only because he/she suffers objectively from these problems (note the number of peasants who have died from pesticide poisoning in Brazil), but also for reasons which have more to do with values and subjectivity. The idea of the poor worker as a slave to the rule of need, often cultivated by the left itself, underestimates the complexity of the system of symbolic representations which make up popular culture. Militants of the Brazilian Green Party who come from the upper middle class, whose values might well be understood within a theory of post-materialism, are frequently surprised to discover a common language with popular groups imbued with prematerialist values, such as Catholic communitarianism or the deep sense of relationship with nature characteristic of Afro-Brazilian religions.

To summarise the discussion, we might say that the problem of sociological prerequisites for green politics is not a simple one. Although the genesis and initial evolution of this current occurred among the affluent, nothing impedes its appearance in different universes. We need to be open, in this case, to the possibility of conceptual re-readings, changes in emphasis and organizational impacts which might be surprising. This should not prevent us from thinking about the objective conditions which facilitate the rise of green politics in each specific area, or even from theorising about more or less universal prerequisites. It is important, however, that we not fall into linear evolutionism, that we not lose sight of the living dynamics of history. Here the question of diffusion enters the picture.

Green politics was born in a historical context, at the end of the twentieth century, in which communication is increasingly planetary due to the speed of communications media and transportation. There is an international system of influence and information, and political life within a country can hardly be isolated from international reference points, or immune to the impact of exogenous material or ideological factors. Collier and Messik, in the article cited above, note two basic patterns of diffusion: hierarchical, among countries more or less developed according to a scale of influence; and spacial, within geographical – historical complexes. Since diffusion within a hierarchy is not necessarily from the top down, it could also occur from less to more developed countries. Moreover, the capacity to produce diffusion is not conditioned on chronological precedence. The British Green Party, for example, is older than its German counterpart, but it was influenced by the latter, even to the point of changing its name.

In analysing the diffusion phenomenon, we need to remain open to the unexpected, to the power of penetration of the life of ideas. In the opening of Alejo Carpentier's masterful novel *El siglo de las luces*, which deals with the impact of French revolutionary ideas in the Antilles at the end of the eighteenth century, there is a sentence which says that 'ideas do not fall into a void'. Ideas take root and spread in complex and living social systems, and their capacity to spread is as surprising as their results are various. Here we need to combine the diffusion of ideas with a sociological study of the arenas in which they appear, investigating, where possible, the objective conditions which make the social terrain more or less propitious for their acceptance and their expansion.

These reflections are necessary because in Brazil, as in the United States, the birth of green politics was directly influenced by the European example. In the case of Brazil, there was an even more immediate factor. Besides the inspiration which came from reporting on European green activities and ideas in the media, the founders and current leaders of the Green Party include a very significant proportion of former exiles, militants of left groups in Brazil in the 1960s who came into contact with green ideas in Europe during the 1970s. The return of some of these exiles, with the 1979 amnesty, was decisive for the creation of the Brazilian Green Party in 1986.

The presence of this exogenous factor in the birth of green politics in Brazil has caused some analysts, especially political opponents, to call it 'an idea out of place', an importation pure and simple of European ideas unsuited to the Brazilian context. This is a narrow conception which imprisons the life of a social project in the sociological context of its birth, without taking into account the open field of historical possibilities for its diffusion and even for its metamorphosis. In addition, the initial performance of green politics in Brazil indicates that there are endogenous factors which favour its presence in that society. This set of factors, however, only signals a possibility; it does not guarantee its continuity. There are also unfavourable factors, and the concrete political behaviour of representatives of green politics will no doubt carry a great deal of weight. Politics is fundamentally a practice, even though it takes place in a structured arena.

II

From the above it should be clear that one cannot understand the birth of green politics in Brazil only on the basis of exogenous diffusion. Part of the complex historical formation of the country, and its international linkages, is the fact that Brazilian culture has always been open to foreign influences, often assimilated and reinterpreted in new cultural syntheses. This receptivity to exogenous ideas and practices, in politics as well, has limits which can only be understood on the basis of endogenous factors, whether structural or conjunctural. The pacifist movement, for example, tried several times to strengthen its organization in Brazil at the beginning of the 1980s. The impressive gains made by European pacifism were certainly important motivations in these efforts. Nonetheless, the visibility of Brazilian pacifism remained quite limited. To understand this differential impact we need to take into account endogenous factors, such as the fact that the country has virtually no experience of war in its national territory and is not, like Europe, at the centre of the East–West conflict. Its position among the ten largest arms exporters in the world is morally and ecologically problematic, but this is a problem with very little transparency in the social consciousness. This is not to negate the importance of the question of peace, even in the Brazilian context, but only to note the limitations of the issue in penetrating public opinion.

Exactly the opposite occurs with the issue of environmental destruction, which has received a great deal of attention in the mass media and on the Brazilian political scene. The ecological problematique is not only highly visible, but is also one of the most basic variables for understanding the nature of Brazilian identity, history and crisis. The exogenous influence, therefore, was an important catalyst for the current emergence of the ecological question in Brazilian politics, helping to bring to public attention a question about which previously little was said but which was of great substantive relevance. This is the important and surprising point: exogenous diffusion did not awaken an idea that was 'out of place', but rather an idea which was very much in place and historically opportune. It became a kind of mirror for the self-knowledge of Brazilian society when confronted with a basic aspect of its national question.

Thus our task is not to determine whether exogenous or endogenous factors were more important, but rather to understand their dialectical relationship. Five endogenous factors appear crucial for analysing the birth of green politics in Brazil:

1. the explosion of socio-environmental problems on the Brazilian national scene, resulting from the conjunction of an ecologically perverse historical formation with an accelerated process of urban industrialisation over the last four decades, producing an extreme ecological crisis in Brazil;

2. the tradition of openness to the issue of nature in Brazilian culture and politics;

3. recent changes in the social fabric of the country, more specifically the rise of the so-called 'new middle class';

4. the space opened up in Brazilian political culture by the emergence of 'new social movements', especially during the 1970s; and

5. characteristics of the Brazilian electoral system.

The causal relationship between the existence of environmental problems and the emergence of green politics has been somewhat neglected in the literature, perhaps because it is so obvious. Several analysts have stressed the need to discuss it more thoroughly (Lowe and Rüdig 1986). In any case, the existence of serious problems of this type as a basic condition for the birth of political ecologism is a basic premise.

In the case of Brazil it is even superfluous to note this. The ecological problematique has been a part of the country's tradition from the beginning. Brazilian space was incorporated into the western world economy beginning in the sixteenth century as a typical colony for exploitation. There was no effort to establish in Brazil a society concerned with its own endogenous development, but rather to organize a series of exploitative activities geared towards exogenous European interests. In addition, as there were no native social formations here whose forms of production were appropriate for the European market, it was clear from the outset that this exploitation would involve direct use of the rich and practically virgin Brazilian nature.

The first element propitious for commercial exploitation, the Pau-Brasil tree, gave the new land its final name, replacing the previous name Terra de Santa Cruz, symbolising the victory of the exploitative meaning over the socio-religious one. The predatory extraction of this tree led to its extinction in only a few decades; thus the stigma of ecological disaster is inscribed in the very name of Brazil. The great economic cycles which followed – sugar cane, gold and diamonds, coffee, etc. – were a succession of ecological disasters provoked by careless and extensive exploitation (Padua 1988).

Nonetheless, the joint impact of pre-industrial predatory activities, with all the deforestation, soil destruction, drought and exhaustion of mineral reserves which they provoked, was still vastly inferior to what we see today. The territory's size and biological wealth meant that many ecosystems – the Pantanal in the Centre-West and the Amazon Forest – survived reasonably intact. To understand the current Brazilian ecological crisis we must examine the process of urbanisation and industrialisation which began early in the twentieth century but accelerated tremendously over the last few decades. The dimension of this change is easy to demonstrate. The urban population went from 31 per cent in 1940 to 67 per cent in 1980. The proportion of the economically active population in the secondary and tertiary sectors, which made up 30·31 per cent in 1940, was up to around 61·04 per cent in 1980 (Santos 1987). The impact of this process went beyond the urban context. In 1950, Brazilian agriculture counted on 8,372 tractors and used 89,000 tons of chemical fertilizers; in 1980 this was up to 527,096 tractors and figures for 1978 show 3,100,000 tons of fertilizers (Graziano Neto 1982).

It is impossible in this chapter to discuss adequately the nature of this historical change and the social costs it generated. Even intuitively, the brutality of the environmental impact is apparent. The Brazilian style of development followed the pattern of western modernity with an economy based on high levels of energy and natural resource consumption; the production of garbage and pollution were aggravated by factors like emphasis on road transport and concentration in scale and geographical distribution of industrial activities (Sunkel 1981). The speed of the process, and the fact that it took place in a politically closed period, were also aggravating factors, facilitating the implantation of socially irresponsible technologies and making it difficult for society to protest about environmental problems. The gravity of these problems increased their visibility, all the more in that there was often a convergence between social and environmental problems. Important collective actions did take place around some of the more glaring cases, which helped to persuade the Brazilian left that the environmental issue was important, helping to legitimate the green current politically.

A second endogenous factor worth mentioning, also with deep historical roots, is that paradoxically, the idea that the natural world possesses intrinsic value has been traditionally present in what we might call the 'Brazilian imaginary'. From the early travellers' chronicles and from colonial art, to nineteenth-century romanticism which influenced the symbolic representation of national independence, we find a long tradition of identifying Brazil with the grandeur of nature. The most important national symbols call upon forests, skies, metals, fauna and flora. This tradition is also evident in popular culture. While difficult to measure in objective terms partly because we are dealing with a fairly schizophrenic dualism, given the real history of devastation, this tradition helps to form a predisposition in the Brazilian mental universe for ecological discourse. At the level of representations in the political realm more specifically, the issues of nature and the destruction of nature have long been important in Brazilian political thought, and are at the core of the work of authors like José Bonifácio, Euclides da Cunha and Alberto Torres, as I have shown elsewhere (Pádua 1988). It is difficult to evaluate the nexus between these historical traditions and Brazilian political ecologism in the 1980s. This is all the more true when we recognise that the ecological component of the debate about natural resources, which remained fundamental in Brazilian politics, was somewhat neglected from the 1930s on, when the focus shifted to nationalism (exploitation of resources by national or foreign firms) and socio-economic questions (private or social appropriation of the wealth generated by exploitation). International analyses which examine green politics through the prism of the history of ideas and political culture are still incipient. The potential richness of this theoretical approach in the case of Brazil needs to be noted and explored further in future research.

A more immediate endogenous variable for the emergence of green politics in Brazil has to do with the idea of a 'new middle class'. Much of the international literature has sought to link the emergence of green politics with changes observed in the social fabric of advanced industrial societies, especially in reference to the question of post-industrial society (Chandler and Siaroff 1986). More specifically, surveys in several countries appear to confirm the hypothesis that the green electoral base is identified with the rise of a new middle class, whose typical individual is young, urban, highly educated, and employed mainly in the tertiary sector (Bürklin 1985). This sector coincides historically with Inglehart's 'post-materialist generation', and in his terms, would be the carrier of new values in politics, largely expressed in political ecologism (Inglehart 1982).

Although Brazilian society diverges from the post-industrial model in various indicators, like the still high proportion of the economically active population in the countryside, over the last few decades it has undergone social transformations analogous to those observed in the model, for example the expansion of the tertiary sector and of the university population (which went from 142,386 in 1964 to 1,399,539 in 1984). The percentage of technico-administrative occupations in the economically active population went from 11·1 per cent in 1960 to 19·1 per cent in 1980. Communications, transportation and leisure underwent a rapid process of technological modernisation. The number of people employed in salaried technical professions, public administration, and public services has grown, while there has been a decline in self-employed occupations of the old middle classes (Boschi 1986). It is interesting to recall that a whole middle-class generation born in the 1950s underwent its basic socialisation in a country with a median GNP growth rate of between 11 per cent per year (1968–74) and 6 per cent per year (1975–9), with inflation under control and with growing job and consumption opportunities. This part of the population, unlike the popular classes, only began to feel the perverse effects of the economic model when the crisis of the 1970s hit them as well. We might hypothesise, in spite of the almost complete lack of empirical studies in this area, that a variant of the 'Inglehart effect' may have occurred in sectors of this new middle class in the large   Brazilian cities, and a cycle of economic security may have helped to awaken new demands on the political scene. Demands for democracy and freedom of expression, for example, began to increase before the resurgence of the economic crisis.

Whether or not this hypothesis is true, over the last decade we have witnessed growing dissatisfaction and political participation on the part of the Brazilian middle class. Many of the demands being raised are typically materialist, involving wages and working conditions. The growing proportion of wage-earners in the old liberal professions generated a powerful middle-class trade unionism. Nonetheless, they also took on broader political demands. Oppositionist sentiment, perhaps to mark differences with the authoritarian regime in power, began to emphasise such values as direct participation and decentralisation, values which were not part of the traditional universe of the Brazilian left. This helped to open up spaces in this universe for the entry of green discourse. The extent to which this new middle class may have flowed into the green party electorate can only be verified by future empirical research. In any case, it represents a potential clientele, and participant observation allows me to claim that it had a significant presence in the composition of the cadre and in the first electoral experiences of the Brazilian Green Party.

This linkage can be further reinforced if we note that, beginning in the 1970s, there were social mobilisations involving the Brazilian middle class around demands normally classified as 'post-materialist'. This is the case for social movements stressing the right to subjective and collective expression of singular social groups. Some of the most important were the movements of women, black people, Indians and homosexuals. Movements also arose around peace, human rights, and, especially, the environment. This leads us to the fourth endogenous factor mentioned: the rise of new social movements in Brazil.

The emergence of these movements in Europe has been noted in the literature as an important factor for the birth of green politics there. According to Galtung (1986), conventional party politics was organized around class interests along a socio-economic axis. The intensification of political demands which fell outside of the class reference (demands by women and ethnic minorities, for example), or even of demands with loose connections with the socio-economic axis (subjective or post-materialist demands), intensified the divorce between the political expectations of society and the monopoly of representation by parties, encouraging the rise of new social movements. Thus the impulse for the birth of green politics would come from the need to aggregate politically these dispersed political demands which do not encounter space in the traditional party framework. The representatives of green politics themselves explicitly embrace this role, adopting, in the words of Mewes (1983), the goal of 'unifying, under the aegis of political ecology, the various groups opposed to contemporary industrial society'.

The rise of new social movements in Brazil during the 1970s is linked to the broader problem of the crisis of the monopoly of political representation by the traditional parties. In the Brazilian context, however, the party crisis had an extra stimulus, which was the continuation of the post-1964 military authoritarian regime. The repressive phase of this regime (1968–74) gave way to a period of informal opening, with greater freedom of the press, of organization and of expression. Nonetheless, the space opened up for political participation was limited due to the obligatory two-party system and other impediments. This encouraged the appearance of alternative channels of participation, configured in a series of movements. It is important to note, however, that these were not only movements of the new middle class; they also included a significant popular dimension. We could include here the movement of base communities, the mothers' clubs, the movements against the high cost of living, etc. The pedagogy of this popular associationalism, largely inspired by liberation theology, also helped to train countless leaders of the new unionism and the new left. Especially significant is the fact that some of these new movements, especially the women's movement and the neighbourhood associations, occurred simultaneously in the popular milieu and in the new middle class, permitting the rise of inter-class alliances around basic principles located in the rights of citizenship. (This is typical of the federations of neighbourhood associations, which brought together associations from poor neighbourhoods with middle- and upper-class ones.) This approximation helped somewhat to circulate new values and political expectations. Thus when we claim that the new social movements helped to open space in the political culture for a dialogue with green proposals, we are not referring only to spaces in the new middle class, but to popular space as well.

This politico-cultural ferment, even across class lines, was also present in the social movement most explicitly linked to green politics: the ecological movement. This movement, in the Brazilian context, is fairly old and has chalked up some successes (Viola 1988). It dates its foundation to 1971, with the creation of the Gaucha Association for the Protection of the Natural Environment (AGAPAN). The Brazilian Foundation for the Conservation of Nature had existed since 1958, but had little public presence, restricting itself to an elite of naturalists. AGAPAN, by contrast, adopted an aggressive posture which brought it notoriety and problems with the authoritarian regime. The exogenous factor was present in the creation of this organization. José Lutzenberger, its founder, became aware of the ecological problem outside Brazil, when he was working for the Swiss firm BASF selling pesticides to African countries. Shocked by the negative socio-environmental results of his professional activities, he resigned and returned to Brazil. His 1976 book, *Manifesto Ecológico Brasileiro*, was a radical philosophical and political (though not partisan) critique, and made him the theoretical reference-point of the movement.

Around 1974, with the relaxation of the repressive climate, a variety of ecological groups began to form all over the country. Some groups focused on the struggle against environmental degradation narrowly defined, confining their ambit of activity to a city, a state, a region, or even a geographical accident (in the case of groups formed to protect a river or a lake). Other groups took a broader cultural position, advocating a change in world view, in personal habits and social behaviour. This existential ecologism was also expressed in the creation, both in cities and in the interior, of a whole 'alternative scene', composed of co-operatives, schools, natural restaurants, rural communities, etc. A survey published in 1983, which included only narrowly-defined environmentalist associations, noted the existence of 503 organizations (SEMA 1983). When a questionnaire was sent to these groups in 1988, however, only 130 responded, probably representing those with a minimum of structure (Landim 1988). More solid empirical research on the social composition of the Brazilian Ecological Movement does not yet exist. It is clear, however, that it is not restricted to the big cities, but extends to the interior and to poorer regions of the country.

However, it would be incorrect to see the ecological struggle in Brazil as restricted to these groups. We can also include in this dynamic three other realities: occasional mobilisations; state environmentalism; and the appropriation of ecological issues by social entities.

The first case includes collective actions which do not become institutionalised in a permanent manner, but rather depend on occasional motivation. This is the case with the wave of demonstrations in defence of Amazonia in 1979, when a highly pernicious exploitation plan developed by the military government became public. Countless committees were formed which dissolved after the government retreated from its position. State environmentalism, on the other hand, is a fairly significant phenomenon in Brazil. The Special Secretariat for the Environment (SEMA) was created in 1972, for basically exogenous motives as a response to criticism of Brazil at the Stockholm conference. It was born weak, marginalised in the state apparatus. Subsequently similar organs were created in states and municipalities (Guimarães 1986). Political marginalisation, however,

often created an ambiguous situation. Technical personnel in these entities began to approach civil society and develop an ideologically ecologist
identity, as a form of justifying their existence *ex parti populi*, since they could
not do so *ex parti princes*. In states where the autonomous ecological movement was fragile, these organs occupied the space of ecological critique,
in spite of their position as part of the state apparatus. The technical personnel formed in this context, whose ambiguous positions remained
unresolved, are important for our story, as many later joined the Green
Party. Another aspect of state environmentalism has to do with the experiences of municipal government after 1977, when opposition politicians
took office in local elections. Some cases of participatory democracy and
ecodevelopment in Lajes, in Santa Catarina and Boa Esperança, in Espirito
Santo, for example, became nationally famous, and were used by the
Greens as an example of the viability of their projects.

The last point to be noted is the appropriation of the ecological issue
by social groups not formally identified with ecologism, a phenomenon
which we might call 'informal ecologism'. The environmental struggle has
been central, for example, for neighbourhood associations. Trade unions
and professional organizations in various areas such as chemical workers,
rubber tappers, architects, agronomists, rural workers, etc. sometimes
adopted explicitly ecologist positions. Recently the indigenous people of
the Xingu area, in their first meeting held at Altamira (February 1989),
claimed to be central protagonists in the struggle for the preservation of
the Amazon forest. In summary, a whole set of forces in civil society participate in the environmental struggle together with the ecological movement *per se*. It is in the universe of informal ecologism that green thinking
has found spaces in which to take root in the popular milieu. All of these
elements indicate the existence of a fertile ecological movement in Brazil,
forming a favourable cultural medium for a green party. The unfavourable aspect, meanwhile, lies in the low level of organization of this movement, and in the fact that most of it prefers to remain at the margin of party
activity. Nonetheless one can state, even if impressionistically, that most
of the activism in the Green Party comes from the ecological movement,
or, to a lesser extent, from other social movements.

One final endogenous factor favourable to the creation of a green party
in Brazil is the electoral system itself. The traditional system of proportional
representation, not by district, with the d'Hondt method for the distribution of remainders, facilitates at least minimal representation of small ideological parties via aggregation of votes dispersed among candidates on the
slate. The barriers set up by the military regime were primarily in the rules
for the legal constitution of party structures (minimum number of members, etc.) and not electoral barriers. The relaxation of these rules in 1979
broadened the range of parties from two to around five, which soon won

legislative representation at different levels. An even more radical relaxation of the rules in 1985 permitted the appearance of dozens of parties, including the Green Party. This possibility of electing a small number of representatives is stimulating for a new party. Today, for example, there are green representatives on the legislative councils of sixteen Brazilian cities, as we will see in the following section.

III

It should be clear from the preceding section that a series of endogenous factors in the Brazilian political universe furnish a rational basis for the presence of a green party, rather than classifying it as an exotic phenomenon. Many of the elements used to understand its appearance in Europe – new middle class, new social movements, relevance of environmental problems, etc. – are present here as well. I think it should also be clear that the birth of green politics in Brazil is part of a broader process of political renewal in the country, within which we find a more substantive approach to the ecological problem in relation to social and democratic questions. In this sense the repercussions of political ecologism, broadly speaking, are much more extensive than the specific activity of the Green Party, which is not its only channel for expression. There is no doubt, however, that the appearance of a party of this kind is important for making the challenges and proposals contained in this discussion more evident.

We have already noted the influence of exogenous diffusion on this dynamic. It is even more evident in the idea to form a Green Party than in the discussion of electoral participation by ecologists. Deputies committed to the ecological movement began to be elected in 1982, before there was any real debate about founding a party. Elected that year were, for example, Caio Lustosa, a leader of AGAPAN, to the Legislative Assembly of the state of Rio Grande do Sul, and Walter Lazzarini, a combative agronomist and ecologist, to the São Paulo state assembly. Both were candidates of a centre-left party (PMDB), and were linked with endogenous environmental struggles, without reference to international green politics. The distinction between legislative participation by ecologists and the constitution of a green current in a global sense began to be traced in Brazil with the election in 1982 of two state deputies in Rio de Janeiro committed to linking ecology and a self-management, libertarian, and countercultural perspective. Liszt Vieira, a lawyer who had returned from exile in France, and feminist leader Lucia Arruda, had run as candidates of the Workers' Party PT. The experience of their two terms in office was an important experiment for showing that green politics was viable in Brazil. It also established the state of Rio de Janeiro as the vanguard of this movement. Green politics was consolidated there first, and later spread to other states.

In 1985, several meetings took place in Rio de Janeiro to discuss the possibility of formally creating a green party, Partido Verde (PV) in Brazil. They were organized by a group of intellectuals, artists, and liberal professionals who had worked for the election of Liszt Vieira and Lucia Arruda. This group included various individuals who were quite well known, had easy access to the media, charismatic qualities, etc., the sort of 'political entrepreneur' whose importance in European green parties was noted by several analysts (Kitschelt 1988). Its core was composed of former exiles like the deputy Liszt Vieira, the writers Fernando Gabeira, Alfredo Sirkis and Herbert Daniel and the geographer Carlos Minc. Other notable personages included the actress Lucélia Santos and the orchestral conductor John Neschling. This group wanted to work for the construction in Brazil of a 'socialist, libertarian, democratic, and ecological society', and some already participated actively in the ecological movement, having helped to organize the anti-nuclear meetings 'Hiroxima Nunca Mais' (Hiroshima never again) in Angra dos Reis (the site of a nuclear power station). A good part of the group had experience in other left parties, like the PT and the PDT, and had criticisms regarding the limitations on developing a green politics in those spaces.

The presence of a founding group composed of famous personalities represented for the Brazilian PV a double-edged sword. On the one hand it greatly facilitated the dissemination of information about the party to society. On the other hand, it created a clear potential for administrative crisis. As Kitschelt pointed out in the article mentioned above, based on the European experience, the anti-bureaucratic characteristics of green politics mean that the power to influence political decisions within parties has less to do with formal decision-making channels and more to do with charismatic capacity and oratory. Public fame, in this case, became a decisive political resource. The party cadre with public activity, deputies or journalists, for example, acquired an over-valued influence in relation to the formal organs of party administration. In this context, the boundary between individual creativity and personalism, or between bureaucratic rigidity and the organization of democratic participation, was not very clear. As a German activist quoted by Kitschelt stated, 'Sometimes political decisions are not made by elected militants, but by informal circles, by certain people who sit down together.' In the Brazilian case this tendency was aggravated by the fact that public personalities identified themselves with the image of the PV from the beginning, as well as by the electoral system, which tends to organize the context more in individual than in party terms. The resolution of this problem is crucial for the Brazilian Green Party, and apparently only its organic growth with a consequential diversification of leadership could attenuate the potential for conflict which this generates.

Returning to the discussion above, it is noteworthy that at that moment the decision to create a political party was not automatic. For organizational reasons a political entity, the 'Green Collective', was created in June 1985 to promote green proposals and discuss the idea of a party. The debate on the PV also occurred at inter-state meetings of ecological groups. The convocation of a National Constituent Assembly to be elected in November 1986, for example, provoked the creation of an Interstate Ecological Co-ordination for the Constituent Assembly (CIEC) in November 1985. This co-ordinating body could not agree on the opportunity of creating a green party. As opinions were divided, however, it considered contacts made to this end legitimate, but resolved to support candidates with an affinity for ecological proposals regardless of their party affiliation.

The decision to create the section of the Green Party in Rio de Janeiro was made in January 1986, and was motivated by two factors. The first was the news that right-wing political groups were organizing to register officially the name PV, with a project to create a conservative environmentalist party. It was thus judged important to fight to maintain for this party name in Brazil the critical and radical identity which characterised the European movement and also the Green Collective in Rio de Janeiro. The second element was the interest which emerged on the part of PT leaders in supporting Fernando Gabeira as gubernatorial candidate in the November general elections. Gabeira was really one of the most famous personalities in Rio de Janeiro; the PT had just experienced a major defeat in the Rio mayoral elections in 1985, where it won 0·9 per cent of the vote, and it thought that an alliance with the Greens could help to broaden its political space.

The PV's organizational process, on the other hand, was at a highly embryonic stage. Green collectives began to emerge in neighbourhoods, in cities in the interior and even in other states, but ideal conditions for running in a majoritarian election did not exist. Besides, it was clear that there would not be time to fulfil the legal requirements and register the party officially for the November elections. It was therefore decided that in spite of the difficulties, forming an alliance with the PT would be an opportunity to use the space of the Gabeira candidacy to spread green ideas for the population as a whole. The idea of a PT–PV coalition gained impetus and was finally adopted. For the PT slate, the PV named the gubernatorial candidate, one candidate for deputy to the Constituent Assembly (Liszt Vieira) and two candidates for state deputy (Carlos Minc and Herbert Daniel). The deputy Lucia Arruda preferred to remain within the PT, in which she was re-elected, and only joined the PV in 1988.

It is interesting that while it was not legally registered, the PV's existence was fully accepted by the press and public opinion in Rio de Janeiro in the 1986 elections. The party itself stressed de facto organization during this period, leaving *de jure* organization for 1987. Collectives were organized around multiple criteria: neighbourhoods, activities, professions, etc. The idea was to create a combative 'Party-Movement' without rigidly-defined organization. A manifesto and a provisional programme were drawn up. The importance of the first of these is that the principal characteristics which distinguish the Brazilian Green Party from its European counterparts were already clearly formulated. The alliance with other political forces on the left, subject to highly polemical debates in Europe, is *de facto* predetermined in Brazil. The logic of this position comes from the very serious social conditions in Brazil, which cannot be resolved by any social force in isolation. There was also a maximum programme to be implemented – the construction of a socialist, ecological, decentralised society, etc. – and a minimal and urgent programme for confronting misery and consolidating democracy. In this sense the manifesto states that the PV is an integral part of a social and political bloc which struggles for a broad set of progressive reforms.

The candidacy of Gabeira, approved in the PT convention on 27 April 1986 in spite of considerable opposition within that party, was a resounding political success. The final result, with 7·8 per cent of the vote, was very significant for several reasons. First, the election was highly polarised, and the PT–PV was situated between two powerful electoral groups: the populist state government and an enormous opposition bloc which ranged from conservatives to communists. Secondly, the result is even more significant if we disaggregate it geographically. In the conservative north of the state, for example, Gabeira had around 1 per cent of the vote. In the Baixada Fluminense, a poor but urban region, the proportion went up to 5 per cent. In the capital it was 11 per cent, and in the southern zone of the capital, with a high concentration of middle- and upper-class voters, it reached 16 per cent. The campaign also met with obstacles. According to the polling institute IBOPE, Gabeira began with 2·5 per cent of preferences in April, reaching 7 per cent in July. In the first televised debate among the candidates, however, on 1 September, Gabeira came across extremely well, winning the debate in the opinion of 34 per cent of the viewers, as opposed to 20 per cent for the candidate of the oppositionist bloc. This provoked euphoria in the campaign, and on 10 September he was already up to 10 per cent in the opinion polls. This growth surprised his two main adversaries, and in the middle of that month a large press campaign began to accuse him of defending free consumption of marijuana (in fact, the PV programme defends decriminalisation of marijuana use). It was a violent campaign, and around 21 September Gabeira had already fallen back to 7 per cent in the polls. The Gabeira candidacy, besides holding on to this percentage, was also notable for promoting creative activities which renewed the image of political action and had a major impact on public opinion, such as the memorable 'Embrace the Lake' event on 26 October. In this election the PV managed to elect Carlos Minc to the state legislature, making him thus the first formally green parliamentary representative in Brazil.

In 1987 the Greens concentrated their efforts on legalising the party. To this end, sections of the PV were created in seventeen states. A second diffusion dynamic, this time internal, greatly facilitated this process. Gabeira's candidacy inspired the formation of nuclei in other states, by demonstrating the viability of green politics in Brazil. From participant observation, the relevance of this catalyst was evident. While there is not yet a systematic study on this, it appears that the origins of the militants of these sections are similar all over the country: former exiles, former militants of left movements, activists from social (especially ecological) movements, technical personnel formed in the ambit of state environmentalism, liberal professionals and students, and some who had not previously participated in politics. Unlike what we would expect from the hypothesis of a linear relationship between green politics and affluence, PV organization was not limited to the wealthiest regions of the country. Sections were organized in three municipalities in the Baixada Fluminense, for example, the most miserable region in the interior of Rio de Janeiro. The party also was organized in six states in the north-east of Brazil and in four in Amazonia.

Finally, one of the central problems the PV faces will be how to reconcile the legal requirements for the organization and functioning of the party with its members' expectations for flexible and innovative forms of action. The organizational freedom and variety initially proposed when the idea of a party-movement was launched (a synthesis between the legal statute of a party and the vitality of a social movement), suffered significant damage when the decision to legalise the PV nationally obliged its militants to dedicate themselves to bureaucratic activities and become organized according to the legally required norms.

At the electoral level, obtaining provisional legal registration in March 1988 enabled the party to participate in its first election in its own name: the municipal elections of November 1988 for mayors and municipal council members. The strategy adopted for this election was modest, taking into account the short existence of the party. There was an attempt to launch candidates in each city, preferably only one, in order to elect at least one representative via a concentration of votes. Another tendency was to participate in common lists with other small left parties, which in the proportional system facilitates the election of representatives through the aggregation of votes of various parties in the coalition. In the elections for mayor the tendency was to support candidates from other parties responsive to green ideas, participating in left fronts.

The results of this first experience were reasonable. The party's candidate in the city of Rio de Janeiro, Alfredo Sirkis, was elected as the individually most voted member of the municipal council, with 43,650 votes. Representatives were also elected in three cities in the interior of Rio de Janeiro, in eight in São Paulo (the councillor Tripoli, in the capital, elected with an ecological discourse by the PMDB, later joined the PV), and in two in Santa Catarina. In addition, council members linked to the party were elected on other slates in Campina Grande (PB), and Alto Paraíso (GO). In the city of Salvador, Bahia, the PV candidate, agronomist Joel Hamilton, was the third most voted; however, he was not elected because the party had not participated in an electoral alliance. While modest, these results show that the party achieved national expression, going beyond its exclusive 1986 base in Rio de Janeiro. As a starting point, they indicate that the party has a potential to continue to exist, even though this potential needs to be confirmed in subsequent elections.

IV

My goal in this chapter has been to discuss, in broad outline, the historical and sociological context in which green politics arose in Brazil. I also sought to present some basic information on the initial moments in the history of the Brazilian Green Party. I did not intend, here, to analyse the history, structure or behaviour of this party in greater detail. This would require an analysis of the sociological composition of its electorate, the theoretical bases of its discourse, the characteristics of its legislative practice, its mechanisms for selecting leaders, etc. The PV has not existed long enough for such investigations to produce satisfactory results, as its official existence only began in March 1988. More relevant conclusions on the characteristics and possible specificities of the Brazilian Green Party can only be drawn when the object is delineated more clearly, and this depends on the continuity of its historical existence, that is, on an accumulation of electoral and legislative experiences, theoretical documents, etc. The future promises many opportunities for research, both in relation to the organizational dynamics of the PV and regarding its multiple interactions with society. (The social invention of a political current, in any case, depends both on the action of its members and on the way in which society accepts it in its space and constitutes it conceptually in the collective consciousness.)

What we can analyse, at the moment, regarding green politics in Brazil, are the conditions of its birth. Here I hope to have made clear in this text one basic premise: if it is true that the PV arose in Brazil through direct or indirect diffusion of the European experience, it is also true that precedents and conditions existed which were favourable to its implantation in the country; these can only be understood by an analysis of endogenous factors.

Even at this embryonic stage of its history, it may be possible to detect a central question which will define the future of this current in the Brazilian political scene: that is the question of its identity. The PV's disposition to ally with other political forces, while understandable in the Brazilian context, could inhibit its growth, and, at the limit, provoke its dissolution. Its challenge is to prove to society, and especially to those sectors of the electorate most responsive to its message, the need for its autonomous existence. It must demonstrate its specificity in relation to other left forces even as it collaborates with them on more general struggles. It needs to be clearly established whether the goal of the PV is only to 'green' the left, or rather is to present society with a new project, involving a new conception of the human being and of social, cultural and ecological relations.

The challenge to the Green Party is not only to affirm this identity, but also to demonstrate it, elaborating theoretically a global project for Brazil which is based on the affirmation of these new paradigms. A mere listing of issues, from environmental problems to minority rights, is not enough, as other parties can absorb them (and effectively do). It is fundamental that its identity be established through a broad and coherent project. This project must make sense in the concrete reality of Brazil, presenting appropriate responses to its enormous social problems. An adequate response to this question evidently implies direct knowledge of and contact with popular sectors in Brazilian society. No Brazilian party today, even if it intended to confine itself to the middle class, can ignore this question. The approximation between green politics and the expectations of the poorest sectors of society could come to represent a significant contribution to the development of this political current on an international scale.

References

Boschi, R. (1986). 'A Abertura e a Nova Classe Média na Política Brasileira,' *Revista Brasileira de Ciências Sociais*, No. 1, pp. 30–42.

Bürklin, W. (1985). 'The German Greens: The post-industrial non-established and the party system', *International Political Science Review*, Vol. 6, pp. 463–81.

Chandler, W. and Siaroff, A. (1986). 'Post-industrial politics in Germany and the origin of the Greens', *Comparative Politics*, Vol. 18, pp. 303–24.

Collier, D. and Messik, R. (1975). 'Prerequisites versus diffusion: Testing alternative explanations to social security adoption', *American Political Science Review*, Vol. 69, pp. 1299–1315.

Dahl, R. (1982). *Dilemmas of Pluralist Democracy*. (New Haven, CT: Yale University Press).

Durning, A. (1989). 'Mobilizing at the grassroots', in Brown, L. (ed.), *State of the World 1989*. (New York, NY: Norton).

Galtung, J. (1986), 'The Green Movement: A socio-historical exploration', *International Sociology*, Vol. 1, pp. 75–90.

Graziano Neto, F. (1982). *Questão Agrária e Ecologia* (São Paulo: Brasiliense).

Guimarães, R. (1986). 'Ecopolitics in the Third World: An institutional analysis of environmental management in Brazil'. (Ph.D. Thesis, University of Connecticut, Datilog).

Hay, P. and Haward, M. (1988). 'Comparative green politics: beyond the European context?', *Political Studies*, Vol. 36, pp. 433–48.

Inglehart, R. (1977). *The Silent Revolution.* (Princeton, NJ: Princeton University Press).

Inglehart, R. (1982). *Changing Values and the Rise of Environmentalism in Western Societies.* (Berlin: Science Centre Berlin).

Kitschelt, H. (1988). 'Organization and strategy of Belgian and West German Ecology Parties', *Comparative Politics*, Vol. 20, pp. 127–54.

Landin, L. (org.) (1988). *Sem Fins Lucrativos: As Ongs no Brasil.* (Rio de Janeiro: ISER).

Lowe, P. and Rüdig, W. (1986). 'Political ecology and the social sciences; the state of the art', *British Journal of Political Science*, Vol. 16, pp. 513–50.

Mewes, H. (1983). 'The West German Green Party', *New German Critique*, No. 28, pp. 51–85.

Pádua, J. A. (1988). 'Natureza e projeto nacional: As origens da ecologia política no Brasil', in Pádua, J. A. (org.), *Ecologia e Política no Brasil.* (Rio de Janeiro: IUPERJ/Espaço e Tempo).

Pizzorno, A. (1976). 'Introduccion al estudio de la participacion política', in Pizzorno, A. et al., *Participacion y Cambio Social.* (Buenos Aires, SIAP).

Rüdig, W. and Lowe, P. (1986). 'The withered greening of British politics', *Political Studies*, Vol. 34, pp. 262–84.

Santos, W. G. dos (1987). 'A pós-revolução Brasileira', in Jaguaribe, H. (org.), *Brasil, Sociedade Democrática.* (Rio de Janeiro: José Olympio).

SEMA (1983). *Cadastro Nacional das Instituições que Atuam na Area do Meio Ambiente.* (Brasília: Sinima).

Sunkel, O. (1981). *La Dimension Ambiental en los Estilos de Desarrollo de América Latina.* (Santiago de Chile: CEPAL/PNUMA).

Viola, E. (1988). 'O movimento ecológico no Brasil (1974–1986): Do ambientalismo à ecopolitica', in Pádua, J. A. (org.), *Ecologia e Política no Brasil.* (Rio de Janeiro: IUPERJ/Espaço e Tempo).

7. Chaos as an Explanation of the Role of Environmental Groups in East European Politics*

BARBARA JANCAR

Department of Political Science, State University of New York, Brockport, New York, USA

Introduction

Eastern Europe is in the process of transition from a Communist one-party command economy system to a democratic free market society. While many countries have been successful in converting from a dictatorship to a democracy and vice versa, history has not one example of the conversion of a Communist system into a pluralistic society. A Hungarian colleague once said it could not be done short of revolution. All over Eastern Europe, the new governments are extremely hesitant to embark upon revolution. Only Poland has taken what has been called the cold-water plunge into a free market. The presidential elections at the end of 1990 indicated how tenuous public endorsement of that plunge was. Even though Poland had experienced a decade of preparation of Poles for democracy and the end to a state-owned economy, the hardships experienced in the transition were almost too severe to sustain the momentum for change. In the other East European countries, fundamental economic change has yet to take place.

It would be wonderful if a country could go through a 'velvet revolution', reclaim its sovereignty, and then pursue a policy which would provide everyone with the same economic benefits of the old system but enhance them with the material riches of capitalism. Overnight, for example, East Germans would have the purchasing power of their West German countrymen, food prices would remain low but food would be abundant, consumer goods would be plentiful, and travel to the West as inexpensive as if the old official exchange rate for foreign tourists still obtained.

Events suggest that such an eventuality is an illusion. The transformation of the East European political and economic systems may yet require a revolution. It may not be a revolution where blood is shed, but a revolution where the existing economic structure is overthrown, some lose their

*This article was completed in early 1991.

high positions, unemployment and job insecurity are rampant; those few who are successful in reaping immediate benefits from the changes appear to be shady characters with little instinct for honesty or integrity. As the authorities cast about for the right decision on the pace, content and extent of the changes, the social order fragments, and governments find themselves looking chaos in the face.

Chaos comes from a word first used by the Greek natural philosopher Hesiod to refer to the universe's initial state of existence, when it was, as he saw it, a confused mass of formless matter and infinite space. Ever afterward, chaos has been synonymous with lack of order, predictability, and measurability. Until recently, chaos was a word which seemed in direct contradiction to science, because science was the study of order in matter. However, since the end of the sixties, chaos has been steadily creeping into the scientific vocabulary. The recognition of chaos theory as an accepted scientific approach is due in large part to the advent of the computer.

Chaos theory developed from research into weather and population growth in closed ecosystems. Both phenomena are not capable of accurate prediction using linear equations. However, it was discovered that when thousands upon thousands of points of a non-linear equation are plotted up with the help of a computer, eventually, a typical pattern emerges. Chaos theory expressed simply is finding the pattern in seemingly formless points. The theory is dynamic. As its point of departure, it hypothesises a constant change in initial conditions. Its focus is dynamic events – the moment when boiling water turns to steam, changing weather patterns, population growth in a pond. James Gleick (1987) popularised the theory for laymen in a book appropriately called *Chaos*. In 1988, game theorist and international relations expert James Rosenau pioneered a chaos model as descriptive of contemporary international politics, with the break-up of the old established order of nation-states and hegemonic stability and the entry of a multitude of new non-state actors on to the world stage. Rosenau's model bifurcates our customary unitary conceptualisation of international politics into 'two worlds'. The traditional state-centric system coexists and interacts with an emerging multi-centric system composed of 'sovereignty-free' actors, who confront an 'autonomy dilemma' that is of an entirely different character than the 'security dilemma' with which states have been historically concerned (Rosenau 1988 and 1990).

The advantage of chaos theory over previous models of world order is its dynamism. Older models have been traditionally concerned with static stability, such as the balance of power, but chaos theory attempts to identify the underlying patterns behind change itself. East European governments may be overwhelmed in trying to assess the impact of ever-changing conditions upon society-at-large. A model of world order which insists on equilibrium or stability may propose an end goal to be imitated, but it is useless in providing understanding of the transition process itself. The utility of chaos theory is that it looks at change, not as an interruption between one static state and another (feudalism or capitalism, communism or democracy), but as an event which may be studied in and for itself. Seen from this perspective, the world as a whole (the macro world) and nations and peoples (micro world) are never in a stable state. All is in chaos. However, chaos has a pattern which can be known. Moreover, chaos theory tells us that the pattern is the same whether one looks at the macro or the micro world. Understanding the pattern as it defines itself in changing conditions enables us to begin to master the dynamics of a world order which never completely is, but is always emerging.

This chapter is an experiment in applying chaos theory to an analysis of the role of independent groups in East European politics, precisely because East European politics are in such an extraordinary state of flux. The type of group selected is the environmental group because it is a transition phenomenon *par excellence*. Its growth and proliferation occurred in the 1980s, during the last years of the old regime. It showed a remarkable ability to subsume other issues under its aegis. It played a key role in the initial stages of the transition. Yet so far it has been unable to translate its admirable record of achievement into political influence. In a study written before the historic changes, the now President of Czechoslovakia, Vaclav Havel (1985, pp. 23–96), investigated the twin problems of dissidence and 'the power of the powerless' under the conditions of what he termed the 'post-totalitarian state' of the old regime in Eastern Europe. Havel postulated the emergence of a parallel *polis* in Communist one-party states distinct from the dominant state structures of the region. He emphasised that the creation of parallel civic structures was not an escape from society, but an act of 'deepening one's responsibility'. Where Rosenau (1988) looked at the development of citizen activist groups from the macro-perspective, Havel viewed the same individual non-state actors from within his society at a time when the state apparatus had become increasingly irrelevant to the needs of its citizens. In the emergence of the dynamic and open informal movements of Eastern Europe, Havel saw the essence of a 'post-democratic' society, characterised by genuine community and a more human dimension. The new society now in the process of formation owes its leadership, thrust and direction to the parallel society which grew in the womb of the old regime. But the victory of the parallel *polis* is not yet secure because it has been unable to depose the old state structure entrenched in its monopoly of economic levers, and fighting to maintain itself in power. The environmental groups played key roles in the emergence of the parallel *polis*.

What is the relevance of the transition politics of Eastern Europe to the 'global village' of world politics? Chaos theory proposes several concepts which define the common pattern in the dynamics of East European developments and those of the interdependent macro world. The first concept is fractal structure. In his model, Rosenau (1988) posits two worlds, the one, state-centric, the other, multi-centric. But within each macro world, there is a micro world. Fractal structure hypothesises that the behavioural dynamics of the macro and micro worlds are identical. If one breaks up a total system, like a coastline, into smaller and smaller units, one will find identically recurring structures (coastal patterns) and behaviour. The growth, during the 1980s, of parallel non-official groups in East Europe acting independently of the state system but of necessity interacting with it, is a 'fractal' of the world-wide growth of NGOs and citizen actors in Rosenau's multi-centric world. They also have sought to maximise their autonomy in their interactions with the world state system. Like subgroups of states which have formed elsewhere, they are the product of what Rosenau terms the changing nature of political authority. The concept of fractal structure enables us to generalise from a study of the behaviour of autonomous groups at the micro, within-state level to the multi-centric world.

One of the most salient features of chaos dynamics is non-periodicity. The movement of an object cannot be predicted, but its seemingly random behaviour is the result of what meteorologist Edward Lorenz first termed 'sensitive dependency upon initial conditions'. Change the initial values and you change the path of the object, but the random path will always trace out the same geometric pattern. In Rosenau's model, the initial conditions are the world-wide breakdown of authority. In Eastern Europe, the breakdown occurred later than in the West, and at a different pace and in varying degrees in each of the East European countries, but nevertheless, the breakdown may be considered a fractal of a global process.

A third characteristic of chaotic behaviour is the 'strange attractor'. By definition, non-periodic motion is non-linear. The attractor or attractors are the lodestones (or magnets) which define the orbital path of an object. Rosenau's model suggests three dimensions of strange attractors. The first dimension relates to the *ordering principle* of his two worlds. For the state-centric world it is security. For the multi-centric world, it is autonomy: the right and, according to Havel, the *obligation* of non-state groups and systems of groups to make policy initiatives. The second is the *decision-rule dimension*. Rosenau posits four types of decision-rules based on four modes of adaptation: acquiescent, intransigent, promotive and preservative. Environmental and peace groups as well as the superpowers fall under the third typology. National movements and small states come under the fourth. Finally, there is the *capability dimension*, which identifies the subsystem in terms of expertise and issue area. In the case of the environmental groups the attractors are the twin issues of democracy and ecology.

The subsystems interact with the state-centric and multi-centric world in a longitudinal sequence called a 'cascade'. Rosenau distinguishes cascades from reciprocal events in that action is propelled from one group to the other within one state, and across states with similar or different political systems, bouncing off one state system and then the other in a manner analogous to the path of white water over rock. The analogy is a useful one, and we shall keep the terminology as long as it is remembered that the process is three-dimensional and that the three attractors function simultaneously, not consecutively.

One may thus visualise three sets of poles attracting the activity of the environmental groups. Where group activity is consistent and relatively well defined we may talk of what chaos theorists call 'basins of attraction'. In our model there are six basins: the security and autonomy basins, the promotive and preservative decision-rule basins and the democracy and ecology issue basins. At the edges of the basins, groups form, make alliances and fall apart. They attempt to strengthen their autonomy by making alliances with other groups or fall apart under state system pressure. Some groups are attracted to the democracy attractor when democracy appears to be the larger issue; others prefer to identify with the ecology attractor. Some groups move too far toward the nationality issue and are pulled into the preservative adaptation basin of attraction. At the boundary of each basin of attraction, one may visualise the forming and reforming of small groups each seeking a mode of adaptation which will facilitate autonomy and a coherent survivable identity. We do not know the names of all the groups which surfaced during the 1980s and are surfacing in Eastern Europe today. Those we do know have evidently moved away from the indeterminate fringes at the boundaries of the basins, and established a firmer identity within the 'gravitational pull' of one or more of the attractors. The three-dimensional model proposed suggests a fluid or plastic variant of a child's six-pointed jack. The attractors are the points. The jack is thrown and tumbles over and over on its points. The points on which the jack lands depends on the initial throw, the rebounds from the first and subsequent landings, and the flow of plastic material into the different basins of the jack resulting from the throw.

Sensitive Dependence upon Initial Conditions: The Changing Nature of Authority in Eastern Europe

Since the advent of Communist power in Eastern Europe, the East European populations have sought to transform the command Soviet-style state system imposed upon them by the USSR into a system more in harmony with their national culture and with what they perceive as the mainstream of European culture. Over the decades, the worst aspects of the Stalinist system, such as terror and legal arbitrariness, disappeared from the foreground of almost all East European countries. Countries with a determined and homogeneous population, like Poland and Hungary, were able to soften the features of Communist rule to where they were scarcely visible to the outside observer. Regimes in other countries did not feel so secure. The Czechoslovak authorities believed they had to crack down on freedom of speech and association up until the very end. They continued to send their most talented artists and writers, such as Havel, to prison, and they broke up their last demonstration on 17 November 1989. East Germany maintained its Stalinist character until the first breach in the Berlin Wall, while Romania and Bulgaria still practise a modified form of one-party rule. The events of 1989 showed that, despite the appearance of political stagnation or rigidity, even the most hardline regimes had been influenced by changes taking place elsewhere in the region.

Khrushchev's speech to the Twentieth Congress of the CPSU in 1956 was the first 'initial condition' which started the process of undermining the authority of the Communist leaderships in Eastern Europe. In Poland and Hungary, the reaction was so severe that Communist authority could only be restored with the threat of troops or by invasion. However, the social contracts made after the revolutions were markedly more lenient and open than those in force before. In 1968, the invasion of Czechoslovakia enforced the Brezhnev doctrine of no retreat from a 'socialist' society. But strikes in 1970 and 1971 in Poland showed that formal Communist rule was insufficient to prevent the emergence of a coexisting popular movement. The second 'initial condition', the signing of the Helsinki Agreements in 1975, speeded up the erosion of Communist authority. Human rights soared to the top of the popular agendas in all the East European countries, which could ignore the issue only at their peril – witness the rise and persistence of Solidarity in Poland and Charter 77 in Czechoslovakia.

Perestroika ushered in the third phase in the deterioration of the authority of the East European regimes. *Perestroika* recognised the incapability of the one-party centrally-planned regimes to promote efficient and effective economic growth. Command economies had become an anachronism. In the effort to shore up its own flagging system, East Germany publicly accepted the principle of different views of socialism and talked of 'socialism in GDR colours' (*Neues Deutschland*, 27 February 1989). Chernobyl, the fourth 'initial condition', completed the process of undermining the Stalinist system. Coupled with the growing sensation of impending ecological disaster throughout Eastern Europe, the event demonstrated the inability of the old system to prevent environmental catastrophe on a global scale. The survival of socialist states was no longer a matter of maintaining security from an outside force, but of providing renewal from within.

Command, conformity and coercion were inappropriate instruments for regimes seeking to rekindle initiative. Hence the need for *glasnost*.Openness in turn gave the unofficial groups an informal guarantee of autonomy and the implicit right to make policy proposals. As events made clear, the key demands of all members of the parallel *polis* were freedom of speech and assembly. In Havel's words, no-one can assume responsibility in a society if his actions are forced to conform to a prescribed pattern of behaviour.

Glasnost must thus be seen as performing two functions in Eastern Europe. On the one hand, it provided the political legitimation for the growth of East European activism as it tore away the ideological under-pinnings of suppression. At the same time, it confirmed the reality of the loss of Soviet control over the economic, cultural and intellectual life of the East European countries. This process was constantly changing in speed and content with each new initial condition from 1956 on. *Glasnost* made it irreversible. Under the new conditions, environmental groups thrived and proliferated. But as in the area as a whole, so in each country (the national fractal), their growth and freedom to operate depended upon the changing conditions of authority. The first groups formed in Poland and Hungary, where the authorities had accepted the necessity for some reform, and antedated Chernobyl. But most environmental groups came into being after April 1986.

The oldest is probably the Polish Ecology Club (PEC). Until the emer-gence of Solidarity in 1980, discussion of environmental problems was taboo in Poland as elsewhere in the bloc. The Club originated in Kracow and was the first ecological group to organize following the Gdansk strikes in September 1980. PEC began publishing a popular monthly and soon claimed a membership of over 1,000 people. Under its sponsorship, the Polish people learned for the first time of the seriousness of pollution in their country. The Club was the motor force behind the drive to close the polluting Skawina aluminium plant near Kracow in 1980–1, and its experts prepared the memorandum demanding the closure of all processes in the plant emitting toxic chemicals. The Club went underground with the imposition of martial law in December 1981 to resurface after Chernobyl. Since 1986, it has been a leading environmental organization in Poland. The work of the Club has been cited in internationally published materi-als (Starzewska 1988) and it was the first East European environmental group to become a member of Friends of the Earth International (FoE) with representation on the international board. We thus see it establishing its autonomy by making alliances in the multi-centric international world, thereby enhancing its capabilities and credibility in environmental exper-tise.

The first Hungarian environmental group was formed in 1983. In 1977, Czechoslovakia and Hungary signed an agreement to build two giant hydro-electric dams on the Danube. The Hungarian dam was to be built upriver from the famous Danube bend at Nagymaros, under the ruins of Visehrad Castle. A group calling itself the Association for the Protection of the Danube Region requested official permission to organize, but was unable to obtain the proper permit from the Hungarian government. In 1983, biologist Janos Vargha founded an unofficial group, the Danube Circle, which became known as the Blues. As the eighties progressed, opposition to the Gabcikovo-Nagymaros Dam drew increasing numbers of Hungarians into a variety of environmental groups seeking not only to halt dam construction, but concerned with environmental issues in general. In 1989, the Communist Party must have realised its time had come, when Kossuth Square in front of the Parliament building filled with over a 100,000 persons demanding the end of the dam and the holding of multi-party elections. The square had last seen demonstrators under Soviet guns in 1956.

After Chernobyl, environmental groups mushroomed in every republic of the Soviet Union and in every East European country. Some formed in response to local environmental grievances: the Danube Circle, the Czech Mothers protesting about polluted drinking water, the local groups in the North Bohemian coal towns, or the Bulgarian group in the Danube city of Ruse which organized to protest the deadly pollution blowing across the river from the Romanian chemical plants on the other side. Other environmental groups emphasised environmental concerns affecting the whole country and/or allied with peace and ecology movements imported from Western Europe. Still others organized a domestic variant of the West European Green Party.

In the Soviet Union, local grass roots environmental organizations have now become a fact of life. It is estimated that there are over 300 such groups in Leningrad alone. Fragmentation has been the chief characteristic of their chaotic development due in large part to the specificity of regional environmental conditions, and the consequent tendency towards the formation of *ad hoc* single-issue groups. A large number of these formed to protest dam or nuclear power construction, but there are many other eclectic cases. One such formed in Gorky to protest subway construction; and another organized in Kirishi to fight pollution from a biochemical plant (*Izvestia*, 6 July 1988). One of the most significant has been the protest against further natural resource exploitation of their homeland by the Nentsy, a small northern people living in the fragile Yamal Peninsula, where oil and gas exploration threatens to thaw the permafrost, and by rendering reindeer pasturing impossible, destroy the Nentsys' traditional way of life. In 1989, for the first time, the Soviet Arctic peoples participated in the Innuit Circumpolar Conference (Perepletkin 1988 and Edwards 1990).

In the union republics, environmental activists have been ingenious in discovering ways to promote their cause. There is a powerful and well-organized anti-nuclear movement in the Ukraine and Belorussia. Led by journalist Yurii Shcherbak's umbrella organization, Zelenyi Svit (Green World), the movement was instrumental in bringing the real facts about Chernobyl to the public,including proof of two-headed cattle, misshapen babies and contaminated food. In September 1990, the Green Party of Ukraine held its founding conference. Among its goals were an independent and economically sovereign Ukraine, the advocation of 'humanism' and the value of human life, and the goal of preventing further environmental degradation in the Ukraine (Marples 1990). In Moldavia, a group of intellectuals first established a section in the national democratic movement called Green Action. In February 1989, the same group attempted to form a Green Party, but the authorities refused to let them hold a constitutive conference (Socor 1989a and 1989b).The group has since formally constituted itself a party. In the Baltic republics (Devvatkin 1988), ecological groups have chosen to work within rather than alongside the national democratic movements.

Dimension 1 – Security vs. the Right to Make Policy Initiatives

All the environmental groups formed with the express purpose of influencing the state system in two major ways. First and foremost, the aim was to save the environment. But the second was linked to it: the promotion of democracy. While these two goals may seem totally different, in fact the very existence of unofficial groups rested on the premise that the state organs authorised to take charge of environmental management had failed and that the public therefore must see to it that they perform their duty. The connection between ecology and democracy in socialist state systems is qualitatively different from what it is in pluralist systems. In western democracies, the rights to speak and to organize are constitutional guarantees, preconditions of the political system. Under socialism, the single party's exclusive right to govern was premised upon its ability to promote economic and social well-being. Silence on the extent of environmental damage, rampant environmental pollution and events such as Chernobyl challenged the party's exclusive right at its base. Contrary to all pronouncements, socialist systems performed demonstrably worse than democratic systems in containing and preventing environmental decay. Charter 77 specifically called for the publication of environmental data and popular monitoring of environmental regulations precisely because the large, state-administered polluting industries were incapable of controlling themselves.

The failure of the socialist system to assure environmental well-being provided the argument for the formation of grass-roots movements in Eastern Europe and the Soviet Union. Because socialised industry could not regulate its behaviour to prevent pollution, the public organized to see that it did. Human rights was the prerequisite to modify the ineffectual system which the Czechs termed *totalita*, not an a priori condition of society itself. The right to make policy initiatives was premised upon state system failure.

The point needs to be emphasised. In the West, the ecological movement in the eighties joined forces with the anti-nuclear and peace movements. There were two assumptions behind such action. The first was that nuclear war might produce nuclear winter, the ultimate in environmental catastrophes. The second was that the military-industrial complex was hand-in-glove with big government to continue polluting modes of production and to escape bearing the full cost of 'environmental marginalities' as long as possible. The right of environmentalists to promote policy was never challenged, although the content of that policy was. By contrast, ecological activists in Eastern Europe have had to argue both for their policy and for their right to promote it. The differences between the two points of view were clearly demonstrated at the conference on International Peace and the Helsinki Agreements which took place in Warsaw in May 1987. The conference was the first independently-sponsored meeting of its kind in Eastern Europe and was organized by a group of young peace activists who called themselves Wolnosc i Pokoj (Freedom and Peace) or WiP. The meeting united 250 activists from East and West for discussion on the connections between the Helsinki Agreements, peace and human rights, non-violent struggle in East and West, and post-Chernobyl environmental issues. While the western participants were emphasising peace as absence of war, and nuclear war in particular, the East Europeans were urging Charter 77's objective of 'democratic peace'. The final memorandum was the product of a year's intense negotiation between the East and West European peace groups, and on the East's insistence, underscored the indivisibility of peace and human rights (Duncan 1987).

Glasnost went a long way in recognising the right of individuals to speak out under the old regime, but this right was not guaranteed until the transition to democracy, and it still is not guaranteed in the USSR, Bulgaria or Romania. Until the change, not only the autonomy but the very survival of the East European environmental groups rested on a tacit agreement between the state system and the unofficial parallel system on the way the grass-roots game could be played, with the state reserving its unencumbered right to promote its security. One way, for example, the Soviet government first tried to handle the numerous local environmental initiatives was to group the various local organizations under an official umbrella organization. In June of 1987, a new subcommittee of the Soviet Peace Committee called Greenpeace came into being, largely through the efforts of Soviet writer, editor and journalist, Sergei Zalygin.

Its two functions were the co-ordination of all domestic grass-roots activities and to serve as the channel for ecological activism directed abroad. To lend international credibility to the subcommittee, David McTaggert, Chairman of Greenpeace International was present at the founding meeting (*Pravda*, 5 June 1987). The Polish government attempted a similar move. But events moved too quickly for these efforts to be successful. By 1990, the capabilities of Moscow to orchestrate events had significantly diminished and democracy had come to Poland. As the security attractor decreased in coercive drawing power, the independent groups naturally gravitated towards the autonomy 'basin of attraction'.

To maintain and increase their autonomy prior to the transition, the environmental groups had essentially three options: to join an internationally recognised environmental or peace movement – Greenpeace, Friends of the Earth, or Peace and Ecology; to join a coalition of independent groups with a nationalist orientation; or to forge an alliance with human rights groups, such as the WiP in Poland. Which option was chosen depended on the strength of the 'strange attractors' on all three dimensions. Joining an international group ensured increased activism at home through international publicity. Joining a national movement ensured group perpetuation but not necessarily environmental activism. Indeed, group survival could overshadow activism. Forging an alliance with peace groups also tended to diminish the environmental component. The autonomy attractor does not operate independently of the other attractors in the process.

Dimension 2 – The Decision Rule

Rosenau's model of the adaptive orientations of whole systems (states) and subsystems in the multi-centric world proposes four modes of adaptation with corresponding sets of decision rules. Environmental groups along with the multinationals, ideological political parties, and the superpowers, fall in his third category, promotive adaptation. Systems and subsystems in this group are characterised by a global scope of concern, willingness to undertake innovative policies, heightened readiness to form temporary coalitions, a manipulative rhetoric and a high degree of resistance to systems with superior capabilities (Rosenau 1988, p. 349).

At the beginning of *perestroika*, the environmental groups in the Soviet union republics were on the same system orientation wavelength as the USSR all-union authorities, but in an entirely different mode of adaptation from the republican and regional authorities which were oriented towards preserving their bureaucratic power. Indeed, Gorbachev may have initially encouraged grass-roots environmental groups to mobilise public pressure against the deadweight of bureaucracy. By the end of the eighties, environmental protests had become commonplace in virtually every part of the Soviet Union. Environmental activists enthusiastically exposed the bureaucracy in the name of a cleaner and healthier socialist community. In many union republics environmental groups were perceived as threatening republican security, witness the authorities' response to the Moldavian attempt to organize a Green Party. The advent of multi-candidate elections in the Soviet Union radicalised republican political environments. Almost overnight the modes of adaptive behaviour were reversed. The republican governments became the focus of innovative action, and found in the environmentalists ready allies, while the all-union government, including Gorbachev himself, retreated into the fortress of preservative adaptation, in the central bureaucracies' futile effort to hold the old Soviet empire together.

In Eastern Europe the old regimes also viewed the environmental movement with suspicion. In the more liberal socialist states, environmentalists were barely tolerated, while in the hardline countries, like Czechoslovakia, people were imprisoned for environmental activism (Krivan 1986). Hungary and Yugoslavia provide instructive examples of environmentalist versus regime behaviour.

In Hungary, the Danube Circle naively thought its focus on environmental issues was apolitical, but the Blues immediately ran into politics. In 1985, the Blues sent a letter protesting the construction of the dam to the Hungarian National Assembly and Council of Ministers. Fifty leading cultural and scientific figures agreed to sign it. The letter was then circulated among the general public. Reportedly, 10,000 signatures were secured, but only 6,000 accompanied the letter, because the rest had been seized by the police. The government requested a blue ribbon committee of the Hungarian Academy of Sciences to give its evaluation of the dam project. When the committee reported back with a negative proposal, the government put pressure on the committee members to quash the report. The academicians never revealed their part in the dam controversy until after the country had held its first democratic elections.

In 1985, the Danube Circle was awarded the alternative Nobel Peace Prize. Thoroughly embarrassed, the Hungarian government only permitted Vargha to accept the prize. The Danube Circle insisted it did not seek confrontation and invited the Hungarian Academy of Sciences to supervise the use of the prize money. The invitation was rejected by the Hungarian authorities. By this time, the environmentalists had generated sufficient support among the public that signatures were secured for a petition demanding a referendum on the subject. This request was also rejected by the government ('Special report' 1987 and Konrad 1988). In my conversations in 1987 with officials from the then Hungarian Environmental Administration, the most common perception of environmental activism was that it was a threat to the existing system of expertise where science gave advice through channels and responsible officials made the decisions.

The dam issue ultimately brought the old regime down. In February 1986, the police turned on Hungarian and Austrian protesters during the wintry 'Danube Walk'. Opposition to the Hungarian variant of *totalita* increased. In October 1989, 200,000-strong marched through the streets of Budapest. In January 1990 the government promised free elections, and in the spring it abandoned the Nagymaros Dam.

In Yugoslavia, tensions between the mass anti-nuclear movement which sought a moratorium on the building of nuclear plants and what was termed the 'nuclear lobby' ran very high. The movement ran head-on into establishment values from its very beginning. In 1986, Aleksandar Knezivic, a student at the Mosa Pijade High School in the Belgrade district of Starigrad, wanted to start a petition to ask the government to postpone construction on a second nuclear power plant. At first the idea was enthusiastically supported by the district's League of Yugoslav Youth (SOJ) conference. Then the conference president was replaced and the incoming president apparently did not want to get involved in such a sensitive issue so early in his tenure. Support for the project quickly died. Knezivic began getting phone calls at night, some threatening him with two months in jail, others predicting his parents would lose their jobs. Knezivic's school principal was called to the Starigrad Committee of the League of Yugoslav Communists (LYC). The committee rejected the idea of a petition, but approved the reading of a letter in all the schools of Serbia. Each class would then decide whether to support the proposal to cease construction of the proposed nuclear power plants. According to the Belgrade weekly NIN (13 April 1986), of 464 schools in Serbia, 110 responded and letters came from schools in three towns in Croatia. There were now 70,000 signatures in all.

The success of the petition raised the objections of officials involved in the planning and management of the nuclear power industry. Specialists from the Machine Building Faculty of Belgrade University invited themselves to the Mosa Pijade School to lecture the students on the benefits of nuclear power. The Serbian SOJ became increasingly uneasy about the initiative. Then the Ljubljana Peace Group issued a statement calling for the Soviet Union to pay reparations for damage done to Slovenia from the fallout from Chernobyl, and demanding a moratorium on nuclear power and a referendum on the construction of a second plant.

Throughout the summer of 1986, the anti-nuclear movement gathered momentum as more people joined in protests. Youth groups were not the only ones concerned about the dangers of nuclear power. Chernobyl occasioned much soul-searching among the scientific community, and many scientists who had previously been in favour of it changed their minds (Jancar 1987a, Chapter 9). In June, the veterans' organization, SUBNOR, indicated its support of a moratorium on nuclear energy until the year 2000. That same month, the first Congress of the Anti-Nuclear Movement was held in Belgrade. In a press interview during the Congress, writer Mijana Robie put her finger on the political nature of the movement. In her words, it was 'the little people' of Yugoslavia who were protesting nuclear power. Moreover, she continued, 'this is the first time a truly important and strong public opinion in the real sense of the word, has been expressed which seeks for itself the right to speak, think, and inquire' (*Danas*, 17 June 1986, p. 60).

The mass outcry was unexpected by the authorities who launched a not very convincing counterattack. The 'nuclear lobby' included top government leaders. Two former Prime Ministers, Milka Planinc and Branko Mikulic, who resigned at the end of 1988, exerted their influence on behalf of the nuclear industry. In Slovenia, the government organized public meetings to deal directly with people's concerns. Planinc and Mikulic took the case for nuclear energy before the LYC Central Committee (Jovanovic 1988). By the time the moratorium was adopted at the end of 1988, nuclear power had become the symbol of what was perceived as an entrenched, uncaring and deaf bureaucracy, while the anti-nuclear movement saw itself as the harbingers of a new day of people power in Yugoslavia.

In both the Hungarian and the Yugoslav case, the activists first thought environmental issues could not be matters of national security. But in each case, the promotive orientation of the movement ran into the preservationist orientation of the authorities. By the summer of 1988, the crisis of authority in Yugoslavia had so deepened that the federal and republican governments were forced to accede to the anti-nuclear demands. Moratoria were pronounced in Croatia, Slovenia and Serbia.

The success of the anti-nuclear movement was an important step in the erosion of Communist Party authority in Yugoslavia, but the movement was too unstructured to withstand the impact of party decay. By 1989, the cross-republican alliance of anti-nuclear groups had splintered into republican 'fractals' struggling to adapt their tactics to rapidly changing local conditions of authority. In the summer of 1989, the environmental group within the Slovenian SOJ broke away to form a Green Party. The party had no official permission to organize, but it had a well-developed network of local groups and a comprehensive political programme, and hence thought itself ready to run candidates for office. In January 1990, the Slovenian Communist Party mounted its autonomy challenge against the centralising state system advocated by Serbia by announcing there would be free elections in March. The announcement flung wide open the already half-opened door of Slovenian politics. The Greens showed themselves particularly adept at taking advantage of the promotive atmosphere. They promptly joined the democratic coalition, DEMOS, and promoted their programme as the only one that was truly global in scope. They won over 8 per cent of the popular vote and 13 per cent of the DEMOS vote (Kusin 1990).

In Croatia, the elections also were oriented toward nationalism, but of a more conservative kind. The environmental groups were not organized to innovate against a preservationist nationalism, but against a preservationist Communism, and so were unable to take advantage of the new conditions of authority. The decision to organize politically came too late for the spring elections and the environmentalists succeeded in winning only one seat in the legislature. In Serbia, nationalism is decidedly conservative, and national self-preservation is the dominant concern. The environmentalists' decision to retain non-governmental (NGO) status and not run candidates for office in the December 1990 elections reflects their approach to maintaining autonomy in the face of strong central power in Belgrade.

Events show then, that over the past several years, as central authority has broken down and the Yugoslav federation has fragmented, the environmental movement has successfully adapted its tactics to the political climate of the fractal units. As in the Soviet Union, wherever the republican governments in Yugoslavia have themselves adopted decision rules based on promotive adaptation, the environmental groups have been adept at taking advantage of a politically fluid climate. Where the republican governments have adopted preservationist decision rules, the environmental groups have had to improvise strategies to oppose them.

The Blues and the Yugoslav environmental movement are instructive examples of the flexibility, manipulative attitude toward authority and resilience of the environmental groups. Neither took negative regime response for a final answer. Each sought to win over other groups within their country and to seek additional support abroad. According to Judit Vasarhelyi, one of the founders of the Danube Circle and now at the East Central European Centre for Environmental Information in Budapest, the Danube Circle was forced to be innovative because of dangerous circumstances. The slightest mistake could bring harm to a member of the group. In the development of a survival strategy, the Blues pioneered in introducing protest actions, many of them derived from the West, such as petitions, letter writing, distributing leaflets, everything by samizdat. In 1985, they mobilised a group of West German Greens to lead a parliamentary delegation to the Hungarian parliament to protest the dam. The 'Danube Walk' was jointly sponsored by the Blues and the Austrian Greens. And thirty Hungarian intellectuals were censored for putting a notice in the Austrian Die Presse petitioning the Austrian parliament to review the terms of their agreement to help finance construction of the dam. There were ten years of fighting a seemingly unending, spiritually wearing, uphill battle. Again to quote Vasarhelyi, 'We were exhausted from the struggle. Everything was sacrificed for it. Our children became orphans of the movement.' The limbo which the Hungarian environmental movement is experiencing today may be the consequence of the Blues' victory. Success in innovating against a strong state bureaucracy has given the environmentalists little experience in manipulating weak democratic institutions, whose dominant concern is economic.

In Yugoslavia, the anti-nuclear movement proved itself surprisingly successful in making officially recognised organizations such as the SOJ adopt its policy initiative on the moratorium, and then seeing to it that the SOJ proposed this initiative to the federal Skupsina. The movement continued this demonstration of flexibility in its rapid adjustment to the erosion of power in the country and its development of tactics suited to the volatile political conditions in each republic.

Dimension 3 - Capabilities: Peace and Ecology Issues

The foregoing discussion suggests a division of environmental groups in Eastern Europe and the Soviet Union into three categories, each with its characteristic capability and expertise. The first is the group exclusively devoted to environmental issues. The group may be involved with environmental problems confined to one area, such as the *ad hoc* environmental group which organized in Moscow's Tushina Borough to protest the cutting down of a local wooded area (*Izvestia*, 6 July 1988), or with one environmental issue such as the Danube Circle. Second, the environmental activist may identify with a broader nationalist or peace and ecology movement. And finally, activists may choose a more overtly political posture and form a green party. Each type of group is pulled toward both the environmental and democratic attractors for the reasons given in the discussion of dimension 1, but the degree of attraction toward the two poles is not the same over all categories.

The first group's primary focus is on environmental issues. If the issue is local, it may require the expertise of a resident scientist to inform a body of concerned citizens. In many local groups, scientists may exercise leadership, witness the early days of the Polish Ecology Club, because their expertise is needed to provide the technical evidence of environmental damage. If the issue is national or international, as with the Nagymaros Dam, it may require the expertise of a whole community of scientists. But essentially the arguments for policy initiatives are based on science with a minimum of normative judgement about politics. Vargha once said, 'The environment recognises no political system.'

The second group is a half-way house between a social movement and a political party. It retains the ideological enthusiasm of a pre-political movement. Its programme is highly normative, critical not only of proposed or implemented official policies but of the values such policies appear to promote. This second type is further politicised in that its interactions with the state system are focused on penetrating the system. One subset of this type is the informal environmental scientific lobby which operated so effectively in the Soviet Union to oppose the pollution of Lake Baikal, and to bring an end to the era of vast engineering projects and big dam construction(Gustavson 1981, Chapter 7). In Czechoslovakia, this lobby took the name of the Environmental Sector of the Biological Section of the Czechoslovak Academy of Sciences. Not surprisingly, many of its members now hold prominent positions in the environmental governmental institutions formed after the fall of Communism. Nor is it surprising that the first chapter of the report issued by the new Czech Ministry of the Environment on the status of the environment in the Czech Lands should explain why *totalita* caused such ecological degradation (Moldan 1990, pp. 7–39). In this 'expert' variant of the second group, the pro-environmental scientists never went into open opposition against the regime, but chose to work behind the scenes to undermine the most negative consequences of arbitrary state power.

A second form of this group is less expert and more value-oriented. It thus tends to enter into a broader coalition, and to gravitate toward the democracy attractor. In Leningrad, four of the 300-odd environmentally-oriented groups, Salvation, Peace, Ecology of Culture and the Cultural Democratic Movement, united to form a Council of Ecology and Culture in 1987 (Sundijev 1988).The Council immediately tried to propose candidates for the first election to the Leningrad district soviets. Its attempt failed because it did not secure official recognition as an organization in time. However, in northern Uzbekistan, environmental activist Roza Baltaeva was selected as a candidate to represent the town of Berunik's environmental movement (TASS, 18 January 1989), and was elected deputy to the Congress of Peoples Deputies in March 1989.

As the 1980s came to an end, the broader coalitions increasingly sought identification with western peace and ecology movements and, like them, called for a new kind of alternative politics. The Llubljana Peace Group's platform is a good example of the totally political philosophy which inspired these organizations. The group posited a clear separation between state and society by distinguishing between two kinds of peace. 'State peace' was guaranteed by state dictatorship over society, while 'civil-social peace' was the demolition 'of the boundaries between civil societies' or 'the internationalisation of civil society'.The Llubljana group established links with like-thinking groups in Western Europe, convinced that contacts with the West were vital to the achievement of its domestic goals. To frame its position according to our model, the group held that the state system's concern for security could only be broken down by a corollary independent multi-centred thrust from below. More explicitly than other coalition movements, the environmental movement in Slovenia consciously sought to create an organic link between dimensions 1 and 3.

The Peace Group's political purpose initially was trans-republican in scope. In 1987, sociologist Tomas Nastna, a fellow of the Institute for Marxist Studies of the Slovenian Academy of Arts and Sciences and a spokesperson for the group, stated that given Yugoslavia's federal composition and national rivalries, an independent peace and environmental movement might be the only type of movement that could unite people across Yugoslavia's many borders. Ties with the West, he said, were essential because the country lacked a democratic tradition and 'popularly shared memories of a strong and independent civil society'. In his view, issue-oriented campaigns could fill this gap and help produce a democratic culture in Yugoslavia. The new forms of activism would not be direct borrowings from the West, but rooted in local conditions (Helsinki Watch Committee 1987, pp. 181–5). Nastna's philosophy was instrumental in launching the Greens of Slovenia toward republican prominence in 1990. But its trans-republican thrust foundered on the upsurge of inter-nation distrust, as central authority broke down.

Green parties have had difficulty in getting off the ground in both the Soviet Union and Eastern Europe. In the Soviet Union, most of the environmental groups at first preferred to join national democratic movements in support of national sovereignty. But as *perestroika* wore on, environmental political parties began to emerge from the fragmenting political landscape. There are green parties in the Baltic republics, the Russian Republic, in Moldavia, Georgia, Armenia, and the Ukraine, with the Ukrainian Green Party probably having the most chance of success. Revelations of the extent of the Chernobyl disaster and of the severity of air and water pollution problems have shocked and angered the public, pushing environmental issues to the top of the national agenda.

In 1990, Eastern Europe held its first free elections in forty years. Yet the saliency of environmental issues did not translate into a green victory at the polls. The results indicated that environmentalists fared best when they joined the leading coalition (democracy attractor). In the Polish, Hungarian, Czechoslovak Federal, Czech National and Bulgarian legislatures, there is no separate green representation. In Hungary, the Czech Lands, and Croatia, the nascent Green Party suffered from accusations of accepting too many ex-Communists into their ranks, and did not receive the necessary 5 per cent of the vote to qualify for a seat in parliament. However, Czech ecological groups ran several candidates under Civic Forum who were elected, while the 3 per cent qualification rule in Slovenia enabled the Green Party there to obtain six of the 150 seats in the Slovak National Council. In Bulgaria, Ecoglasnost registered with the victorious coalition group, the Bulgarian Union of Democratic Forces and won fourteen seats in the 400-member assembly. In Romania the Romanian Ecological Party, allied with the opposition to the ruling National Salvation Front (NSF), won a total of nine seats in the bicameral legislature, while the Romanian Ecological Movement which supported the NSF won thirteen seats overall. The electoral victory of the Greens of Slovenia won them a seat in the Slovenian Presidency, a vice-presidency in the Slovenian Executive Council and Parliament, three ministerial offices, one of them the Ministry of Energy, and nine seats in the three houses of the Slovenian legislature (Kusin 1990).

There are several points to note about the pattern of success and failure in the development of the green parties. First is the fundamental division, which the author has discussed in depth elsewhere (Jancar 1990), between environmental activists over how to achieve environmental goals. The majority are highly sceptical of competing for political power. They believe that environmental issues are essentially technical and politically neutral. The best way to resolve them is by mobilising pressure from the civil society outside the state system upon the wielders of political power. A second group insists that environmental degradation is inherent in the economic–bureaucratic structure of the modern state. The way to environmental integrity is through a political struggle which would transform the power of the 'bureaucratic-technocratic-intelligentsia' into a new democratic form of power, which Barry Commoner (1990) calls 'ecodemocracy'. At the basis of this division lies the question of how to translate the experience of the parallel *polis* created under Communism into effective action under the new political conditions. The NGOs support the first position, the Greens the second.

Second, while the parallel *polis* is a concept native to the former Communist countries, the inspiration for the ecology movements came almost totally from western models of non-traditional party activism. In their search for an appropriate autonomy model, the PEC and the Russian ecology movement have allied with Friends of the Earth and Greenpeace. In an unprecedented move, the 1988 annual meeting of FoE International was held in Moscow. NGOs have also taken the lead in the Hungarian movement. The World Wildlife Fund helped the Danube Circle and other unofficial Hungarian environmental groups in September 1988 to sponsor a three-day conference on the Nagymaros project (*Magyar Nemzet*, 5 and 12 September 1988; *Die Zeit*, 15 September 1988; *The Economist*, 12 September 1988). In July 1990, the East European Centre for Environmental Information opened in Budapest with US backing. One of its functions is to serve as an information and co-ordination headquarters for NGO environmental activity throughout Eastern Europe. Environmentalists in Poland and the Czech Lands also are leaning toward NGOs, while events are too uncertain in Bulgaria and Romania to know which course of action the environmentalists will choose there. Only in Slovakia and Slovenia has the idea of Greens in political power received any real popular support, and leaders of those parties are doubtful whether they will long retain it.

No matter which western model the domestic environmental movements eventually adopt, all share two convictions: that Eastern Europe and the Soviet republics should be reintegrated into the 'normal' process of democratic development of Western Europe; and that alternative politics should adopt modes of organization and rules of interaction with the new state systems that are not perceived as threatening to their security. A key function of the environmental groups is to move across the frontiers of the state-centric world and, through the twin pulls of the autonomy and democratic attractors, influence the state systems to a pro-environmental politics, whether NGO or party driven.

A second feature of the environmental movements is their susceptibility to internal redirection and reformation (reaggregation in Rosenau's terminology). There is an undisputed link between nationalism and environmentalism in the Soviet Union which goes back to before *glasnost* with the efforts of official republican environmental organizations to preserve national landmarks and scenic vistas (Jancar 1987a, pp. 194–211). In the Russian republic, the so-called village writers tied national tradition to specific landscapes. Foremost among this group, writer Valentin Rasputin became a leader in the fight to preserve Lake Baikal and to stop the project to turn the Siberian rivers southward. In an interview with *Literaturnaya gazeta* in January 1988 (*Literaturnaya gazeta*, 1 January 1988, pp. 5–6), Rasputin made no secret of his association of environmental values with the preservation of Russian culture and history. The adherence of environmental groups to national movements after 1985 was a logical outgrowth of the earlier developments, with the nationalist organization, Pamyat, representing one extreme of in the spectrum. In all the union republics, environmental activism has been linked with protests of national discrimination and failure to preserve national historical and cultural monuments. The most visible of the environmental groups have been the Georgian, Armenian, Estonian, Azerbaijani, Moldavian and Ukrainian. In 1987, 350 Armenian intellectuals issued a *samizdat* report accusing the Soviet authorities of 'biological genocide'. It was thus no coincidence that the demonstration for the return of Nagorno-Karabakh began in Erevan the day after thousands took to the street, for the second time to protest environmental pollution in Armenia, shouting that Moscow was promoting ecological genocide (Jancar 1988). In the Ukraine, Zelyenyi Svit first was organized as a single-issue environmental group. It subsequently joined forces with the broad-based national alliance, Rukh. By 1990, political conditions had so changed that Shcherbak decided to found a green party to compete openly for political power.

Aggregation/reaggregation among the East European environmental groups has followed a similar pattern in every country. In Bulgaria, environmental groups were unknown until 1987 and 1988. The first major event was in February 1988 in Ruse, when 2,000 demonstrated against chlorine pollution from a Romanian chemical plant across the border. The Committee for the Protection of Ruse formed to place pressure on the authorities to take action. That committee evolved into the first full-fledged independent environmental organization in Bulgaria, the Independent Committee for the Protection of the Environment. Environmental groups then began to form in other Bulgarian cities and towns. At the end of 1988, a schoolteacher from Vratsa in north-western Bulgaria and a member of the unofficial Association for the Defence of Human Rights attempted to form a Party of the Green Masses. The founders were arrested and put in prison. By 1989, one organization established earlier in the year led the independent groups: Ecoglasnost. In November 1989, Ecoglasnost sponsored a series of protests in Sofia during the Helsinki conference on environmental co-operation. The subsequent imprisonment of the demonstrators contributed in no small part to the fall of the Zhivkov regime (Le Quotidien (Paris), 13 January 1989; AFP (Vienna), 20 January 1989; and Liberation (Paris), 19 January 1989, p. 33). By 1990, Ecoglasnost had become the roof organization for the many smaller groups struggling to stay in existence.

Slovenia's first independent organizations emerged in 1983 as separate single-issue groups of environmentalists, peace workers, gay rights activists and feminists. These groups merged into the Slovenian Peace and Ecology Movement registered within the SOJ under the Slovenian Socialist Alliance. The Movement subsequently joined the unofficial opposition alliance, the Slovenian Democratic Alliance (Viestnik (Zagreb), 16 January 1989). In the summer of 1989, the environmentalists broke away to form their own Green Party and, just prior to the elections, allied with the pre-electoral democratic coalition, DEMOS. In Croatia, local environmental groups joined together in the spring of 1990 to form the Croatian Environmental Alliance. The Alliance is threatened with a rupture by the strong green group in Split. In Serbia, environmental groups also work together under an environmental umbrella organization.

In Hungary, the Danube Circle and other environmental groups joined an umbrella organization of diverse independent groups which formed in May 1988 under the name of Network of Free Initiatives (Reuter (Budapest), 2 May 1988). As elections approached, the environmentalists themselves split into an NGO and a Green Party. There is now an umbrella environmental association which hopes to gather all the environmental groups under its aegis. However, it is by no means certain the Greens will choose to join.

The path of the Czechoslovak independent environmental movement has the least in common with the other movements. During the seventies and early eighties, Charter 77 dominated the alternative political scene in Czechoslovakia, publishing several statements on the state of the Czechoslovak environment (Jancar 1988). At its tenth anniversary, the Charter assumed the mantle of spokesman for the environment (Jancar 1987b), while steadfastly protesting that its message was cultural and moral, and favoured no political position (Havel 1985, pp. 23–7). With perestroika, Czech and Slovak civil society began to revive. In 1988, five new unofficial groups were formed. Only one of them, however, was environmental, the Independent Ecological Society, a surprising commentary for a country with such severe environmental problems. Under the leadership of Ivan Dejmal, a committed layman, the Society began publishing an underground journal, Ekologicky bulletin. Unfortunately, the Bulletin never attained more than a limited circulation. The Society opposed the Nagymaros Dam, nuclear power, destruction of the Czech forests and similar environmental issues. Another of the new groups formed in 1988, the Independent Peace Association, stated its general support for all 'values which make life more humane', but its primary agenda, ending of the draft (RFE 1988a), gave it more immediate visibility (RFE 1988b), than the Ecological Society ever achieved.

As events in Czechoslovakia rushed toward 17 November 1989, participation in environmental demonstrations increased. A new group, the Czech Mothers, called for an end to unclean drinking water by parading their babies in baby carriages through the streets of Prague. On 11 November 200 people in the North Bohemian town of Chomutov braved police attacks to protest the toxic level of air pollution. Immediately following the resignation of the Communist leadership, the Ecological Society met with representatives from the official Czech mass environmental organizations, environmentalists from Charter 77, and members of the Ecological Sector of the Biological Section of the Czechoslovak Academy of Sciences. It was decided to found a green umbrella organization, Green Circle, to co-ordinate environmental programmes and campaigns. Green Circle quickly lost importance as the country moved further toward freedom, and environmental groups found themselves badly in need of money. Although the Circle continues to exist, the environmental movement has fragmented as individual groups search for a raison d'être. Green parties have sprung up in different parts of Bohemia and Moravia. But they have enjoyed the greatest popularity in Slovakia, where they adopted the Slovak nationalist interpretation of environmental degradation in the republic. The fault, they say, lies with Prague (Author interviews with Slovak environmentalists, summer 1990).

The fluid fortunes of the independent environmental groups and parties in the USSR and all of Eastern Europe attest to the chaotic process inherent in the formation and consolidation of the alternative *polis*. At one end of the spectrum lies quick oblivion; at the other may lie either a unified national, anti-imperial opposition, as appears to be happening in the Soviet union republics, a composite democratic opposition as occurred in many countries of Eastern Europe, or a loose more specialised and perhaps more expert environmental coalition. In the case of absorption into a national opposition, the promotive character of the environmental movement confronts the preservationist character of the national movement and risks having its goals subsumed under the cause of national self-preservation. In the event the national goal is achieved, such cries as 'biological genocide' perforce subside, depriving the movement of its emotive nationalism. In the case of alliance with the democratic opposition, the goals and decision rules of democracy and ecology run parallel. As a result, the environmental movement risks submersion into the democratic ideology, as is happening during the transition period. A distinct pattern emerges from this 'turbulence'. While environmental parties and groups in the Soviet union republics increase in strength under the aegis of nationalism as the old empire disintegrates, environmentalists in Eastern Europe are seeing their constituency dissolve in the triumph of democracy.

Environmental Cascades

Environmental cascades as they relate to Eastern Europe have two basic forms. The first is the cascade deriving from an environmental problem with social, economic and political spin-offs; the second is the cascade containing an environmental problem but deriving from economic and/or political mismanagement. In the first cascade, the environment is the primary issue; in the second, it is political economy. While both cascades are global in scope, the intensity of the second cascade is stronger, but in our opinion it can be more contained and is of shorter duration than the inherently environmental cascade. Examples will illustrate the differences in behaviour.

The first example is Chernobyl. Until the accident, large sections of the East European public were unconcerned about environmental issues. A few environmental groups, like the PEC and the Hungarian Blues, were fighting battles which remained relatively unpublicised. Chernobyl was the greening of Eastern Europe. Overnight, groups sprang up everywhere, some 200 in Poland alone. Even the Catholic Church organized its environmental group, the Society of St Francis of Assisi. The anti-nuclear protest in Poland set back the development of nuclear power in Poland by years. In Yugoslavia, the movement turned into a virtual moral crusade against the Communist authorities, breaking across republican lines with the aid of a sympathetic press. Nuclear protest also swept across Western Europe and crossed the Atlantic, where an informal moratorium on the further development of nuclear power dating from 1978 was reconfirmed and supported by the governors of the states of New York and Massachusetts (Rossin 1989).

The initial intensity of the cascade was of relatively short duration, lasting a year or so. But the basic problems of nuclear power are far from being solved in a manner acceptable to the public. 1989 and 1990 witnessed the publishing of additional information about the damage caused by Chernobyl, turning denuclearisation into a matter of national self-preservation in the Ukrainian and Belorussian republics. The duration of the cascade is thus unpredictable. And it may be expected that wherever nuclear power is an issue, including the disposal of nuclear waste and reactor safety or shutdown, the intensity will boil up to engulf the globe.

Moreover, nuclear power implies nuclear weapons. Indeed, the peace and ecology groups in the West do not distinguish between the two. Hence intensity will also flare up wherever and whenever nuclear disarmament and conventional arms reductions threaten to be reversed. It is significant that Gorbachev's initial proposal to take nuclear missiles out of Eastern Europe came after Chernobyl. Soviet willingness to reduce conventional arms is also a post-Chernobyl phenomenon. While the need to turn around the USSR's economic decline was doubtless the major rationale for Gorbachev's military decisions, the fact is that 'no nukes' is a global demand that will only cease when the fear of nuclear bombs ends. The nuclear cascade is then of long-term duration. As it bounces back and forth between Europe, Asia and America, and between the individual sovereign states and economic groups, its intensity will vary as all the actors continue to try to solve those aspects of nuclear power which endanger life and health (the environmental attractor) and to move toward a less dangerous-seeming world (the security attractor).

A second global environmental cascade is acid precipitation, since air pollution knows no frontiers. Environmental groups have formed everywhere in Eastern Europe to fight air pollution. Some, like most of the local groups or the 200 demonstrators in Chomutov, have utilised a serious local situation to focus public attention on a national problem. Others, like Poland's PEC, Zelenyi Svit in the Ukraine, and the committee in Ruse have gone on to embrace the totality of environmental issues. In general, the intensity of the cascade has remained low, but it has flared up whenever air quality is perceived to have seriously deteriorated. In East Germany, Bulgaria and Czechoslovakia, public protests against air pollution played significant roles in ending the Communist regimes. State system response to the demand for cleaner air through plant closures in Poland, or the promulgation of a new environmental policy in Bulgaria (Xinhua (Sofia), 9 May 1988) may have temporarily reduced the intensity of activity, but gave new life to the environmental crusade. By 1988, the acid rain cascade had spilled over East European borders, as environmental groups reached out to their counterparts within the bloc, and to Austria, Germany and the international environmental organizations. The expanded networking of environmental groups in 1989–90 drew international organizations (Greenpeace, Friends of the Earth) into the discovery of local East European pollution problems, thereby globalising them. The severity of trans-boundary air pollution in turn helped break down the borders of the East European state security system by mobilising adjacent state systems to action. In 1989, the GDR embarked on its first publicised effort to reduce sulphur dioxide emissions (Donovan 1989), and the East European nations moved towards their first serious attempt at regional environmental co-operation within CEMA (Sobell 1989). The democratic change speeded up government efforts to find western assistance for the acid rain problem.

Like nuclear power, acid precipitation is a long-term problem. Its close association with global climate change, which is just beginning to become a public issue in Eastern Europe, adds further turbulence to the cascade, prolonging its 'chaotic flow'. Like the nuclear cascade, the air pollution cascade bounces back and forth between the macro and micro levels of world politics and within the geographic fractals of these levels. As the East European environmental groups, supported by an increasingly well-knit international network, urge their governments toward participation in the globalisation of information and standardised solutions (autonomy dilemma), the intensity of the acid precipitation cascade will doubtless vary with the degree to which these governments are able to find the financial and technical means to implement solutions (security dilemma).

Environmental cascades sparked by the nature of political–economic decision-making are typified by giant projects: cases in point in the Soviet Union are the turning of the Siberian rivers and the development of the gigantic phosphate lode on the Estonian coast (Jancar 1987a, pp. 162–3, 206). Under glasnost, both projects were abandoned in the face of a huge public outcry. A proposal to construct the Caucasian Mountain Railway through some of the most impressive scenery in the Soviet Republic of Georgia was similarly revised and the railroad built through less nationally sensitive territory (Jancar 1988). Environmental consciousness may be said to have been born in Yugoslavia when the people learned that the federal government planned to build a hydro-electric dam across the Tara River Canyon, one of the most scenic gorges in Europe and protected under the United Nations Man and the Biosphere Programme. For many Slovenians, the nuclear plant at Krsko was the symbol of Communist monopoly control, as nuclear power came to be for people across Yugoslavia. Nagymaros is a classic example of Communist regime gigantomania. For Czechs and Slovaks, the proposed ten-unit nuclear power plant at Temelin in South Bohemia and the Gabcikovo Dam are the two main symbols of old regime economic and environmental irresponsibility. Interestingly, the new government has no plans to stop the projects. The Gabcikovo hydro-electric station is scheduled to go into operation with a modified water flow, while the number of units planned to go on line at Temelin has been reduced to three.

In all these instances, the scope of the cascade remained contained with a very high intensity. The cascade lasted until the decision was rescinded or modified, or the project abandoned. The role that these projects played in reifying the shortcomings of the Communist system cannot be overestimated. However, once disposition had been made of the problem, the cascade seemed to dry up overnight. In interviews across Eastern Europe in the summer of 1990, I found environmentalists and environmental officials alike concerned about the disappearance of environmental activism from the East European scene. People seemed to have lost interest in what were once very passionate issues. All over the area, the environmental movement was in disarray as the public returned to its private concerns. The movements founded on system inefficiency seemed to have faded away, their marginal utility gone.

With the drying-up of the most popular type of environmental cascade, the East European environmental movements today face a decision point. One course of action is to disband completely, and many appear to have done so. A second is to transform themselves into some low-intensity but permanently organized NGO under a roof environmental organization. And the third is to take the path of political power like the Greens. The Soviet groups are not yet at that decision point since reform is still not a reality. Those environmental groups who make the NGO decision are indirectly expressing their conviction that the democratic changes which have taken place do in fact provide sufficient opportunity to influence public decision-making. They will focus on getting laws passed and regulations implemented. The party decision implies a belief that the environment can be saved only through a radical transformation of western society. Taking the first option effectively contains the system-induced environmental cascade in its native East European and/or Soviet setting. Taking the second means the merging of a system-induced cascade typical of a particular area into the global flow, through the transformation of the East European problems of gigantomania and inefficiency from localised regional issues into problems characteristic of a whole industrial era.

The second option broadens the scope, increases the intensity, and prolongs the duration of the cascade indefinitely.

Conclusion

This chapter has sought to demonstrate the relevance of chaos theory to a specific international problem. It has shown that understanding the independent environmental movements in Eastern Europe as fractals of the multi-centred world enables us to posit a parallel pattern of behaviour whose parameters constantly shift, depending on changes in macro and micro conditions of authority, but the points of whose orbital path always fall between the security/autonomy, promotive/preservationist and ecology/democracy attractors. Whether the environmental groups' objectives explicitly included the development of democracy or the promotion of alternative politics, their insistence on autonomy from the state system as well as their belief in their right to make policy initiatives on one of the key problems of the day, made them important players in the parallel polis which developed in the former Communist states and correspondingly took root in world politics through the proliferation of non-state actors. Given the permanency of environmental cascades, the environmental movement is in a position to utilise the experience gained from the old regime, not only in Eastern Europe's transition to democratic, market-oriented societies, but in the world at large. Chaos theory in turn posits that environmentalists from other parts of the world seeking autonomous and active global roles will function within similar parameters as their East European and Soviet colleagues, as will the global environmental movement as a whole.

Defenders of the single international world of hegemonically organized nation-states may deplore the emergence of these highly activist non-state actors and dismiss chaos theory as non-applicable to the power concerns of nation-states. However, the world is becoming both more interdependent and more fragmented. Chaos theory enables us to identify the dynamic yet episodic patterns (cascades) in whole and fractal sets of seemingly unrelated political, economic and environmental events. Identification is a first step toward managing them.

References

Commoner, B. (1990). 'Environmental democracy is the planet's best hope', Utne Reader, No. 40 (July/August), pp. 61–3.

Devvatkin, D. (1988). 'Report from Estonia: An interview with a leader of the Green Movement', Environment, Vol. 30, No. 10 (December) pp. 13–15.

Donovan, B. (1989). 'New resolve to combat ecological decay in the GDR', RFE. RAD Background Report/31 (German Democratic Republic), 21 February.

Duncan, P. (1987). 'A new generation of opposition', *Sojourners*, Vol. 16, No. 9 (October), pp. 14–16.

Edwards, M. (1990). 'Siberia, in from the cold', *National Geographic*, Vol. 177, No. 3 (March), pp. 2–39.

Gleick, J. (1987). *Chaos: Making a New Science*. (New York: Viking Press, Penguin Books).

Gustavson, T. (1981). *Reform in Soviet Politics*. (Cambridge: Cambridge University Press).

Havel, V. (1985). *The Power of the Powerless*. (Armonk, NY: M. E. Sharpe, Inc.).

Helsinki Watch Committee (1987). *From Below: Independent Peace and Environmental Movements in Eastern Europe & the USSR: A Helsinki Watch Report*. (New York: Helsinki Watch, October).

Jancar, B. (1987a). *Environmental Management in the Soviet Union and Yugoslavia: Structure and Regulation in Communist Federal States*. (Durham, NC: Duke University Press).

Jancar, B. (1987b). 'Environmental politics in Eastern Europe in the 1980s.' Presented at Conference on Environmental Problems and Policies in Eastern Europe, Wilson Center, Smithsonian Institution, Washington, DC, 15–16 June.

Jancar, B. (1988). 'Testimony before the US Commission on Security and Cooperation in Europe', Washington, DC, 25 April.

Jancar, B. (1990). 'The East European environmental movement and the transformation of East European Society.' Paper delivered at the World Slavic Congress, Harrogate, UK, 21–6 July.

Jovanovic, D. (1988). 'Konacno-Moratorijum' (Finally – the Moratorium), *NIN*, 11 December, p. 70.

Konrad, G. (1988). 'The prerequisite of friendship', *Across Frontiers*, Vol. 4, Nos. 2 & 3 (Spring–Summer), pp. 30–1, 51.

Krivan, J. (1986). 'Ecology as deviance: The case of Pavel Krivan', *Across Frontiers*, Vol. II, Nos. 3 & 4 (Spring–Summer), pp. 15–18.

Kusin, V. V. (1990). 'The elections compared and assessed', RFE, *Report on Eastern Europe*, Vol. I, No. 28 (13 July) pp. 38–47.

Marples, D. (1990). 'The Greens and the "Ecological Catastrophe" in the Ukraine', Radio Liberty, *Report on the USSR*, II, 44 (2 November), p. 23.

Moldan, B. and Collective (1990). *Zivotni prostredi Ceske republiky* (The Environment of the Czech Republic). Czech Ministry of the Environment. (Prague: Academia Praha, pp. 7–39).

Perepletkin, Y. (1988). 'Attack on Yamal Suspended', *Izvestia*, 10 October, p. 2.

RFE (1988a). Czechoslovak SR/8, 3 June.

RFE (1988b). Czechoslovak SR/17, 21 October.

Rosenau, J. N. (1988). 'Patterned chaos in global life, structure and process in the two worlds of world politics,' *International Political Science Review*, Vol. 9, pp. 327–64.

Rosenau, J. N. (1990). *Turbulence in World Politics: A Theory of Change and Continuity*. (Princeton NY: Princeton University Press).

Rossin, A. D. (1989). 'Forgotten lessons of Three-Mile Island hurt US struggle for energy', *Harold-American* (Syracuse, NY), 19 March, pp. B1, B4.

Sobell, V. (1989). 'New multilateral initiatives in ecology', RFE, *RAD Background Report*/29 (Eastern Europe), 6 February.

Socor, V. (1989a). 'The Moldavian democratic movement: Structure, program and initial impact.' *RFE Background Report*/21 (USSR), 9 February.

Socor, V. (1989b). 'The Moldavian Greens: An independent ecological association in the Moldavian SSR', *RFE Background Report*/39 (USSR), 7 March.

'Special report on environmental politics in Hungary' (1987). *Across Frontiers*, Vol. III, No. 4 (Summer–Fall), pp. 6–13.

Starzewska, A. (1988). 'The Polish People's Republic', in Barbara Rhode (ed.), *Air Pollution in Europe, Volume 2: Socialist Countries*. (Vienna: European Coordination Centre for Research and Documentation in the Social Sciences, p. 9).

Sundijev, I. Yu. (1988). 'Unofficial young people's associations: Attempting an exposition', *Sotsiologicheskiye issledovania*, Vol. 5 (September–October), pp. 56–62.

Comparing Green Parties

WOLFGANG RÜDIG

Department of Government, University of Strathclyde, Glasgow, UK

S. Parkin, *Green Parties: An International Guide.* London: Heretic Press, 1989.
F. Müller-Rommel (ed.), *New Politics in Western Europe: The Rise and Success of Green Parties and Alternative Lists.* Boulder, CO.: Westview Press, 1989.
H. Kitschelt, *The Logics of Party Formation: Ecological Politics in Belgium and West Germany.* Ithaca, N.Y.: Cornell University Press 1989.
H. Kitschelt and S. Hellemans, *Beyond the European Left: Ideology and Political Action in the Belgian Ecology Parties.* Durham, N.C.: Duke University Press 1990.

Green parties have now been with us for almost twenty years. They have been set up in every Western European country, and have been spreading to Eastern Europe as well. Even a cursory glance at individual green parties will show that the differences between them are quite substantial. The size, internal organisation, policy orientation, electoral success, policy impact, to name only a few areas, all show some pronounced variations.

It is thus an obvious challenge to the social sciences to document, describe and explain these differences. The implications are important: some variations, for example in the area of party organisation, form the substance of almost continuous debate within most green parties. A comparative analysis of the variety and impact of different organisational forms could provide some insights of immediate practical importance. From an academic point of view, the rise of green parties in their different forms poses a number of interesting questions. Naturally, social scientists are generally interested in explaining why these parties have emerged, why they are adopting particular forms and strategies, and whether they will quickly disappear again, or not. More fundamentally, the phenomenon of the greens provides an excellent opportunity to test a range of theories of the development of party systems, the effects of different electoral laws, or the idea of an 'iron law of oligarchy' sweeping away any pretence of genuine inner-party democracy, to name three of the most popular areas. It is really only the comparative analysis of green parties and their development within different types of political systems which can give us the opportunity to explore these questions systematically.

The empirical analysis of green parties has made some great strides forward in recent years. An internationally comparative treatment of the subject has, however, remained relatively rare. Detlev Murphy and Ferdinand Müller's discussion of the emergence and electoral potential of green protest parties, published in 1979, is probably the first academic treatment of the subject (Murphy *et al.* 1979). A more systematic overview, entitled 'Ecology parties in Western Europe', was first presented by Ferdinand Müller-Rommel to the Fourth Annual Meeting of the International Society of Political Psychology in June 1981, and later published in *West European Politics* (Müller-Rommel 1981, 1982). Another early attempt to compare green parties goes back to November 1981 when E.G. Frankland presented his paper 'Ecology, ideology and party politics: A comparative perspective' to the Northwestern Political Science Assocation (Frankland 1981). Since these early days, the amount of information available has increased substantially, in line with the continuous international spread of green parties around the world. There is thus clearly a need for books providing a general overview of the development of green parties around the world. The first book which genuinely tried to achieve this aim was Patrick Florizoone's book *De groenen* published in Flemish in 1985. In English, we had to wait until 1989 before two contributions tried to fill the gap.

Sara Parkin's *Green Parties: An International Guide* is exactly what it says it is: a very comprehensive and impressively compiled guide to green parties around the world. Ms Parkin, who has played an active part in the British Green Party for at least ten years and who shot to fame during the highly successful 1989 European elections compaign, is not an academic, and her book should not be judged in these terms. She is an insider, having acted as the British Greens' International Liaison Secretary for many years. She was also secretary of the European Greens for three years, and she has travelled the world to meet green activists. She is thus the ideal person to write a book like this, and, overall, she has made a rather good job of it.

Sara Parkin's book mainly consists of individual country chapters in which information on green politics in that particular country is provided in a systematic form. All country chapters follow a set format. Each chapter starts with some basic statistics about the country and its green party (date of foundation and number of members), followed by a brief rundown of the general historical background, usually taken from nineteenth- and twentieth-century history. A statement of the key electoral conditions, such as the electoral system, conditions for gaining access to the ballot, party financing, and access to the media during election campaigns, concludes this first part. The second part looks at the factors affecting the development of green politics and is usually made up of a summary of the main environmental and other post-war conflicts which had an influence on the greens. The third part of each chapter turns to the green party or parties themselves, providing details about their history, electoral record, internal organisations, and general political development. A fourth part gives an assessment of the future prospects of green politics in that particular country. Each country chapter is concluded by an appendix listing party publications, academic and non-academic writings about the party, addresses, a graph of the internal organisation, and a table with the party's election results so far.

The book is a treasure trove of information, and Sara Parkin has used her position at the heart of green politics in Europe to collect an enormous amount of information. Particularly impressive are the frequent listings of non-English publications. Anybody interested in gaining a basic overview of what has happened in green politics in Europe over the last ten to twenty years must read this book, and, at the very moderate price of £4.95 (US: $10.95), it is an extremely good buy.

Apart from this comprehensive overview of facts, is there any interpretation of the reasons for the emergence of green parties, of the condition of durability, of success or failure? The author does not provide us with any final conclusions. Although interpretations of individual cases can be found throughout the book, there is no easily digested round-up of the essence of the experience of green politics thus far. Is there any pattern? Do decentralist parties always fare worse than centralist ones? Does an opening to the left pay-off in electoral terms? What determines green parties' electoral success or failure?

If we want answers to these questions, we are given some scattered clues. The structure of each chapter already gives us some indications about relevant factors. The general history of a country is obviously presumed to have some bearing on the character of green politics, as are more specific factors such as the electoral conditions (including the way votes are counted and processed and the conditions for parties to gain access to the ballot in the first place), the opportunities to claim financial public support for party activity, and the access to the media during campaigns. While these factors can realistically be expected to have some sort of impact, the author clearly falls short in terms of analysing them. The link between the 'general history' and the account of green politics often appears to be non-existent and is rarely made explicit. Equally, relatively little use is made of any of these data in the sections which explain the current and future prospects of green parties.

A more common denominator is an interest in the internal workings of green parties. How are they organised, and has this an impact on their standing? Internal organisation has clearly been at the forefront of British debates, but the book shows how it has also been an important issue throughout virtually the whole globe. Despite this awareness of importance, it is very difficult to reach any type of general conclusion from the experience of various countries. While a lack of effective organisation is given a very high value to explain the problems of the British Greens, for example, Parkin shows an understanding of the highly-decentralised organisational set-ups in Italy and New Zealand, and in the latter case argues quite convincingly that with whatever internal organisation, the external opportunity structures for the Values Party in the late 1970s and 1980s were very bad and that a different organisation would not have made any difference.

Here we are at a point where social scientists should be involved: Parkin has provided us with a very useful database and attempts to explain each individual case. Looked at as a whole, it is clear that different types of explanations are competing with each other. How important are electoral systems, party financing laws, and, indeed, internal organisation? We need a more systematic and truly comparative analysis: looking at individual cases often can lead us astray. This is particularly relevant in this case where the author has been personally involved in some of the most ardent discussions.

An 'insider' writing about his or her daily concerns always faces the danger of remaining too close to the subject matter, obscuring independent judgement. Overall, Sara Parkin has been remarkably successful in avoiding this pitfall. The accounts of the development of individual green parties are generally fair and balanced but at specific points the more laid-back style makes way for some strong statements. For example, Parkin was strongly involved in the international debate about the Dutch 'Small Left' parties claiming to make use of the label 'green', and the passion felt is still evident in the passages on this episode. Also, the author does not shrink away from making fairly outspoken comments on the actions of fellow-party members in the case of the 'Maingreen' initiative of 1986.

Fortunately, this type of writing is rather rare. If one looks for comprehensive explanations, one will not find them here but instead the book provides a valuable round-up of the main developments of green parties around the world. As so much has changed in the world since publication of this book in 1989, a second edition, with full details of new developments in Eastern Europe, would be highly desirable.

The second major publication attempting to provide a general overview of green politics, this time limited to a consideration of Western Europe, is the book *New Politics in Western Europe: The Rise and Success of Green Parties and Alternative Lists*, edited by Ferdinand Müller-Rommel.

The core of this volume consists of country case-studies which are written by leading specialists on the particular national parties. Case studies are provided for Austria, Belgium, Denmark, West Germany, Finland, France, Great Britain, Italy, Ireland, Luxembourg, Sweden, and Switzerland, and a separate chapter is devoted to the organisation of the Greens in the

European Parliament. Unfortunately, there is no chapter on the rather interesting case of The Netherlands. Each individual case study has the same structure. It starts with a brief summary of the development of green politics before turning to the parties' organisational structure, electoral support, programmatic profile, and record of government participation. A look into the future concludes each of these chapters. It is obvious that the editor has required individual contributors to present their material in a comparable form. He has been largely successful in this, although some case-study authors look at the points in a difference sequence or leave out certain aspects. For a volume of this nature, the degree of conformity is quite high and this certainly enhances the usefulness of the book.

Outside the realm of influence of any editor is, of course, the nature of the research results available on each party: here there are some major imbalances. Some authors are able to provide new data, sometimes previously unpublished or not available in English: this makes such chapters particularly useful. Other chapters provide little, if any, new information. Nevertheless, these case studies are quite useful and provide the reader with a state-of-the-art report which was fairly up-to-date at the time of publication. (All case studies were completed in 1988.)

Beyond the provision of basic data on the development of green parties, *New Politics in Western Europe* also aims to provide an impetus for the theoretically-inspired explanation of the green politics phenomenon. In his introduction, Ferdinand Müller-Rommel provides not only a general, albeit very brief and necessarily simplistic, overview of the standing of green parties around the world, he also broadly endorses an Inglehart-inspired, 'value change' – oriented explanation which sees the rise of green parties in terms of the emergence of a new cleavage in which the post-materialist 'new politics' confronts the materialist 'old politics'. Müller-Rommel merely states the main tenets of this position which has dominated much of the writing on green movements and parties; he does not engage in any discussion of alternative propositions or possible limits of such an approach. Disappointingly, the definition of 'green parties' as 'new politics parties' is thus rather uncritically accepted. There is no real discussion about what exactly constitutes a 'new politics party'. Are there 'new politics' parties which are not green parties for example? Or green parties which are not 'new politics' parties? And how about the distinction between 'green parties' and 'alternative lists' alluded to in the book's subtitle, a matter which is not identified explicitly as a topic worthy of further discussion in the book itself? It is perfectly defensible to classify green parties as 'new politics' parties, but it would have strengthened Müller-Rommel's position if a little more care had been taken to define these concepts and then discuss them more explicitly.

Admittedly, the introduction's theoretical ambitions were very limited, and the main theoretical contribution to the debate was intended to come from the two concluding articles, by Thomas Poguntke and Jens Alber. These two chapters present interestingly contrasted views: Poguntke argues within the 'new politics' framework, and Alber suggests a rather different approach, focusing on the career opportunities of young university graduates.

Essentially, Poguntke's article seeks to provide criteria to allow a more sophisticated classification of green parties into 'new politics parties' and what Poguntke calls 'conservative "green" formations' which do not share a 'left-wing, emancipatory' outlook going beyond 'mere' ecology. In other words, Poguntke concedes that there are two basic types of green parties, 'new politics' parties and non-'new politics' parties. By implication, he also suggests that there are 'new politics' parties who are not green parties, presumably parties such as the group of 'new left' parties in Norway, The Netherlands, Switzerland, and Italy, although he never discusses this and concentrates instead solely on explicitly 'green' parties. Poguntke proceeds to define criteria in three areas: programmatic outlook, unconventional political style, and electoral profile. He concludes that the Austrian United Greens and the Swiss Green Party could not be classified as 'new politics' parties. Overall, I think the design of this classification and the way it is used is rather frustrating. First, the range of parties subjected to the analysis is rather limited. Given the proliferation of green parties throughout the world, it is an important theoretical and practical problem to distinguish 'real' green parties from those who adopt a green mantle for purely opportunistic reasons. Poguntke's approach seems to make it very easy for 'left-wing' parties to claim to be green, a position which would certainly be rejected by many mainstream green parties. Secondly, the analysis does not focus at all on differences between the mainstream green parties which are seen as 'new politics' green parties. For example, while the German Greens' identity as part of the 'Left' would surely be shared by a large majority of activists, the British and French green parties have always rejected, in very strong terms, any such association.

Undoubtedly, the most interesting and challenging theoretical piece in this volume is provided by Jens Alber's chapter entitled 'Modernisation, cleavage structure, and the rise of green parties and lists in Europe'. Essentially based on a paper published in 1985 in German, Alber argues that the rise of the Greens is related to the emergence of new cleavages which are defined in rather different terms than Inglehart and his 'new politics' followers surmise. The key structural change he sees is the 'educational revolution'. According to Alber, the arrival of mass education led to a situation where a large number of highly-educated graduates could not be absorbed by the labour market, particularly at a time when the public

sector expansion had come to an end. It is this group of young, highly educated people who are not integrated into the system either economically
or politically which provides the protest potential from which the Greens
draw their main support. It could thus be expected that it is 'students and
other groups outside the labour force' who form the backbone of the
Greens. Alber cites results of surveys in Germany, France and Austria in
support of this thesis but concedes that the international data situation does
not allow a proper empirical test of this hypothesis. (Recent comparative
analysis of green voting does find some support for this thesis but only in
Germany and not in other European countries; see Franklin and Rüdig
1991.)

In addition to this hypothesis about the social composition of green
supporters, Alber briefly tries to explain international differences between
green parties by looking at other variables. In addition to the electoral
thresholds for representation, Alber proposes three other variables char-
acterising the political 'setting' in which green parties have to operate: the
strength of the old labour–capital conflict, the strategy of established left-
wing parties (co-operation or conflict), and the position of the main left-
wing party in government or opposition during the formation phase of
green parties. Alber predicts that green parties will be more successful
where the labour–capital conflict has decreased in importance, where the
main left-wing party has engaged in co-operation rather than conflict, and
where it has been in government during the formation phase of green parties. A quick survey of various European countries leads to the conclusion
that conditions for green parties are best in West Germany, Switzerland, and
Austria: all countries in which green parties have enjoyed some electoral success. On the other hand, countries such as Belgium do not fit this model.

Alber thus provides a number of hypotheses, but they are not necessarily moving into the same direction. Each of the variables which Alber
suggests is associated with the rise of green parties could quite plausibly
contribute to an explanation. But how, if at all, do they combine, and
which variables are the really important ones? It is comparatively easy to
find support for bivariate relationships of various types, either at the individual or aggregate level: it is rather more of a challenge to combine these
various factors in a proper model which can be tested at multivariate level
and which should then lead to more complex explanations. Some of the
ingredients for such an attempt are there, but Alber does not pursue it any
further. (It should be noted that other comparative studies have shed
major doubt on the value of Alber's theory of green parties as a 'representation of highly-trained age cohorts with blocked mobility chances' (p.
205). For data on green voters, see Franklin and Rüdig 1991; for aggregate cross-national analysis of the success of green parties, see Kitschelt
1988 and Müller-Rommel 1990.)

Overall, Müller-Rommel's book is a useful addition to the literature on comparative parties in that it provides both basic information and some good (and not so good) theories about the comparative analysis of these parties. This, however, is all it does. It provides an entry point for the real social science analysis, but not the analysis itself.

Parkin and Müller-Rommel are raising a lot of questions about various aspects of green parties. How and why are they formed, what is their organisational structure, what is the socio-economic background of their members and voters, what determines whether they are electorally successful, are they able to influence policy making, and so on. But if we look beyond the mainly descriptive studies providing a broad overview, we find rather little in terms of systematic comparative analysis. There are quite a number of individual country case-studies, and not surprisingly, studies of the German Greens are most common (for example, Hülsberg 1988, Kolinsky 1989). But even here the coverage does not live up to expectations for a profound, empirically grounded and theoretically sophisticated social science analysis.

The exception to this dearth of serious comparative analysis is the work of Herbert Kitschelt whose two pioneering books on the German and Belgian Greens provide an inspirational analysis which will hopefully stimulate more serious empirical work of a comparative nature. Kitschelt's *The Logics of Party Formation: Ecological Politics in Belgium and West Germany* (1989) and Kitschelt and Helleman's *Beyond the European Left: Ideology and Action in Belgian Ecology Parties* (1990) provide the first cases of incisive empirical analysis of green parties on a comparative basis.

Kitschelt's *The Logics of Party Formation* makes a major contribution to the literature, combining theoretical sophistication with profound empirical inquiry. Kitschelt looks both at the macro- and the micro-political level, seeking to explain both the behaviour of individual activists and the differences between regions and nations. Quite apart from the theoretical contribution, his analysis of the internal workings of green parties is immensely perceptive. Anybody familiar with green politics in Germany, Belgium, or probably any other country will easily recognise the phenomena he is describing, and it is not just academics but also those engaged in green politics who could benefit from reading this book, despite its highly academic and sometimes inaccessible style. Unfortunately, it is only published in hardback at a rather forbidding price ($49.45) by a US university press and therefore not readily available to green activists in Europe.

The major contribution of this book is the description and analysis of the internal workings of the German Greens and the two Belgian ecology parties, mainly based on intensive interviews with 134 German and Belgian green party activists carried out in 1985. After an analysis of the international development of what Kitschelt terms 'left-libertarian' parties, a consideration of various theories, and a brief introduction to the historical development of green parties in West Germany and Belgium, Kitschelt presents his results in six densely-written chapters on the process of getting involved in party politics, local activism, the internal functioning of the parties, the recruitment of 'leaders', the links to social movements, and the debate about participation in government. A chapter on the future of left-libertarian parties concludes the volume.

What holds this book together and makes it important is its great theoretical sophistication. Not only do a number of themes run through the book, but the author also draws on his knowledge of a wide variety of other theories to discuss individual aspects of green politics. The most basic starting point is his theory of 'left-libertarianism'. This is the idea that there is a new group of parties, of which the German and Belgian green parties are members, characterised by a combination of traditional left-wing concerns for social justice and redistribution of wealth, and libertarian concern focusing on individual autonomy and citizen participation. Kitschelt thus defines what others have called 'new politics' movements and parties predominantly in terms of the form which characterises them rather than the substance of their concerns – in other words the issues, such as environmental issues – on which they are mobilising. The mobilisation of these 'left-libertarian' concerns in the 'new social movements' forms the most important independent variable that Kitschelt employs. He carefully distinguishes between areas of high and low mobilisation of left-libertarian movements and seeks to show that this has a major effect on the internal workings of these parties. The other major categories he relies on stem from a classification of party activists. He identifies three types of activists: there are ideologues, mainly identified with the 'fundamentalists' in the German context, who want a participatory party, a broad programme and who favour a radical strategy; lobbyists are characterised by a more narrow, programmatic (for example environmental) concern; the third group are the pragmatists, or 'realists', who want a broad programme but a moderate strategy and a party organisation geared towards electoral effectiveness. Ideologues primarily have a background in 'New Left' politics of the 1960s and 1970s as well as involvement in 'left-libertarian' movements; lobbyists are more narrowly-based on movement activists, while realists, predominantly, come from other established parties or are complete political novices.

What are the most important results of Kitschelt's study? Overall, I think that it is the ideal of 'grass roots democracy' which is most comprehensively dismantled by this book. Kitschelt shows very convincingly that the ideas about the internal structure of green parties are mostly misplaced. Radicals, Kitschelt argues, have no proper conception of the forces which commit individuals to an organization and which make them become active in it. As a result they build internal structures which try to avoid any formalisation of power relations by means such as placing restrictions on the length any elected position can be held by any individual and, most importantly, by the allocation of decision-making powers to a plethora of bodies which are relatively independent of each other. However, individual members have very different resources which they can devote to party activity. Inevitably, it is those with the greatest resources, such as spare time, political experience, oratory skills, and so on, who play a greater role than others, and who relatively quickly form an 'informal' elite running the party. With its delegation of power to a wide variety of bodies at various levels, the structure of the party works against this natural force and restricts the exercise of any power or control by these informal elites. Referring to Eldersveld's notion of 'stratarchies', Kitschelt describes green parties' internal power structure as being highly fragmented and, consequently, the party is largely unable to pursue any effective political strategies. Kitschelt thus identifies some major dilemmas. The attempt to create a true grass roots democracy within green parties has several unintentional consequences, among them a weakening of strategic capabilities.

This book clearly has pioneering features, but it also has several weaknesses which should not be overlooked. First, the empirical basis on which this book is based is rather limited. As explained in the appendix, all attempts to gain permission to undertake a survey of Green Party members in Germany have so far failed. Kitschelt thus relies on his intensive interviews with a selected group of party activists as well as studying party literature and direct observation. Such a limitation is rather severe, and many of the hypotheses and theories discussed by Kitschelt ideally would require a much larger database to be properly tested: many of the current results are based on fairly limited evidence. This shortcoming is further exacerbated by a concentration on long-standing party activists. While Kitschelt made every effort to speak to a wide variety of activists with different characteristics, even he does not claim that they represent a random sample of activists. Furthermore, many, if not most, of his hypotheses really require a membership survey, taking into account the views of ordinary and passive party members. While Kitschelt is very careful always to qualify the validity of his results on the basis of his limited data set, the complete lack of data on ordinary party members is a major shortcoming which, I feel, is not sufficiently recognised in the presentation of the results. Therefore, we have to be very careful in interpreting some of the conclusions reached in his book.

A second weakness which has to be addressed concerns the role of theory and its relation to empirical inquiry. It is obvious that this book is theory-driven and, despite valiant attempts to support the choice of categories with empirical data, I cannot help feeling that Kitschelt is running a not insubstantial risk of imposing a theory on the subject, particularly given the limitations of the data-set.

These weaknesses do have some major implications for the central thrust of the book – the attempt to demonstrate that left-libertarian parties are different and will remain different from the established parties. Central to this idea is the distinction between the 'logic of party competition' – parties will change their programme and organisation in order to maximise votes – and the 'logic of constituency representation' typical of left-libertarian parties – parties will reflect the aims and structures of left-libertarian movements. As the form of political discourse is centrally important to left-libertarians, they will continue to press for open, participatory, not hierarchically structured party organisations. Kitschelt argues that a move towards a logic of party competition is by no means inevitable or likely, given the strength of movement-socialised radicals.

However, there are quite convincing reasons for the opposite to happen, even if we take Kitschelt's own reasoning into account. If, as Kitschelt suggests, most activists are socialised by a pre-1979 social movement experience and new members are far less involved and influenced by this socialisation, if social movements have all but disappeared and do not offer themselves as an alternative political outlet, and if the ties of activists to green parties are slight with a great deal of turnover, then it would be reasonable to presume that the drive to what Kitschelt calls the 'logic of electoral competition' would strongly increase. It would have been interesting to see to what extent passive members were already geared towards a logic of electoral competition in the mid-1980s. The developments in the last six years suggest that internal party structures are by no means as untouchable as might have been thought, and that the moves towards a logic of electoral competition is growing stronger and stronger. Since 1985, the experience of political failure (mainly in Germany) and the cumulative experience of internal party decision-making seems to have pushed the party inexorably away from a logic of constituency representation, quite apart from the fact that the 'constituency' of left-libertarian movements has also weakened in strength substantially. In a sense, then, it seems that Kitschelt is reluctant to draw the obvious conclusion, that, after going through an inital transition period, green parties may end up looking not so politically different after all.

Such a conclusion would, however, go right to the heart of Kitschelt's notion of left-libertarianism. It would mean that green parties are prepared to change their principles about the form of conducting politics in order to maximise their material political impact or, perhaps more realistically, to survive as a viable political force. The original premise on which the theory of left-libertarianism is built would thus have disappeared.

On other grounds, I am not convinced that the notion of 'left-libertarian' movements and parties as the key generic term makes sense. It is indeed strange that all theorists of green politics discussed in this article, Poguntke, Alber, and now Kitschelt, ignore the material aims and issues which brought them to the fore – concern for the environment (for more on this point, see Rüdig 1990). The term 'ecological' is used in the book's subtitle, but this is of no theoretical consequence, and the German and Belgian Greens are thrown together with other New Left parties. Indeed, there seems to be very little, if any, difference between the theory of left-libertarianism and that of the 'new politics'. A focus on the specifically ecological element of green politics, the tie which binds green parties of various types together, would perhaps be an analytically more fruitful starting point.

The breadth and complexity of this book makes it impossible to do justice to it within such a brief review. There are other achievements to be recognised, but also many other critical points which could be made. For example, the title is rather strange as there is very little in the book which is, specifically, concerned with the formation process of green parties. More importantly, perhaps, the comparative element is not as prominent as might have been expected. Most important points could be made with reference to the German Greens only.

Nevertheless, despite the problems, this book is a great achievement and will surely remain a standard point of reference for any future work on green politics.

Kitschelt and Hellemans' *Beyond the European Left* can be seen as a sequel to *The Logics of Party Formation*. Contrary to their experiencies in Germany, Kitschelt and his collaborator were successful in carrying out a survey of activists of the two Belgian green parties, AGALEV and ECOLO. A structured self-completion questionnaire was handed to about 400 party members attending the 1985 AGALEV and ECOLO national conferences. A total of 256 questionnaires were returned to the authors, a response rate of more than 60 per cent. This database opened up the opportunity to test some of the hypotheses developed in the first volume, and also to look at other areas more closely. The basic theoretical framework chosen is exactly the same as in the previous volume.

Do they succeed? The volume presents a wealth of interesting, and sometimes fascinating, empirical data which, as the authors quite rightly point out, were completely unique and unmatched by any other survey of this kind when the book was published. We learn quite a lot about the socio-economic profile of members, their previous political activities, current political views, and so on. At the end of the volume, however, I could not help being somewhat disappointed.

One of the main problems with this study is that the authors find it very difficult to get hold of any major significant variances in their sample. This is not entirely surprising as AGALEV and ECOLO are rather more homogenous than the German Greens. Furthermore, this study is still dealing with national activists and excludes passive party members. Kitschelt and Hellemans do their best to find variances, but they are forced to concentrate most of the time on the difference between the Flemish Greens, AGALEV, and the Walloon Greens, ECOLO. In Kitschelt's terminology, 'left-libertarian' movement mobilisation was somewhat more pronounced in Flanders than it was in Wallonia, and this, again, is the main independent variable which is employed countless times to explain, to a greater or lesser degree, the often quite minor variances between the two parts of the country.

Even with such a survey, the small size of the sample makes it very difficult to say much about differences between sub-samples, particularly if we are looking at each of the parties separately. The authors struggle valiantly, mobilising multivariate techniques such as multiple regression and factor analysis. Rather than focusing so much on the difference between the two parties, emphasising macro-political variables, a greater concentration on differences between individual attitudes and forms of behaviour might have been preferable. The authors do cover these aspects, but only relatively briefly, and they make no great attempt to develop more complex theoretical perspectives. But to some considerable extent, these problems are again linked to the types of data they have available.

Herbert Kitschelt's work on the German and Belgian Greens has given us ideas which will guide empirical research on green politics for many years to come. The quality of this work again highlights the large gaps that still remain to be filled in our understanding of the comparative development of green parties.

References

Alber, J. (1985). 'Modernisierung, neue Spannungslinien und die politischen Chancen der Grünen', *Politische Vierteljahresschrift*, Vol. 26, pp. 211–26.

Florizoone, P. (1985). *De groenen: Ideën, Bewegingen en Partijen* (Kluwer Politieke Bibliotheek).

Frankland, E. G. (1981). 'Ecology, ideology and party politics: A comparative perspective', Paper presented at the Annual Meeting of Northwestern Political Science Association, Newark, N.J., November.

Franklin, M. N. and Rüdig, W. (1991). *The Greening of Europe: Ecological Voting in the 1989 European Elections*. Strathclyde Papers in Government and Politics, No. 82 (Glasgow: Department of Government, University of Strathclyde).

Hülsberg, W. (1988). *The German Greens: A Social and Political Profile*. (London: Verso).

Kitschelt, H. (1988), 'Left-libertarian parties: Explaining innovation in competitive party systems', *World Politics*, Vol. 40, pp. 194-234.

Kolinsky, E. (ed.) (1989). *The Greens in West Germany: Organisation and Policy Making.* (Oxford: Berg Publishers).

Müller-Rommel, F. (1981). 'Ecology parties in Western Europe', Paper presented at the round table on The Politics of Environmental Concern, Fourth Annual Meeting of the International Society of Political Psychology, Mannheim, 24–7 June.

Müller-Rommel, F. (1982). 'Ecology parties in Western Europe', *West European Politics*, Vol. 5, pp. 68–74.

Müller-Rommel, F. (1990). 'Political success of green parties in Western Europe', Paper presented at the Annual Meeting of the American Political Science Association, San Francisco, August–September.

Murphy, D., Rubart, F., Müller, F. and Raschke, J. (1979). *Protest: Grüne, Bunte und Steuerrebellen.* (Reinbek: Rowohlt).

Rüdig, W. (1990). *Explaining Green Party Development: Reflections on a Political Framework.* Strathclyde Papers in Government and Politics, No. 71 (Glasgow: Department of Government, University of Strathclyde).

Developing Green Political Theory

ADRIAN ATKINSON
Development Planning Unit, University College, London, UK

Andrew Dobson, *Green Political Thought*. London: Unwin Hyman, 1990.

In 1973, Hans Magnus Enzensberger published a lengthy essay entitled 'A critique of political ecology'. In it he laid out an initial analysis of a new social movement that had arisen intent upon taking action to head off impending environmental catastrophe as outlined in a series of writing in the early seventies. The essay was prescient in the seriousness with which it took both the problems and the nascent movement, and predicted that a long process of politicisation and maturation lay ahead of the movement. Almost twenty years have elapsed since that essay was written. The kinds of environmental problems which 'The limits to growth' and other environmentalist writings warned of have shown more definite signs of emerging and the movement has, indeed, gone through a long process of maturation, emerging latterly as the 'Green Movement'.

Following a long phase of campaigning and pamphleteering, the movement entered more seriously the political arena and also took to providing more substantial published statements of its contentions and intentions. Meanwhile, academic analysts initiated attempts to define the movement in terms of social purpose and structure. A series of books appeared in the UK in the later 1970s and early 1980s – notably by O'Riordan (1976), Lowe and Goyder (1983), Sandbach (1980), Cotgrove (1982) and Pepper (1984) – attempting to analyse, within various frameworks, aspects of what they saw as important about the movement.

In general it is necessary to note that none of these was able satisfactorily either to subsume the movement into the existing conventional sociological wisdom or to understand the inner coherence of the movement itself; there was discussion of a 'New ecological paradigm', but no sense of what that might amount to. As the 1980s wore on, generally sympathetic acknowledgement of the existence and even the importance of, albeit ill-defined 'new social movements', subsuming the Green Movement, slipped into the mainstream of conventional sociological analysis.

However, during the second half of the 1980s more substantial approaches, in English, to analysing the structure and purpose of the movement were more or less restricted to attempts from politically orthodox right and left positions – notably those of Frankel (1987), Mellos (1988), Bramwell (1989) and Denitch (1990) – to defame and/or dismiss the ambitions of the Green Movement. Raymond Williams' *Towards 2000* (1983) provided the one major contrasting view, emphasising the importance of green concerns and projects to any viable future and noting the way in which these were being effectively jammed by the prevailing politics and culture. It is quite remarkable, in spite of the now widespread representation by Greens at all levels of government in Europe, if not yet in the UK, how, with the exception of a few monographs specifically on green parties – notably Capra and Spretnak (1984), Hülsberg (1988) and Parkin (1989) – conventional political science continues to avoid altogether more than passing acknowledgement of their presence.

There can be little doubt that a major problem that has stood in the way of an adequate academic theorisation of the Green Movement lies in the incommensurability between the purpose of the movement and the methods of academic analysis. Although social analytical method has, in recent years, been evolving rapidly out of its earlier iron positivist mould that only concerned itself with behaviour and refused to acknowledge social aspirations or intentions, there still remains a significant level of unwillingness to accept the theoretical validity of views and attitudes – and indeed to a degree even actions – that are generated outside, in the broader society, rather than internal to the academic process. Academia jealously guards its prerogative to produce theory on behalf of society, to 'explain' society to itself.

Perhaps the appearance of Andrew Dobson's *Green Political Thought* is an indication that the walls between academia and the real world are crumbling. On the other hand, this book may remain an isolated case. The point is that we now have the first sympathetic attempt to look for coherence and consistency within the theory and practice of the Green Movement itself, relating this more loosely to certain wider theoretical contexts rather than subjecting it to any procrustean theoretical analysis. It should be added that Dobson has been very much assisted, in contrast to the analyses of the movement in the early 1980s, by the great increase in books written by participants in the movement stating more coherently what they think the movement is all about.

The general structure of Dobson's approach is clear and straightforward. The introduction outlines a few of the main points of the argument and in particular states two contextual contentions as follows: 'ecologism', sometimes referred to in the book as 'political ecology' and referred to throughout the book as Green with a capital 'G', cannot be subsumed into other major political ideologies but is a discrete political ideology in its own right; and ecologism, as a political ideology, is not the same as environmentalism – referred to in the text as green with a small 'g' – which is a concern to improve the technical management of the environment. Ecologism challenges in a major way the Enlightenment foundations of the modern world-view.

There are just five main chapters: the first sets the scene, analysing the motivations and main concepts around which ecologism is organized; the second looks at the philosophical ideas generated, or otherwise subscribed to, by the ecologists; the third looks at the kind of 'sustainable society' which the ecologists seek to build; the fourth looks at the strategies which the ecologists pursue towards achieving their goals; and the fifth looks at the connections and contrasts between ecologism, socialism and feminism. There is also a brief conclusion.

Ecologism arises from the conviction that economic growth cannot continue indefinitely and if we are to head off dire consequences from continuing with this, it will be necessary for us radically to change the structure and mode of functioning of our society. Improved environmental management alone will not work: we need a new view of our relationship with nature and with one another. Ecologists believe this message is not aimed at any particular interests but has universal appeal: we are all part of the holistic ecological process and must respect this and act accordingly.

So ecologists believe that they lie neither to the political right nor the political left. An analysis of their policies and attitudes reveals that, in view of their challenge to Enlightenment ideology, they can be seen in some respects as left wing and in others as right. An important point made by Dobson here is that whilst the green perspective involves in many respects a reworking of old ideas, such as Malthusianism, 'history defines the context within which ecologism operates (and therefore helps to define ecologism itself), and provides the ground on which old themes acquire new resonances, coalescing to form a full-blown modern political ideology'.

In looking at the philosophical foundations of ecologism, Dobson starts by noting how the ecologists have looked for the reflection of egalitarianism and holistic modes of organization in nature to justify their views about an appropriate form of society and our relationship with nature. This they have found in Capra's reinterpretation of particle physics and in the science of ecology. But their attempt to find justification for their attitudes and actions in Lovelock's notion of Gaia – that the biosphere as a whole is a sentient organism – raises problems because, whilst the ecologists are concerned to reorganize society so that mankind can survive, Gaia, in Lovelock's view, may be quite happy to extirpate humanity if this ensures her own health. This introduces the problem of environmental ethics.

Dobson investigates at some length the ideas of the 'ecophilosophers' and their theories of 'deep ecology'. A very extensive debate arose over the desire to adjust the relative importance of man and nature within the framework of ethical discourse and belief. Initially this revolved around the issue of the 'intrinsic value' of nature, the extension of 'rights' to non-human species and to develop a notion of 'biospherical egalitarianism'. Foundering on the problem of operationalisation – in theory, let alone practice – the emphasis of the debate shifted to a concern for 'states of being' and 'changes in consciousness'. The debate has, however, suffered badly from a lack of rootedness in social conditions and practice which might motivate and maintain any 'change of consciousness'. Indeed, this failure to address practical questions has brought it into sharp contradiction with much of the development of green policy and hence 'ecophilosophy's failure to address the issue of social practice will disqualify it from ever formulating a satisfactory solution to the problems that have given rise to it'.

In analysing the nature of the sustainable society which the ecologists seek, Dobson notes that their rejection of purely technological solutions, derived directly from 'The limits to growth', already sets them apart from environmentalists. The Greens' fundamental commitment to the principle of scarcity and a scientific, rather than romantic, approach to nature are defining ideological characteristics. Dobson cites O'Riordan's typology with respect to possible reactions to the scarcity thesis: new global order, centralised authoritarianism, authoritarian communitarianism and anarchist self-reliant communitarianism. Dobson asserts that the green position approximates closest to the last of these. The green sustainable society is a decentralised communal world involving a fundamentally liberal-left political position.

But the key to the sustainable society lies in changed patterns of consumption and in general consuming less. Redefining needs is one aspect; reducing population is another; thirdly, Greens would radically change our relation to technology: this is not an anti-technology stance so much as one which preaches caution and appropriateness. Reduced need for energy and production from renewable sources is important. Greens also hold the unfashionable view that trade and travel should be radically reduced in order to minimise dependency, to help control the proliferation of 'needs', to extend control over resources and the terms of trade. It is an important principle that: 'The sustainable society is substantially about living "in place" and developing an intimacy with it and the people who live there; travel, on this reading, is too expansive and too centrifugal an occupation.'

The ecologists' attitude to work is that it can be fulfilling but that we need a much looser relation to it. This means that everyone should receive enough income to live by – a guaranteed basic income – regardless of work and that the worth of non-paid employment should be recognised. Dobson notes that, judging by the attempts of social democratic regimes, such a system may be more difficult to achieve that the ecologists imagine; furthermore, the administration of such a scheme would seem to require centralised mechanisms quite contrary to the decentralised polity which the Greens otherwise advocate.

The extreme statement of the green sustainable society is that of the bioregionalists who see the reorganization of society into self-sufficient polities defined by natural boundaries and with a local culture that relates directly to the particular ecological setting. Whilst not overtly espoused by rank and file ecologists, this concept 'will certainly inform many of the postures struck by even the least mystical of the Green movement's members'. Organic agriculture in such regions becomes the praxis of green politics. Dobson notes at this point that whilst the bioregionalists emphasise that different regions will have very different political arrangements, many ecologists may have misgivings concerning the potential outcome of this, suggesting possibilities for localised petty tyranny .

Dobson now looks at various green proposals for the administration of decentralised polities. These range from emphasis on the commune, through more conventional arrangements of local politics and participatory democracy to the complex arrangements that appear in the British Green Party Manifesto. In the latter case, it sometimes appears that a parody of the heavy-industrial command economy is being advocated, rather than the decentralised polity which elsewhere seems to be the green norm!

Concerning green change, Dobson starts by asserting the inadequacy of the green notion of the universal appeal of their message and general weakness of their strategies to bring about the changes they advocate. In the UK, efforts to enter politics are stymied by the electoral system, and green policies generally fail to recognise the dynamics of real economic and political power that would lead to investment strikes, capital flight and so on in the event of any attempts at enactment. The experience of the German Green Party in the legislature demonstrates the power of co-optation intrinsic to such institutions. The result is that environmentalism makes progress at the expense of the broader green programme.

It is to combat this that Greens advocate lifestyle changes. Whilst recently 'green consumerism' has demonstrated the suddenness with which lifestyle changes can be adopted, there nevertheless remain problems, firstly of obtaining sufficient change to make a real difference, and secondly the dubiousness of appealing to consumerism to achieve genuine change: in this case we are talking of environmentalism rather than ecologism. Nevertheless, Greens do see radical changes in lifestyle as a potentially important aspect of strategy. However, rather than individual lifestyle change, ultimately the intention is to achieve change by reorganizing community life, and alternative communities, such as the Centre for Alternative Technology, have attempted to demonstrate this. The difficulty here has been to maintain over a comparatively long period the spirit of opposition in a hostile world.

Dobson goes on to focus considerable attention on the problem of class. He is sceptical that calls for a general change in consciousness are sufficient, and asserts that 'it is simply not in the immediate interests of everybody to usher in a sustainable society'. At this point, reference is made at some length to Marx's critique of the utopian socialists and the way in which Marx sought, and found in the new industrial working class, an agent of sufficient weight, in whose interest it was to bring about an egalitarian society. However, in a post-modern world where all is difference and diversity, 'it would be foolish and unwarranted for class theorists to make any universalistic claims for any agent they might identify'. Nevertheless, various theorists have been looking for relevant agents, identifying variously 'the middle classes', 'new social movements' and the 'socially marginalised' – particularly in the form of what Gorz has referred to as the 'non-proletariat' centring on the unemployed. Dobson has problems with all these approaches and wonders how effective political action for change might be organized around any of these agents.

Dobson notes that ecologism might be compared and contrasted with a number of different politico-ideological positions, but those of immediate interest are socialism and feminism. In general, ecologism can be seen as being to the left of current mainstream 'socialist' politics. However, socialist theorists have attacked the Greens for paying insufficient heed to questions of economic and social structure: to capitalism, the problem of the poor and to class analysis. Much of this criticism has, however, talked past, rather than to the ecologists as their focus of attention is upon different causes and different solutions to those identified by the socialists. Some socialists believe Greens are insufficiently critical of the capitalist camp, whilst others find few material differences in stance; but ecologists on the whole pay insufficient regard to existing traditions and common heritage within socialism as a radical movement for change. There is, however, a fairly general recognition of common traditions in William Morris and perhaps other utopian socialists, albeit perhaps relating more closely to anarchism than to socialism as conventionally understood.

The ecofeminist debate takes place within feminism rather than between feminism and the Green Movement. On the one hand, there has been a strong assertion that male oppression of women and of nature are indissolubly bound together. Women are closer to nature and a revaluation of the feminine together with nature is required. On the other side, however, some feminists argue that the acknowledgement of the commonly-held belief that women are closer to nature only reinforces the domination of women by men. In this view, the women's movement is about undoing the modesty and humility which is a feature of the assumed identity of women with nature.

In concluding the book, Dobson confirms the contention that ecologism is a distinct political ideology. But he then illustrates how the recent emergence of a very broad concern for environmental despoliation has not made space for the emergence of ecologism to broader public debate, but rather that Greens have been encouraged to assert environmentalist views. This represents a very grave problem for the movement. It nevertheless appears that the general public is dimly aware of the distinction between 'light green' and 'deep green'. As Dobson puts it: 'Act One of the Green movement's paradise play is over, and it is time that the curtain was lifted on Act Two.'

By way of preface to the short commentary on Dobson's text which follows, it must be stressed that his analysis comprises a milestone in academic theorisation about the Green Movement and its ideology. Whilst the approach is clearly academic, in the sense of arising from a position of uninvolvement in either the theory or praxis of ecologism, it nevertheless succeeds in grasping the inner coherence of the ideology, providing a good balance of exposition between the various facets deemed to be important by the movement itself. The critique which Dobson offers is constructive both for the movement and for future academic analysis directed towards ecologism. Rather than provide any general criticism of the book, the following paragraphs aim to comment on certain problematic issues that are likely to require extensive further thought and debate both within the movement and on the part of academic analysts.

First a brief word on ecophilosophy. Dobson does not make reference to the fact that ecophilosophy has been almost exclusively generated by and debated within the walls of academe. As an essentially conservative force within our society – true also of academic Marxism – the natural focus of academic debate tends to be ignorant, even contemptuous of praxis. Whilst the shift within the ecophilosophy debates from 'intrinsic value' arguments to those concerned with 'change in consciousness' may be a tribute to the walls of academe crumbling away, and with this a dawning awareness of the whereabouts of practical relevance to the debate, as Dobson notes this is still very far from providing any philosophical insight of real use to the movement. My suspicion is that the copious ecophilosophical literature will, in time, prove to be scholastic, and that as green theory develops and matures it will find its own way much more directly out of the movement, via social praxis, to an ethics relevant to the needs of a sustainable society.

Dobson has effected a considerable service in the way in which he has opened up the debate between Greens and the Left about class and agency in an agnostic manner. Whereas in continental debates on the Left (even in the Australian Frankel's leftist critique of the Greens) the considerations of agency are tending towards abandoning a strict adherence to faith in the 'working class' and looking wider afield, in the UK, for reasons of the configuration of the socialist movement and its place in the wider social and political conjuncture, this debate has been more difficult to raise. Nevertheless, there have been some attempts and it is unfortunate, given the importance – rightly in my view – which Dobson attaches to the differences between Green and Left analysis on social issues, that he makes no reference to this debate.

Since the mid 1970s the Socialist Environment and Resources Association (SERA) has organized discussions and run a journal in which a socialist green position on a whole range of issues has been sought. The Conference of Socialist Economists (CSE) has also run workshops on green issues, including debates on 'industrialism' versus 'capitalism', in some of their annual conferences. The advent of the now annual Socialist Conferences, in which Green Party members have been involved from the outset, triggered an intensification of these debates and the formation of a group, initially calling itself the Association of Socialist Greens inside the Green Party, explicitly aimed at engaging in clarification of a green socialist position. Subsequently a Green and Red Network formed as an umbrella for this debate, running two very high-profile weekend conferences and now established as a more permanent organization with a newsletter, aimed at extending and advancing the debate. Besides the books of Ryle (1988) and more recently Wall (1989) and Kemp and Wall (1990) that have emerged from this debate, there is a large volume of 'grey literature' to which Dobson could have referred.

There is no doubt that elements in the Green Movement do have a serious analysis of the role of class that is significantly at variance with that of the conventional Left, and which ties in with a coherent view both of the kind of society we are aiming to achieve and how we should go about achieving it. There is a genuine problem on the Left in Britain, contrasting with other industrialised countries, to acknowledge the possibility that a critique of the Marxist reliance on the working class as sole or even central agent of social change might be fruitful. This attitude, bordering on dogmatism, on the Left and its grip upon 'progressive' intellectuals in Britain more generally is, in my view, a major reason for what Dobson considers to be the weak development of green strategy for change.

There is a urgent need for the development of theory here which would be assisted greatly by the Left shifting its commitment to social change more willingly out into the fluid arena of post-modern debate. I think that by accepting a more pluralistic notion of agency, the question of the universalistic appeal of the green message would come into sharper focus. Prima facie, the Green Movement is at least as reasonable in its prediction of environmental catastrophe, given the continuation of our current social trajectory, as was Marx in his prediction of universal immiseration of the working class given continuation of early capitalism.

But theory is (and very easily to the point of scholasticism) concerned with the consistency of a set of propositions, rather than simply reacting to one dimension of events in the outside world. This does not, however, mean that a consistent green political theory as powerful as that of Marx is unavailable, and we might speak of the urgent need to elaborate a coherent 'green critique' of Marxism. Here are a few suggestions.

If we look back to Hegelian-Marxist theoretical foundations we can see, in Marx's *Economic and Philosophical Manuscripts*, how progress in social praxis and praxis in relation to nature were sundered at that time for pragmatic reasons; the natural sciences and the development of technology went their own way, whilst society appeared to be heading for an insoluble crisis.

The concept of political ecology – the inner functioning of natural systems including our species – set against the background of what Dobson refers to as a 'new resonance' deriving from our growing confrontation with absolute scarcity as a consequence of developments in science and technology *as well as* society, opens the way to fruitful theorisation concerning what Marx referred to as an eventual 'single science of man and nature'. Greens assume that the universalistic appeal of political ecology will become increasingly stronger as intractable environmental problems reveal themselves. Under these circumstances, the process of utopia-building can be expected to proceed in a more forthright manner and, symmetrically, the question of agency can afford to develop in a much more pluralistic and contingent fashion – in Feyerabend's words: anything goes! The theory of political ecology is thus wedded to the praxis of the green way of life – the Green Utopia – in contrast to the instrumentalism of Marxism that separates the machinery for bringing about change from the kind of end product we hope to achieve, and then focuses all its attention on the former.

So, focusing this on Dobson's argument, I contend the following: he has underestimated the power of the argument for universalist appeal; his critique of the Green Movement by reference to Marx's critique of the Utopian Socialists is weakened in the light of his own reference to the 'new resonance' which the emerging reality of absolute scarcity brings about; and he does not take his own acceptance of post-modern relativism seriously enough in insisting on the importance of a more precise definition of agency and its role.

Finally, to the question of bioregionalism. There can be little doubt that the realisation of this Green Utopia would fly directly in the face of the whole inner structure of the Enlightenment and its liberal ideology. As the Greens become more coherent and insistent about their utopian solutions, the sharpness of the leftist critique will increase rather than diminish as it becomes evident that socialism today has lost its commitment to the communitarianism of the early socialists, adopting instead the liberal individualistic ideology that underpins modern social democracy. Indeed, the central problem is not simply theoretical or ideological – about freedom of the individual versus communitarianism – it also has some very obvious practical ramifications. The 'excesses' of the great Maoist experiments and of the Khmer Rouge are a graphic illustration of the dynamic that can take hold once the path to a communitarian utopia is embarked upon.

The Green Movement is certainly going to have to develop new forms of wisdom as it moves in that direction if it is genuinely to nurture diversity of human self-expression within relatively small communities. The problem will be particularly intractable amongst people (the European Enlightened middle classes) whose cultural expectations revolve around the freedom of the individual to abscond from any potentially problematic social encounter. The communes movement is pioneering these questions on all our behalf and it is a pity that Dobson did not take a closer look at what is going on in that field. In my view, practical experiment in commune living is the most important facet of green praxis currently under development.

References

Bramwell, A. (1989). *Ecology in the 20th Century: A History* (New Haven: Yale University Press).

Capra, F. and Spretnak, C. (1984). *Green Politics: The Global Promise* (London: Hutchinson).

Cotgrove, S. (1982). *Catastrophe or Cornucopia? The Environment, Politics and the Future* (Chichester: Wiley).

Denitch, B. (1990). *The Socialist Debate: Beyond Red and Green* (London: Pluto Press).

Enzensberger, H. M. (1973). 'Zur Kritik der polititischen Ökologie', *Kursbuch*, No. 33, October, pp. 1–42 (English translation: 'A critique of political ecology', *New Left Review*, No. 84, March/April 1974, pp. 3–31).

Frankel, B. (1987). *The Post-Industrial Utopians* (Cambridge: Polity Press).

Hülsberg, W. (1988). *The German Greens: A Social and Political Profile*. (London: Verso).

Kemp, P. and Wall, D. (1990). *A Green Manifesto for the 1990s* (London: Penguin).

Lowe, P. and Goyder, J. (1983). *Environmental Groups in Politics* (London: George Allen & Unwin).

Mellos, K. (1988). *Perspectives on Ecology* (London: Macmillan).

O'Riordan, T. (1976). *Environmentalism* (London: Pion)

Parkin, S. (1989). *Green Parties: An International Guide* (London: Heretic Press).

Pepper, D. (1984). *The Roots of Modern Environmentalism* (London: Croom Helm).

Ryle, M. (1988). *Ecology and Socialism* (London: Radius).

Sandbach, F. (1980). *Environment, Ideology and Policy* (Oxford: Basil Blackwell).

Wall, D. (1989). *Getting There: Towards a Green Society* (London: Green Print).

Williams, R. (1983). *Towards 2000* (London: Chatto and Windus).

Green Reflections and Sustainable Visions

DANIEL NEAL GRAHAM
Department of Political Science, North Carolina State University,
Raleigh, N.C., USA

Lester W. Milbrath, Envisioning a Sustainable Society: Learning Our Way Out. Albany,
N.Y.: SUNY Press, 1989.

The subtitle of this thoughtful and important book, Learning Our Way Out, highlights the many strengths, as well as the one inherent limitation of this much-admired work. This culmination (so far) of Dr Milbrath's long career in the environmental policy field as Director of the Research Program in Environment and Society (State University of New York) incorporates a wide range of scholarly insights with a refreshingly personal approach that bridges the typical gap between academics and political activism. Although some scholars may complain that Milbrath 'wears his beliefs on his sleeve' in rude contrast to the proclaimed goal of social science 'objectivity', the personal one-on-one style of this book reflects his epistemological critique of the process of social learning – a major concern of this entire project. Claims for social science objectivity are rejected by Milbrath. Science is inherently value-based – an understanding that motivates the attention given to education and 'learning our way out'. The minor drawback of this focus will be discussed below. The importance of values, socialisation, education, and paradigm debates for a sustainable future makes this contribution essential reading for those who want to help create human societies which can live in harmony with our home – the planet Earth. Perhaps the attention this book received at the 1990 American Political Science Association meeting (a special roundtable panel) is one indication that discussion of values and survival questions within the academy is beginning to echo the concerns usually heard outside the ivy walls.

In his previous book, Environmentalists: Vanguard for a New Society (1984), Milbrath explored and discussed the shifts in elite and popular values from the Dominant Social Paradigm (DSP), which promotes 'progress' defined as unlimited economic growth and material accumulation, to a New

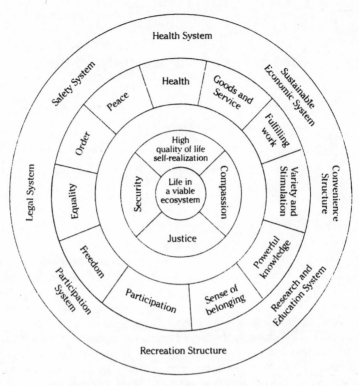

Figure 1 Milbrath's proposed value structure for a sustainable society

Environmental Paradigm (NEP) which is challenging such assumptions. *Envisioning a Sustainable Society* examines the vital role of values, social learning, and political changes which can bring about conditions for a sustainable future. As stated in the preface of this book,'Any society,especially any new society, must first exist in the minds of the people' (p. xi). Radical change requires unlearning false or outdated political and social assumptions and the values which underlie them. It also helps to have a vision of what a new society might look like and which values accompany and support such changes. Paine's *Common Sense* contributed to the debunking of social values which propped up monarchies. Literary contributions like Callenbach's *Ecotopia*, and the lyrical visions of John Lennon's 'Imagine' can sometimes affect popular culture and value systems more deeply and more quickly than many of the well-researched studies produced by groups like the Worldwatch Institute. Milbrath's approach combines the straightforward logic of Paine with the scholarship of Lester Brown, within a framework that acknowledges the vitality of envisioning a different society. His focus on education, social learning and value change is sharp. Outside this lens – in the field of political strategy – the situation becomes more fuzzy. How to overcome the structural and systemic barriers of institutionalised vested interests and class-dominated political economy receives less attention. *Envisioning a Sustainable Society* helps us to see the inherent cracks in old declining social models and contributes to the foundations of new societies based on a harmonious and sustainable relationship with our environment.

Milbrath's goal is 'to design a new society that provides a decent quality of life while coexisting in a long-run sustainable relationship with the natural environment that nourishes it' (p. xi). He begins in Part I with a critique of contemporary society and an epistomological examination of thought structures necessary for a sustainable future. Here he examines power and domination and how they are embedded in culture and its values, along with a discussion of the most basic values that unite the human species. His proposed value structure is visually shown in Figure 1 – a circular diagram with the value of a viable ecosystem as the centrepiece, surrounded by four core values: high quality of life, security, compassion, and justice (p. 72). This core ring is surrounded by a third ring of instrumental values which are designed to lead to the realisation of the core values.These include: freedom, equality, peace, order, health, participation, knowledge, fulfilling work, sense of belonging, and goods/services. The fourth ring lists societal systems which serve instrumental and core values. This section concludes with an examination of how social learning, paradigms, and political ideologies contribute to thought structures.

Part II elaborates Milbrath's vision of a sustainable society by examining natural systems, and how human institutions can be designed to fit in harmony with them. Topics explored here include: modern agriculture; the nature of work; income and employment; the role of material goods for life quality; the role of science and technology; and the need to design politics and government to help society learn to become sustainable. He suggests the need for more reliance on transnational institutions and the appointment of a domestic 'Council for Long-Range Societal Guidance' with advisory powers and legal status (pp. 288–93). His political strategies focus on the importance of education, enlightenment of elites, and mass socialisation, while giving too little attention to the structural barriers of vested interests and class positions in the political economy.

Part III concludes with a comparison of the two scenarios (paths) that might be taken. He rejects the first as the unsustainable present course based on the DSP. The alternative path is based on the value structure examined in Part II. Although he sees this 'green' alternative as desirable and necessary for survival, he also realises that 'most of the traditional methods for educating and arousing people will not be sufficient because most people will not be listening' (p. xiv). Those who have most of the power – the elites – may not want to listen to plans which challenge their present position of domination. Those who may be inclined to listen don't occupy positions of power to make structural change.

The debate over human cleverness is examined early on in this work – a reply to the technological optimists who assume that anything humans mess up, they can clean up . Whether ozone layers can be easily repaired, or whether global warming can be prevented, remains mostly a scientific debate. For Milbrath the issue is not so much how clever humans might become, as much as with the problem of unintended consequences (p. 19). The tall smokestacks designed to deal with air pollution have made the acid rain problem more dangerous and more global in its effects. In Milbrath's view we should temper our cleverness by studying and emulating nature rather than trying to conquer it. Because we can 'never do merely one thing', we should develop the habit of asking, 'And then what?' (p. 21). The lack of holistic thinking and the false assumptions based on so-called value-free science underlie this problem of human cleverness. For example, we may know too much about nuclear science (enough to kill ourselves) and too little about our limits (what do we do with all the radioactive wastes). For Milbrath it is clear that 'Science that pretends to be value-free will serve the values of those who rule "the establishment"' (p. 65). The claim of scientific 'objectivity' should be replaced by the goal of 'intersubjectivity' (p. 61). The related problem of overspecialisation is discussed in his reform suggestions. Some other important themes addressed include:the Gaia Hypothesis of Lovelock; debates between deep ecology and social ecology; the difference between simplicity and poverty and how they relate to affluence; world order and decentralised bioregionalism; and the limitations of our existing institutional structures.

The incomplete analysis of structural barriers and their political clout emerges in Chapter 7, where he discusses ideologies – specifically the similarities and differences between capitalism and socialism. He argues that these modern industrial models have more in common with each other than either one has with the green alternative. The subtitle of this chapter is 'Please do not label me!' Many greens don't like to be labelled along the traditional left/right spectrum. This is a major reason why ideological pronouncements are rejected in favour of 'value-based' politics in their philosophy. Although it is evident that the important issues of economic growth, power, anthropocentrism, and the role of science/technology do cut across the traditional left/right axis, it remains an over-simplification to claim that green politics is 'neither left nor right' on most other issues. Concerns with peace, equality, freedom, co-operation, and social welfare have been generally associated with left, feminist, and green political movements. Marx's early works on alienation and commodification of humans and resources has been extended to include other species by many greens. As Milbrath notes, control over economic activities is more important than outright social ownership (p. 141) – a position embraced by greens and many democratic socialists alike. Incorporation of social-use and environmentally sound criteria for investment decision-making blends classical left and green positions, in stark contrast to the narrow capitalist focus on private short-term profits. Milbrath explicitly embraces 'the middle way' (social democratic) found in Scandinavian systems – one that blends market distribution with social control. This middle way, or 'third way' between state-socialism (Communism) and corporate capitalism is a stated goal of both greens and democratic socialists. Democratic public control over economic decisions is a necessary, but hardly sufficient basis for an ecologically sustainable future. I think Milbrath fudges on this point.

In his discussion about political strategies for radical change Milbrath's work also comes up a bit short. In Part III he grapples with the realisation that social change tends to be slow. He acknowledges the problem of 'the dominant patterns of socioeconomic-political activity' which leads to status quo socialisation (p. 339). He seems to attribute our rejection of slavery and colonialism to changes in thinking patterns, while giving scant attention to the role which wars and struggle played in eliminating these practices. This point is brought up by Joel Kassiola in his recently published The Death of Industrial Civilization – a book published by SUNY Press in their Environmental Public Policy Series, which Milbrath edits [Cf. the separate review of this book in this volume: the Editor]. In Kassiola's words, 'What if the powerful postindustrial elite do not change their views and values, holding on to their control of society and its bases for power; government institutions, economic wealth and the mass media?'(Kassiola 1990, p. 163). Indeed, and what if the entrenched military–industrial complex refuses to be swayed by environmental education? As important as changing thought structures might be, it is equally important to change the political, and especially the economic structures and their control mechanisms, to either force elites to operate in an environmentally sustainable manner, or to allow a shift in power from these elites to democratic control.

Milbrath's politics are hardly utopian. It is clear that simply educating elites will not be sufficient. It will be necessary to topple those leaders from power who cling to DSP models which press for economic wealth and growth. His most complete review of political strategies is enumerated in Chapter 18, 'Learning our way to a new society'. These include: logical persuasion as an important first step; power-coercive approaches (revolutions, new laws, lawsuits, strikes, boycotts, civil disobedience and violence); elite change; social inventions, like the writing of new constitutions; formation of social movements (civil rights, feminism, anti-war, environmental, etc.); and normative re-educative approaches directed more at individuals than societies (pp. 354–5). Common to all of these approaches is the process of social learning, which is Milbrath's major concern. He realises that 'education alone is insufficient for social learning' (p. 358). Once socialised into a particular paradigm, people are highly resistant to critical challenges. This is a particular problem for environmental activists who bring to people a rather negative analysis of our world's present condition. The necessity of offering a positive alternative vision is a major motivation for this book.

At the tactical level, greens have been grappling with the transition from movement politics to party development – one 'fraught with difficulties' (p. 362). This is especially true in political systems with 'winner-take-all' elections as practised in Great Britain and the United States. Green electoral success has been easier in systems with proportional representation voting. Watering down party ideology to woo votes is another inherent problem for green parties. These remain unresolved debates, and Milbrath doesn't pretend to have the enlightened answer, nor does he completely despair over these difficulties. The overthrow of right-wing dictatorships in Spain, Portugal, Argentina and the Phillipines gives him hope (p. 368). Recent reforms in Eastern Europe could also be mentioned. There is a significant difference, however, between these examples and the green challenge to the present DSP. Though suppressed by force and habit, the ideas of freedom, democracy, and self-government have had a long socialisation period along with existing models of political democracy (both conservative capitalist and social democratic) which gave people alternative examples to their established orders. This is simply not the case for the NEP green alternative. As Milbrath himself points out, 'The Green Party challenges capitalism more fundamentally than the Marxian parties do [in Germany]' (p. 363). I am sure that he would agree that the NEP and green politics challenges all models of industrial societies, and the DSP which supports them, even more fundamentally than Marxism ever has. No existing society yet offers an example of a green alternative. This challenge faces much steeper barriers than was the case in the democratic political revolts which Milbrath cites.

Perhaps it is these strategic difficulties which lead the author to entertain the possibility for massive changes in social thinking described in Rupert Sheldrake's work on 'morphic resonance' which suggests the possibility for people to tune in to the mental activities of others without verbal communication (p. 375). It is not clear whether this possibility is merely hopeful thinking on Milbrath's part, or whether he is simply acknowledging the existence of fields of study which may yet prove helpful in overcoming the barriers to social learning in time to save our planet and ourselves.

More plausible is Milbrath's point that nature itself will be the spur to new thinking. Climate change and many other feedback indicators of threats to life-support systems should shake up even the most stubborn defenders of the DSP. But will this happen in time? Will our life-support systems pass beyond critical thresholds before we make the social and industrial change necessary to slow their demise? Milbrath is not overly optimistic: 'we should expect the physical transformation of our infra-structure and patterns of daily activity to take decades, perhaps a century or two. That transformation cannot make significant headway until our thinking (our belief paradigm) changes' (p. 377). He is very clear about the political responsibility of those who are in the forefront of creating a sustainable alternative to our present condition. 'Those given the gift of understanding will become the conscious mind of the biocommunity, a global mind, that will guide and hasten the transformation. Those who understand what is happening to our world are not free to shrink from this responsibility' (p. 380).

Although it would have been helpful to see more attention paid to the structural and class barriers which uphold our present social order, this book succeeds in its stated goal of challenging the underlying thought patterns which support the DSP and in helping to create a vision of a sustainable alternative – one that links harmony within the human species with harmony between humans and the rest of our living planet. I certainly plan to use it and its many valuable insights in my classes. I have already incorporated them into my political thinking. Much obliged!

References

Kassiola, J. K. (1990). *The Death of Industrial Society: The Limits to Economic Growth and the Repoliticization of Advanced Industrial Society* (Albany, N. Y. :SUNY Press).
Milbrath, L. W. (1984) *Environmentalists: Vanguards for a New Society* (Albany, N.Y.: SUNY Press).

The Ubiquity of the Environment: Comments on a Recent Upsurge of Environmental Directories

ELEANOR McDOWELL

Department of Government, University of Strathclyde, Glasgow, UK

Brackley, Peter (ed.), *World Guide to Environmental Issues and Organizations* (Harlow: Longman 1990).

White, Graham (ed.), *The Scottish Environmental Handbook* (Edinburgh: The Environment Centre 1990).

Cowell, Sara (ed.), *Who's Who in the Environment: Scotland* (rev. ed.) (London: The Environment Council, 1989).

Cowell, Sara (ed.), *Who's Who in the Environment: England* (London: The Environment Council 1990).

Milner, J. Edward; Filby, Carol, and Board, Marian (eds.), *The Green Index: A Directory of Environmental Organizations in Britain and Ireland* (London: Cassell 1990).

Frisch, Monica, *Directory of the Environment: Organisations, Campaigns, and Initiatives in the British Isles.*, 3rd ed. (London: Green Print 1990).

In the last two years, the 'environment' has received unprecedented public attention. Environmental issues have been popularised, politicised, and consumerised to become something of a fixture in everyday life. One reflection of this is the wave of 'green' literature, books, specialist journals and magazines, encyclopaedias, directories and dictionaries published in 1989 and 1990.

Collectively, this 'green' literature fulfils a double role. In the first place it may be used as a source of reference to guide readers who seek factual information on various aspects of the environmental movement. Second, it acts to promote an 'alternative' society which advocates the adoption of a new set of moral principles in our approach to technology, development, health, education, peace, politics, ecology, feminism, spirituality and consumerism. The latter, in particular, has become a popular slogan as well as a powerful commercial force, with green consumer guides among some of the best selling paperbacks in Britain. Practical advice is given on A–Z listings of 'environmentally friendly' merchandise, covering everything from detergent to organic foodstuffs. Additionally, given the growth and diversity of the environmental movement referred to by Jonathon Porritt in the forward of *The Green Index* as 'one of those proverbial broad churches', one might reasonably assume that the current spate of directories have been compiled largely as a source of information and contacts for all those interested in or concerned about conservation and the environment.

What brings these books together in this review is their central aim to compile a list of local, regional, national, and in some cases international organizations, groups, statutory bodies, companies and institutions which form part of the environmental movement. All six offer much that is useful, although inevitably there is a degree of overlap between them. Nonetheless, it is fitting to review them all together because, as one might expect, there are variations among them in presentation, price, comprehensiveness and style

Some of the directories are sponsored by business; others are written by academics, for example, the *World Guide to Environmental Issues and Organisations* is produced by a team of leading specialists and academics who discuss some of the major environmental issues and organizations of various countries. By contrast, the *Scottish Environmental Handbook* seeks to encourage a more individual approach to environmental issues in Scotland, through participation in practical projects, local initiatives and campaigns. The directories listed above have all been published in 1990 (with the exception of *Who's Who in the Environment: Scotland*, which was published in 1989), and they should all be suitable for a diverse readership, ranging from the novice to the established environmentalist.

The *World Guide to Environmental Issues and Organizations* is, as the title suggests, an ambitious attempt to provide an analytical account of the major environmental issues, organisations, and debates of the world today. The breadth of scope of this book, both in a geographical sense and in terms of the diversity of subject matter, differentiates it from the other books under review.

After a Foreword and an Introduction, the main body of the book is divided into four sections. Part 1 (Issues) incorporates a selection of essays on a variety of topics. These are intellectually challenging and relevant to contemporary environmental issues. The topics cover acid deposition, the Antarctic, deforestation, the greenhouse effect and global warming, land degradation and desertification, the loss of biological diversity, marine pollution, nuclear power, ozone depletion, renewable energy, vehicle emissions and water quality.

Generally speaking, any collection of essays may be evaluated from at least two points of view; the quality of the articles taken separately, and the quality of the collection as a whole. From the first perspective, the essays differ in terms of style, some owing to the nature of the topic: acid deposition, the greenhouse effect, global warming and water quality are generally more technical than other topics. At another level, other issues such as trans-boundary pollution have greater international (as opposed to national) implications. Finally, in the case of nuclear power and renewable energy, the policy implications, remedial options and alternative strategies are stressed.

As a unit, there are underlying themes tying the various essays together: the recognition of the need for greater scientific research and more information; and the call for a change in attitudes at the individual, national, and international level. Dr Mostata Tolba underlines this point in the Foreword: 'There is not much point in individuals taking action unless the government is responsive, and there is not much point in nations taking steps to conserve energy or protect coasts and rivers unless their neighbours do likewise. No country – no matter how mighty – can protect its own patch of sky' (pp. xiii).

Collectively, the essays stress the magnitude of the environmental crisis, and anticipate the potential threats to the planet unless appropriate action is taken.

The second section of this book, Part II (Politics) provides an analysis of environmental or 'green' politics. This section opens with a consideration of various philosophical principles and criteria for being green, followed by an overview of established green parties around the world describing the events and problems that have coloured their development. The section concludes with a visionary perspective which considers the prospects of green political parties in the future. A number of key factors are considered pertinent here: the general state of the environment and the level of public concern; the ability of other political parties to deal effectively with environmental issues; the extent to which green parties can overcome their internal fractions and constraints; and their capacity to improve their organization and resources in an attempt to survive and to maintain credibility in the political arena.

The penultimate section of this book, Part III (Conventions, Reports, Directives and Agreements) presents a detailed account of treaties and other regulatory machinery, such as multilateral and bilateral arrangements which have been formed to promote a more integrated and co-ordinated international approach to the problem of the environment. The results and implications of such treaties are set out under the same subject issues as in Part I of this book.

Finally, Part IV (Organisations) lists directory entries for the major environmental monitoring and pressure groups throughout the world. However, given the knowledge that there are thousands of organizations active in the environmental field (as acknowledged in the introduction of this book), only a selection of organizations have been listed. It seems that the environment has become too big an issue, even for this comprehensive volume. Overall, the *World Guide to Environmental Organizations and Issues* is an innovative analysis of the major environmental issues and organizations of our era, which subsequently minimises jargon at no expense to scholarship. The editor also adds to the unity of the book by including a list of acronymns, a detailed index, a bibliography, suggested further reading and references. The only criticism is that it lacks a conclusion; such a successful blending of disparate environmental issues into a coherent framework calls for a concluding epilogue.

On a more local/national level, The Scottish Environmental Handbook, published by the Environment Centre in Edinburgh and funded by the Shell Better Britain campaign, is a sort of how-to-do-it-book specifically aimed at the 5 million Scots who are not members of any environmental or green movement of any kind. The intention here is to encourage more people, particularly those with little environmental or conservation background, to become further involved in local environmental activities. The handbook is organised into eleven chapters, each relating to different aspects of the environment: lifestyle and consumer issues; resource use; pollution; training and careers; and getting involved.

The information presented to the reader is threefold in structure, relating to a given environmental topic. First of all, a historical overview is given of the way in which particular aspects of the environment in Scotland have developed, leading to a focus on more contemporary issues. Second, a number of key agencies, contacts, resources and educational materials are listed. Third, examples of successful conservation projects and awards are outlined, principally with the intention of inspiring similar activities and initiatives within the wider community, encouraging involvement at the local, regional and national level. A secondary aim of the handbook is to bring the 960 active groups in Scotland closer together. According to the Handbook's author and editor, Graham White, 'the challenge for existing environmentalists is to try to get the message across to ordinary people in Scotland that environmental problems are not just fringe issues, but central to the quality of life that they and their children will enjoy or suffer in the coming decades' (p. 4). If a book such as this, which provides a valuable source of information and contacts, makes individuals more aware of existing environmental problems and, equally important, of the potential for a more positive approach in dealing with them, it will have served its purpose. The Scottish Environmental Handbook (albeit long overdue in terms of a recognition of the Scottish environmental dimension) deserves the widest possible readership.

The only other directory in this review to deal specifically with Scottish environmental organizations forms part of a series of the Countryside Commission's free publications of Who's Who in the Environment directories covering the United Kingdom. The revised edition of Who's Who in the Environment: Scotland (1989) follows the successful distribution of over

10,000 copies of the original (1988) publication, which suggests that a valuable service is being provided. In browsing through the Scottish directory and its English counterpart *Who's Who in the Environment : England*, the reader is presented with a useful inventory of details in so far as the entries are listed by way of name, address, telephone number and date of formation, along with contact (group representative) and their position. Moreover, the status of the organization (for example, voluntary, charity or government body), its publications, number of staff and volunteers, membership (including cost), and details of local branches are given. Finally, a summary of aims and activities completes this resumé of practical information, which in broad terms amounts to a well-researched and balanced source of guidance. With this in mind, the future proposals for similar publications in Wales and Northern Ireland are to be thoroughly recommended.

It is worth noting that all of the preceding directories (excluding the *World Guide to Environmental Issues and Organisations*) have been supported or funded by major oil companies. The two *Who's Who in the Environment* volumes are, in fact, distributed free of charge. It appears that the vogue for environmental concern has few boundaries as multi-nationals are increasingly drawn into the green arena and want to be seen as champions of the environment. Whether or not it is a matter for concern that such 'environmentalist' publications are sponsored by multi-nationals (as the less sanguine and accommodating environmentalists may believe) is open to question. What is clear is that to be considered ' environmentally friendly', particularly in the present green climate, is instrumental in forging good public relations.

The unsavoury truth is that wholly altruistic motives are not symptomatic of our age. The reality of the situation is that we do not live in a utopian world without vested interests. As a result, multi-nationals and environmental agencies are brought together in some sort of reciprocal arrangement which presumably benefits them both. The implication here is that the striking shift in awareness and concern over environmental issues has elicited a series of pragmatic responses from various quarters, ranging from industry, commercial interests, the mass media and the government. Although this is not the place to explore this issue at length, one might reasonably assume that it is often preferable to have the opponent within and co-operating, rather than outside and conspiring.

The final two directories in this review, *The Green Index* compiled and edited by J. Edward Milner, Carol Filby and Marion Board, and *The Directory for the Environment* by Monica Frisch are both extensive in their coverage of environmental organizations and contacts within Britain and Ireland.

The Green Index has been compiled largely to meet the requirements for a single-volume comprehensive directory. As such, it is a worthy credit to the collaborative efforts of those who contributed in drawing together virtually all one needs to know about environmental organizations throughout the British Isles. It provides the reader with a definitive and concise account of over 5,200 environmental organizations, groups, institutions and companies. The main list in the directory (pp. 1–258) arranges alphabetically the names of all the organizations concerned, along with the basic information for contacting them. Subsequent lists include a useful geographical index arranged by county or region (pp. 261–40). Finally, details are given of a number of organizations which offer information and act as 'umbrella' bodies (pp. 341–52). The primary intention here is to inform, and the wide scope of organizations prevent any detailed account of the entries listed. The include: government and statutory bodies; voluntary organizations; pressure groups; academic, educational and research establishments; trade and professional associations, and commercial and industrial bodies. All reports are brief and concentrate on relevant factual details; the aims and activities of organizations are excluded. On a practical level, The Green Index is well researched and factually written, and should benefit readers who require a comprehensive reference manual.

In a similar vein, The Directory of the Environment, now in its third edition, provides a useful service by assembling a completely revised guide to over 1,500 organizations, campaigns and initiatives in the British Isles. While previous 'pioneering' editions of the directory published in 1984 and 1986 do not appear to have been great commercial successes, the current edition of The Directory of the Environment is said to have been virtually sold out a few months after its publication, an indication that the recent demand for environmental or 'green' literature extends particularly to factual, 'practical' information rather than theoretical treatises.

Reference to the more comprehensive directories affords an opportunity to consider what rationale is applied in the selection of groups from a vast array of organizations. To stress a point made above, it is necessary to consider the heterogeneous character of the environmental movement. Difficult decisions have to be made concerning the criteria for inclusion in or exclusion from any directory. In the case of The Green Index, J. Edward Milner confirms in the Foreword that 'we felt it important to cover as wide a range of groups as possible, using finite space to include more entries, rather than give too much information about each group'. In The Directory of the Environment, by contrast, organizations have been selected on the basis that they are

> involved in activities that relate in some way to the natural, physical, or human environment, particularly those that seek to promote alternatives to the detrimental use or exploitation of the earth and its resources ... the primary concern is the maintenance and management of the global habitat and secondary concerns are all those activities which affect the non-human inhabitants. (pp. xv–xvi)

This excludes the areas of human rights and welfare. Whilst not disputing such groups' relevance, Frisch rightly suggests that 'some boundaries have got to be drawn somewhere' (p. xvi).

The Directory of the Environment includes, where possible, all the national organizations, most regional ones, and prominent county and local organizations. However, with respect to Scotland only national organizations are included in order to avoid a duplication of the sources already available in The Scottish Environmental Handbook. As with the previous directories, an A–Z of local and national environmental organizations comprises the bulk of the book. In addition, the inclusion of a subject index, a bibliography of relevant environmental literature and a selection of periodicals are especially welcome, particularly for those not well versed in environmental affairs. The Directory of the Environment is a bonus for those who seek information on the range and variety of organizations which make up the environmental movement.

The collection of directories listed above are books to browse through and refer to and should be a valuable tool to guide those concerned with recent environmental developments. As more people become interested in and concerned about conservation and the environment, so the amount of information dramatically increases. In this respect the directories are a timely addition to an already fertile field of environmental literature. They should provide a useful service not only to confirmed environmentalists, but to teachers, field workers, community and youth groups, voluntary associations, and above all to a patchily informed public.

However, I am moved to record one fundamental criticism. There is a general propensity in these directories to juxtapose a variety of environmental organizations (albeit alphabetically) in a manner bereft of efficient categorisation. The environment movement is comprised of a host of groups and organizations as diverse in their aims and objectives as they are in their operating styles, working at local, regional and national levels. Given the complexity of organizations which come under the broad banner of environmentalism, there are strong grounds for a more coherent system of classification. One solution might be to arrange environmental groups into specific categories and headings, such as charity; voluntary; government body; privatised industry; commercial enterprise; action group; animal welfare organization, and so on, in an effort to facilitate ease of reference and to differentiate amongst the plethora of organizations and groups currently involved in various aspects of the environment.

The unifying theme of the directories is their aim to inform, and although they are not all of equal value, it would be a difficult task to select 'the' reference book among them. In this instance the reader must decide, for the choice depends largely on individual requirements. Some directories are primarily concerned with one particular region such as Scotland or England; others incorporate the whole of the British Isles or indeed undertake an international/global perspective. One can only advise the reader to familiarise himself or herself with the growing environmental literature before coming to a decision.

Book Reviews

McDonagh, Sean, The Greening of the Church. London: Geoffrey
Chapman, 1990.

Sean McDonagh is an Irish Columbian missionary who has worked in the
Philippines for a number of years. He has written a book which tries to
incorporate a number of themes. Unfortunately, his efforts have not been
very successful. The first section, incorporating three chapters, is concerned to examine 'the relationship between environmental issues and
Third World poverty' (p. 4). This objective is achieved reasonably well by
a discussion of the impact of the international debt burden on developing
countries, a discussion of the implications of rapidly increasing
populations in Third World states, and an examination of the importance
of the rainforest. This is undertaken with many references to the situation
in the Philippines with which McDonagh is familiar and to the Catholic
Church's attitudes and actions towards these issues. This first section is a
useful contribution to the literature and is written in an accessible way.

The author's major problems arise when he tries to reinterpret the
Hebrew and Christian scriptures to provide a reorientation which fits in
with the contemporary environmental consciousness. McDonagh is caught
in a non-man's-land between, on the one hand, Christianity which believes
in God the creator, who gave humans a privileged place in that creation,
and whose tripartite nature of God the Father, Jesus the Son and the Holy
Spirit are all emphatically male, and on the other hand, a pantheistic green
spirituality in which all is part of God and in which the feminine is to be
elevated above the masculine. The following examples should illustrate this
problem.

After referring to the Wisdom literature of the Old Testament and the
Apocrypha, McDonagh says that in

> the New Testament, the wisdom theme becomes fused with that of
> the spirit of God who brings forth life ... The same spirit who guided
> and moulded Jesus for his mission is active within the Church. There
> she is the source of life, unity, strength and creativity (Acts 2: 1–13).

She is the one who inspires all fruitfulness and creativity ... From her comes the present-day urge to heal what is broken, re-unite what is separated and recreate the face of the earth. (p. 157)

This rapid transformation of the Holy Spirit into a feminine wisdom is not based upon the teachings of the Bible.

In another problem area, McDonagh argues that we 'are beginning to realise that the parameters of the body of Christ [which in the Bible represents the Church] are expanding to include not just Christians or all humans but the totality of creation' (p. 161) (section in brackets added), that the 'redemption wrought by Christ which is experienced primarily by people is also extended to all creation' (p. 163), and that 'God's salvific power triumphs over sin and brings wholeness to individuals, human communities and the totality of creation' (p. 164). The pantheism which is implied here in the extension of Jesus' sacrifice to the material world does not sit well with the scriptures which say that he 'was put to death for our trespasses' (Romans 4: 25) and that he 'died for our sins' (1 Cor. 15: 3).

McDonagh's ambivalent attitude towards the paganism which much of the New Testament warns against is clear in a section in which he says that the 'Celtic experience can help guide the Christian Churches for an appropriate spirituality for the ecological age' (p. 170). This Celtic experience 'was centred on the heavenly bodies and the cycles of nature. Imbolc ... was celebrated to mark the end of winter. Beltane (May Day) ... Lugnasad (Lammas in England) ... Samhain also dealt with the natural elements of light and darkness' (pp. 168–9). Again, this syncretic approach to religion is one which is at odds with biblical teaching.

The book has been written to open a debate within the Catholic Church on the merits of a green perspective within that Church. The debate to which it is more likely to contribute is that concerned with the relationship of Christianity both to other spiritual traditions and to emerging social and political theories and their associated lifestyles. This debate is likely to develop further as individuals located within the various component parts of the Green Movement search for forms of spirituality appropriate to their beliefs. McDonagh's book is a useful contribution, but its arguments are more likely to appeal to those seeking to reassess God from the perspective of nature than to those seeking to reassess nature from the perspective of God.

Alistair McCulloch
School of Public Administration and Law
Robert Gordon's Institute of Technology
Aberdeen, UK

Dalton, R. J. and Kuechler, M. (eds.), Challenging the Political Order: New Social and Political Movements in Western Europe. Cambridge: Polity Press/New York: Oxford University Press, 1989.

'The challenge that new movements pose to the political order in Western democracies springs from within. It is not a revolutionary attack against the system, but a call for democracies to change and adapt' (p. 3). This guiding hypothesis represents an underlying thread which runs through the otherwise diverse contributions to this volume. In order to assess such a hypothesis thoroughly, three key issues are particularly discussed: a) what are the origins (historical, structural, cultural) of new social movements (NSMs); b) what is their relationship to institutionalised forms of politics, where by this term are meant from time to time the state; established political and social actors, ranging from parties and interest groups to other social organizations; conventional styles of political action: c) whether these movements and the parties which have sprung from them have exerted any substantial impact on the party system, in terms of 'partisan dealignment' as well as 'partisan realignment'.

A specific section of the book is devoted to each of these issues. In the first thematic section, Karl-Werner Brand, Ronald Inglehart, Frank Wilson and Max Kaase propose different and sometimes (Brand and Inglehart) overtly conflicting interpretations of the connection between the spread of NSMs and broader transformations at the macrosocial and/or cultural level. In the second section, Thomas Rochon, Bert Klandermans, Joyce Gelb and Dieter Rucht discuss links between 'new' and 'old' forms of political participation, 'new' and 'old' political actors. Finally, Herbert Kitschelt, Ferdinand Müller-Rommel, Claus Offe and Sidney Tarrow investigate the relationship between NSMs and political parties, in terms of both the role of new parties and the impact of NSMs on established ones.

The editors' conclusions identify the dominant characteristics of NSMs as follows. The nature of a movement may be detected in the nature of its belief system (what the authors call 'ideological bond'). In the case of NSMs, this bond consists of two aspects: 'a humanistic critique of the prevailing system and the dominant culture, in particular a deep concern about the threats to the future of the human race, and a resolve to fight for a better world here and now with little, if any, inclination to escape into some spiritual refuge' (p. 280). Consequently, these movements can not be conceived of as further examples of cyclical upsurgences of middle-class 'anti-modernism'. In contrast to previous middle-class movements, such as the romantic 'ecological' reactions to the growth of industrialism, contemporary movements do not indulge in any form of retreatism but want instead to achieve a transformation of substantial mechanisms of social and political domination. These movements also differ from traditional class movements which had characterised previous phases of intense social and political unrest. In contrast to them, they do not represent specific group interests, nor do they mobilise on behalf of economic, material demands. Second, while the specificity of NSMs has to be located in their non-institutional nature (along lines close to Smelser's once influential formulation), they are by no means wholly anti- or extra-institutional phenomena. On the contrary, contributions in the second section of the volume converge to a large extent in highlighting the intermingling of institutional and anti-institutional aspects which these movements actually display. While maintaining a fundamentally sceptical view of political institutions and established actors, new social movements are ready to start co-operations and alliances whenever possible and compatible with their goals. Rather than reflecting a mere trend à la Michels from revolutionary purity to institutional compromise, NSMs are marked by the persistent, unresolved tension between fundamentalist and pragmatist orientations.

Finally, new social movements and related (green and alternative) parties have so far proved unable to start a process of partisan dealignment and realignment. They have obviously affected the composition of several party systems as well as the behaviour of many their members of theirs on several key issues and policies. At the same time, however, their efforts to lay the ground for a new cleavage, strong enough to displace the existing ones, have so far fallen well short of the target. Green parties have, with the partial exception of Germany, failed to achieve a consistent political influence, expecially but not exclusively in countries with an unfavourable electoral system. Even worse, they have been unable to capitalise on the large support which public opinion seems to assign to their favourite issues. Last but not least, there is some evidence that the links between movements and parties might be weakening, thus undermining the parties' primary source of support.

The volume provides an excellent and updated introduction to many important controversies of recent debates on social movements. Moreover, it is fairly balanced (in spirit perhaps more than in strict quantitative terms) between supporters and opponents of the thesis of the 'newness' of contemporary movements. While the editors stand in the last analysis for this perspective, they do not fall prey to an 'evangelical' mood and offer a fair discussion of different points of view. Finally, and more substantively, the book rejects the clear-cut and somewhat simplistic division between social movements and institutional forms of political activity, in favour of a relationship between the two which is not only more complex, but also more realistic and more aware of the impact of social and political fluctuations on movements' characteristics. In other words, the book offers an account of NSMs which, while emphasising the newness of these phenomena, does not predict from it the imminent disappearance of conventional forms of political participation but rather highlights their   interplay.

Mario Diani
Department of Sociology
Bocconi University, Milan, Italy

Kassiola, J. K. , The Death of Industrial Society: The Limits to Economic Growth and the Repoliticization of Advanced Industrial Society. *Albany, N.Y.: SUNY Press, 1990.*

This book argues that the cause of the current environmental crisis lies in the adoption, around the time of the first industrial revolution, of an economic model based upon the attainment of limitless growth and the subservience of social and, ultimately, political life to this goal. This economic model, it is argued, denied the existence of the earth's biophysical limits and, as a consequence, the environment now faces unprecedented stress. Unless humankind undertakes an urgent reappraisal of the centrality accorded to economic growth, then the very life-support system of the planet may fail.

The thesis that there are biophysical limits to the earth's development capacity has already been well developed by the 'limits to growth' theorists. However, Kassiola's book makes an important new contribution to this literature in its focus on the underlying values and beliefs, or what he terms the 'normative roots', of the limitless economic growth models. This provides the central theme of the book, namely, that the environmental crisis is of such a magnitude that post-industrial society must, as a matter of urgency, undertake a fundamental re-examination of its values and beliefs. This, the author argues, means that we must engage in nothing short of the design of a new social order. Of crucial importance in this undertaking is the replacement of the centrality of economic activity with that of political and moral affairs, or what he terms the 'repoliticisation' of advanced industrial society. This use of political philosophy to engage in a critique of the underlying assumptions of economic theory is welcome; especially so because of the promise it holds for those concerned with the reconstruction of a new world order based upon a sustainable approach to the earth's resources.

Kassiola argues that the current crisis presents us with a 'dangerous opportunity to improve things' and he proceeds to examine what type of social order should take the place of our current system, and how the process of replacing the post-industrial social order should occur.

The move to a 'trans-industrial' social order means a fundamental re-appraisal of the materialist value system which links non-material states, such as happiness and fulfilment, to the possession of material goods. This capitalist ideology sustains the current economic order by legitimising the spiral of ever-increasing consumption and production. Recognising this for the dangerous illusion that it is gives a firm base to Kassiola's moral imperative to change our way of thinking about, and interacting with, the world's resources. The capitalist ideology of growth not only results in eco-logical stress but deflects attention away from the politically and morally necessary task of dealing with the current problem of injustice in the global distribution of wealth. Policies aimed at the redistribution of wealth can be side-stepped using the claim that the benefits of economic growth will eventually trickle down to benefit all. Recognising that economic growth holds out only the illusion of equality strengthens Kassiola's moral imperative to change.

Nevertheless, Kassiola's discussion on the process of the replacement of materialist social values is weak. In particular, his use of Rousseau to develop an alternative view of humankind with which to ground a new set of values is uncritical. Furthermore, no attempt is made to draw upon the wealth of scholarship that has been produced since Rousseau, especially the recent literature dealing with the idea of nature, the notion of the social contract and the position of human beings vis-à-vis the natural world. It is here that the book is the most disappointing. It is true that it is easier to criticise an existing belief system than it is to construct a path to an alternative one. Furthermore it is, perhaps, unrealistic to expect the pages of a book to provide us with a 'blueprint' for a new civilisation. However, this section lacks imagination, especially when it limits its horizons pri-marily to a few Western philosophers (Rouseau, Hegel), and ignores the depth of thinking on the environment found, for example, in Eastern phi-losophies and among indigenous peoples. Despite the recognition of the global nature of the current environmental crisis, the construction of a new approach to the environment is based exclusively on a Western-centred understanding of the crisis and relies upon Western thought for its solu-tion. This is both limited and parochial.

Despite this shortfall, Kassiola's is a very interesting book. It does not provide original insights but is, rather, a good synthesis of current philo-sophical thinking on the environmental issue. For example, the author's discussion of the ecological consequences of Adam Smith's separation of economic science from political economy and ethics is insightful and thought-provoking. So, too, is his critique of the theoretical use of the Pareto optimality criteria in economic science. These strengths go some way towards mitigating the weakness of his discussion of the transition to trans-industrial society.

Kassiola is right when he draws attention to the underlying problems of the economics of limitless growth. The reader, however, should be aware that adoption of the model of unlimited economic growth is but one of the causes of our current environmental crisis. There are other equally important factors to be considered, including the mechanistic view of science and society found in Enlightenment thinking, the system of patriarchal domination, and Western estrangement from the spiritual dimensions of existence. The construction of a new approach to the world is a multi-dimensional undertaking and must involve an all-embracing critique of the total set of beliefs, values and ideologies that constitutes contemporary thought.

Susan Baker
Faculty of Social Sciences
Erasmus University, Rotterdam
The Netherlands.

Notes on Contributors

Adrian Atkinson is Senior Lecturer at the Development Planning Unit of University College, London. His main research interests are the problems of environmental planning and management in developing countries, and green political theory. He is the author of two books, Principles of Political Ecology (Belhaven Press, 1991) and Green Utopia (Zed Press, forthcoming).

Susan Baker is Lecturer in the Social Sciences Faculty of the Erasmus University, Rotterdam, The Netherlands. She is currently writing a book on the Irish environmental movement.

Russell J. Dalton is Professor of Political Science at the University of California, Irvine, USA and Director of the UCI Research Programme on Democratization. He is author of Citizen Politics in Western Democracies (1988) and Politics in Germany (1992); co-author of Germany Transformed (1981); and editor of Electoral Change in Advanced Industrial Democracies (1984), Challenging the Political Order: New Social and Political Movements in Western Democracies (1990) and Germany Votes 1990 (1992). He is now completing a book-length study of the environmental movement in Western Europe.

Mario Diani is Lecturer in Sociology at the Bocconi University, Milan, Italy. He has published widely on new social movements and green politics in Italy and is currently researching a book on the networks of action in the Italian ecological movement.

Andrew Flynn was Research Fellow at the Bartlett School of Architecture and Planning, University College, London, and is now a lecturer in the Department of Geography and Earth Science, University of Hull.

Mark N. Franklin is Professor of Political Science at the University of Houston, Texas, USA. He is author of The Decline of Class Voting in Britain (Clarendon Press, 1985), co-author of Green Party Members: A Profile (Delta Publications, 1991) and co-editor of Electoral Change (Cambridge University Press, 1992).

Daniel Neal Graham is an Adjunct Professor of Environmental

Politics, Political Theory, and American Government in the Department of Political Science, North Carolina State University, Raleigh, North Carolina, USA. He has written several articles on Green and Left politics and is currently completing a Ph.D. thesis on the 'Politics of Ecology and Equality'.

Peter R. Hay is Lecturer in the Centre for Environmental Studies at the University of Tasmania, Hobart, Australia. He has published widely on green political theory and is co-editor of *Environmental Politics in Australia and New Zealand* (1989). From 1989 to 1991, Dr Hay worked, on secondment, for the Tasmanian state government in the Office of the Minister for Environment and Planning.

Barbara Jancar is Professor of Political Science at the State University of New York, Brockport, USA, and author of *Environmental Management in the Soviet Union and Yugoslavia* (Duke University Press, 1987).

Philip Lowe is Reader in the Bartlett School of Architecture and Planning, University College, London. In 1992, he will move to a chair in Rural Economy at the University of Newcastle. He has published widely on environmental politics in Britain and, *inter alia*, is co-author of *Environmental Groups in Politics* (George Allen & Unwin, 1983).

Alistair McCulloch is Lecturer in the School of Public Administration and Law at the Robert Gordon's Institute of Technology in Aberdeen, Scotland. He has published several articles on green politics in Britain and green political theory, and is currently engaged in a research project on business responses to the rise of environmental concern in Britain.

Eleanor McDowell is a postgraduate student in the Department of Government of Strathclyde University, Glasgow, Scotland. She is currently researching the development of the Scottish environmental movement.

José Augusto Pádua is co-ordinator of Environmental Studies at the Brazilian Institute for Social and Economic Analysis (IBASE), Rio de Janeiro, Brazil.

Stephen Rainbow just completed his Ph.D dissertation, 'The Unrealised Potential of Green Politics: A Study of Four Green Parties' at the Victoria University of Wellington, New Zealand, and is currently preparing a book manuscript on the history of green politics in New Zealand.

The Editor

Wolfgang Rüdig is Senior Lecturer in the Department of Government of the University of Strathclyde, Glasgow, Scotland. He is author, or co-author, of *Energiediskussion in Europa* (3rd ed., Neckar Verlag , 1981); *Anti-Nuclear Movements: A World Survey of Protest against Nuclear Energy* (Longman, 1990); *Green Party Members: A Profile* (Delta Publications, 1991) and *The Green Wave: A Comparative Analysis of Ecological Parties* (Polity Press, forthcoming). He is also editor of the book series Environment, Politics and Society (Edinburgh University Press).

Index

Acid rain, 18-9, 22, 27-8
Alber, J., 39, 190-1
Alternativbewegungen (Alternative
    Movements), 63
Anti-nuclear Movements, 3
Anti-Vietnam War Activities, 5
Arruda, L., 148
Ashdown, P., 26
Australia
    Tasmania
        Australian Labor Party (ALP), 88,
        91, 95-6, 103, 106, 108; Franklin
        Dam controversy, 87-91, 95, 102;
        Green Independents, election of,
        90; Green politics, 86-110; Labor-
        Green Accord, 91; Lake Pedder
        controversy, 86, 89-90, 108;
        Liberal Party, 88, 91, 95-6;
        Tasmanian Wilderness Society
        (TWS), 89; United Tasmania
        Group, 87-90
Austria, 170

Baxter, J. K., 120
Belgium
    Environmental groups:
        Amis de la Terre, 62; Bond Beter
        Leefmilieu, 62; Greenpeace, 62;
        Inter-environment Wallonie, 62;
        National Union for Conservation,
        62; Raad Leefmilieu te Brussel, 62;
        Reserves Ornitologiques, 62;
        Stichting Leefmilieu, 62; World
        Wildlife Fund, 62
    Green Parties, 1
Berry, J., 67
Blueprint for Survival, 112-3

Boerner, H, 93
Bonifacio, J., 143
Bracewell-Milnes, B., 10, 11, 18
Brazil
    Brazilian Foundation for the
        Conservation of Nature, 145
    Gaucho Association for the Protection
        of the Natural Environment
        (AGAPAN), 145
    Green Party (PV), 134-55
    New Middle Class, 141, 143-4
    New Social Movements, 141, 144-5,
        148
    Pacifist Movement, 140
    PDT, 149
    PMPB, 148, 153
    Workers' Party (PT), 148, 150
Brooks, P., 30
Brown, B., 89, 91
Brundtland Report, 27
Brunt, T., 112
Bulgaria, 161, 163, 165, 173-6, 179
    Ecoglasnost, 176
Burke, E., 39
Bürklin, W. P., 39

Carbon tax, 34
Carlisle, K., 11, 20
Carpentier, A., 139
CFCs, 22, 27
Chaos theory, 157-60
Chernobyl, 3, 161-4, 168, 178
Civil disobedience, 3
Civil rights activities, 5
Clough, R., 113
Clover, C., 25
Conscience community, ecological, 5